Chinese Research Perspectives on Population and Labor, Volume 1

Chinese Research Perspectives: Population and Labor

International Series Advisors

Cai Fang, Kam Wing Chan, and William Lavely

VOLUME 1

The titles published in this series are listed at *brill.com/crpo*

Chinese Research Perspectives on Population and Labor, Volume 1

Edited by

Cai Fang

BRILL

LEIDEN | BOSTON

This book is the result of a co-publication agreement between Social Sciences Academic Press and Koninklijke Brill NV. These articles were selected and translated into English from the original《中国人口与劳动问题报告2011》(*Zhongguo renkou yu laodong wenti baogao 2011*) and《中国人口与劳动问题报告2012》(*Zhongguo renkou yu laodong wenti baogao 2012*) with financial support from the Chinese Fund for the Humanities and Social Sciences.

This publication has been typeset in the multilingual 'Brill' typeface. With over 5,100 characters covering Latin, IPA, Greek, and Cyrillic, this typeface is especially suitable for use in the humanities. For more information, please see brill.com/brill-typeface.

ISSN 2212-7518
ISBN 978 90 04 27317 7 (hardback)
ISBN 978 90 04 27318 4 (e-book)

This book is printed on acid-free paper.

Printed by Printforce, the Netherlands

Contents

Looking at the Future of China's Population from the Sixth National Population Census and United Nations Population Projections

Cai Yong

The success of the Sixth National Population Census has provided the latest basis for the formulation of population policy and socio-economic development planning. The population census is a comprehensive, systematic survey and registration of the national population carried out in the same time period and according to the same methods, specifications, and questionnaire. The information obtained is the source of fully grasping a country's population and basic situation of socio-economic development and is the fundamental basis for formulating population policy and socio-economic development planning. The Sixth Population Census has provided the latest data on China's total population and its structure. The Sixth Population Census shows that China's fertility rate has been below replacement rate for two decades, that population has entered a phase of slow growth, and that aging has increased rapidly.

Based on the census, population projections are made through the understanding of the laws of population changes. Population projections are an important basis for the world's governments to develop economic and social policies. China's population census, by collecting fertility and mortality information, can be used to understand the trajectory and trends of China's future population changes through population projections. The Sixth Population Census shows that China's population will be facing the issue of aging for some time to come.

United Nations (UN) population projections data is often considered to be the most authoritative. The UN Population Division is an agency devoted full-time to organizing and publishing official calculations and projections of the world population. The agency is responsible for collecting and arranging the most recent population information and the corresponding economic and social information from each country, making comprehensive assessments of the current circumstances of the world population, and using this to make detailed projections for the future trends of the world population and for each country. Every two years, the UN publishes the latest analysis and projections in the form of amendments to World Population Prospects. So far, World

© KONINKLIJKE BRILL NV, LEIDEN, 2014 | DOI 10.1163/9789004273184_002

Population Prospects has been amended and updated 22 times. The UN published World Population Prospects (2010 Revision) on May 3, 2011. That day, the UN Population Division published its latest analysis and projection data for the world population on its website and released a press release titled, "World Population to reach 10 billion by 2100 if Fertility in all Countries Converges to Replacement Level." This press release once again raised public concern and discussion regarding the future of the world population. Also based on this revision, the UN Population Fund set October 31, 2011 as "World Population 7 Billion Day." Not only does the entire UN system use the population information published by the UN Population Division as the foundation of its work and the basis for considering global issues, but many international organizations, governments, and non-governmental organizations large and small use the population data published by the UN Population Division to formulate targets and assess policy choices. The importance and influence of the population data published by the UN Population Division goes without saying. The latest "UN Population Prospects (2010 Revision)" was released basically concurrent with the Sixth Population Census. It should be noted that "World Population Prospects (2010 Revision)" made major adjustments to the assessment and projections of China's population.

Through a comparison of data from the Sixth Population Census and UN population projection, this chapter explores the trajectory and future of China's demographic changes, as well as the role population projections should play in population policy.

I   The Misjudgments and Corrections in UN Population Projections on China

An important change in "World Population Prospects (2010 Revision)" is major adjustments to the assessment and projections for China's population. The adjustments are reflected in two aspects: first, lowering China's current total population; and second, adjusting the judgment of China's future population trends.

Comparing the Chinese population projections in the 2008 and 2010 versions of "World Population Prospects," one discovers that the UN's projection of China's peak population and the long-term trend have undergone major adjustment (See Figure 1.1). "World Population Prospects (2008 Revision)" projects that China's population will reach a peak in 2032 of 1.463 billion, after which China's total population will fall gradually, reaching 1.417 billion in 2050. The 2010 Revision projects that China's population will peak in 2026 at

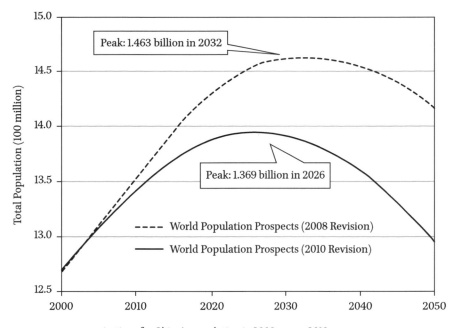

FIGURE 1.1 *UN projections for China's population in 2008 versus 2010*

1.396 billion and fall rapidly thereafter, reaching 1.295 billion in 2050. The 2010 Revision not only lowers China's peak population by 67 million, it also moves the peak forward by six years. By 2050, the difference in the projected values for the Chinese population reaches 120 million. In only two years, the UN judgment of China's population has changed dramatically.

One reason behind the change is that the 2010 Revision adjusted the estimate of China's current population downward. In elaborating on the differences between the 2010 Revision and the 2008 Revision two years earlier, the UN Population Division pointed out that the 2010 version adjusted the 2010 world population downward from 6.909 billion to 6.896 billion, a drop of 13 million. While the UN did not specify, in reality, the 13 million-person reduction came entirely from China. The 2008 Revision estimated that China's 2010 population would be 1.354 billion, which the 2010 Revision adjusted downward to 1.341 billion, a reduction of exactly 13 million. While 13 million is only 1% of China's population of 1.3 billion, the statistical error in the 2000 Census reached 1.81%. This adjustment seems to be technical and not a serious issue. But the question is why the UN adjusted the Chinese population. What is the basis for the adjustment?

The root cause of the major change in assessment of and projection for China's population is a major shift in judgment about China's fertility trend.

Since the early 1990s, except for a very few examples, survey data have shown that China's fertility rate has fallen far below replacement rate (about 2.1 children over the lifetime of each woman). Over the years, there have been two distinct voices in China regarding China's fertility and population situation. One is represented by the National Population and Family Planning Commission (now National Health and Family Planning Commission), which has the responsibility of managing population growth, which holds that China's fertility rate has been around 1.8 for many years, and there is risk of a rebound. The low fertility rates obtained by various surveys, including the Population Census, are attributed to under-reporting or omission, and this school of thought holds that they do not reflect the actual situation in China. Another school of thought is that over the past decade or so, international and domestic population scholars have gradually formed a consensus on the basis of thorough study and public discussion. After analysis and study of different data using different methods, those in this school have discovered that although under-reporting and omission have occurred, China's low fertility rate is a fact. A large number of empirical studies have shown that China's fertility rate had dropped to around 1.5 to 1.6 by the early 21st century (Cai 2008; Goodkind 2011; Morgan et al. 2009; Retherford et al. 2005; Zhang and Zhao 2006; Cai Yong 2009; Guo Zhigang 2000, 2009, and 2010). In 2007, as the official agency responsible for collecting and publishing China's population changes, the National Bureau of Statistics found in assessing China's 2006 population that the country's fertility rate had dropped to 1.6. Research by Guo Zhigang (2001) found that after 2006, the National Bureau of Statistics no longer trumpeted the increasing total number of births found in its surveys each year as it had done during the 1990s.

The one-child policy is not the only thing behind China's low fertility rate. More important are social and economic development, higher levels of education, increasing stress, postponed marriage and childbirth, and other factors (Cai 2010; Chen et al. 2010; Morgan et al. 2009; Zheng et al. 2009; Guo 2000). It is also an inevitable result of China's integration into the globalization process (Wang Feng 2010). In recent years, several other major international population-forecasting agencies like the Population Reference Bureau and US Census Bureau International Programs have adjusted China's birth fertility rate since 2000 to about 1.5. These arguments also influenced the judgment of the UN regarding China's population.

Comparing the last three UN estimates of China's fertility rate, one can see the changes in the agency's judgments. From Figure 1.2, one can see that the 2006 Revision of World Population Prospects determined China's fertility rate between 2000 and 2005 to be 1.7 and predicted that it would rise to

1.85 between 2020 and 2025 and stay there. The 2008 Revision raised the fertility rate, finding it to be 1.77 between 2000 and 2010, but made no changes to the long-term trend given in the 2006 Revision, assuming that the rate would rise to 1.85 between 2020 and 2025 and stay there. While the UN stresses that its estimate for China's fertility rate is an independent judgment obtained from detailed analysis of Chinese population data from multiple sources, the higher fertility rate estimate in the 2008 Revision was obviously influenced by the "fertility rate rebound" argument of the National Population and Family Planning Commission a few years ago. The 2006 "National Population and Family Planning Survey" omitted a number of young women (i.e. 30 years of age and below) due to significant sample bias, which led to the illusion of a recovering fertility rate after 2005 (Guo Zhigang 2009). The National Population and Family Planning Commission, without careful review, hyped the view of "fertility rate rebound and grim situation" based on the results of a survey with a severely biased sample. The State Council issued a decision titled "CPC Central Committee State Council Decision on Fully Strengthening Population and Family Planning Work Planning to Resolve Population Issues" on December 17, 2006, which stressed "doing everything possible to stabilize a low fertility rate." But it was soon found that the "fertility rate rebound" was sheer fiction, which could not be corroborated by other population surveys in the same period or later periods. At the "UN Experts Conference on Recent and Future Trends in Fertility" held in December 2009, Gu Baochang and myself (Gu and Cai 2011) requested an explanation from UN Population Division officials responsible for China's data for the higher fertility rate in the 2008 Revision. We recommended that the UN Population Division estimated China's fertility rate based on the research of scholars, experts, and large institutions in various fields rather than simply using or relying too heavily on data provided by the National Population and Family Planning Commission.

In the 2010 Revision, the UN significantly lowered China's recent and future fertility rates. As Figure 1.2 shows, the UN estimates that China's fertility rate fell from 1.7 for the 2000–2005 period to 1.64 for the 2005–2010 period. In the future, the agency projects that it will decline further to 1.51 for the 2015–2020 period before turning around and rising to 1.77 between 2045 and 2050 and 2.01 between 2095 and 2100 (not pictured). Downward adjustments to estimates of China's current and future fertility rates reflect not only new understandings of China's current population and fertility, but technical progress in the UN's population projections.

One major technical improvement in the 2010 Revision was the use for the first time of stochastic models to predict fertility rates in each country. Previously, the UN used deterministic modeling with empirical data, which is

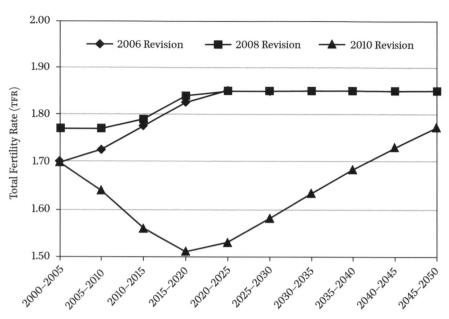

FIGURE 1.2 *Three recent UN projections of Chinese fertility rates*

an estimate of points and lines. However, changes to fertility rates have a high degree of uncertainty. Only by measuring and evaluating their uncertainty and making an interval and surface estimate can one truly understand changes to fertility rates. The 2010 Revision for the first time employed the Bayesian fertility prediction model (Alkema et al. 2011) jointly developed by Leontine Alkema of the University of Washington Department of Statistics and the UN Population Division to make fertility rate projections for various countries. The advantage of the Bayesian model is that it can predict a country's future fertility rate changes by referencing the country's history of fertility rate decline and the changes of fertility rates in other countries. At the same time, the stochastic-variable-based Bayesian model calculate the range of future fertility rate changes through simulations and thereby measure and evaluate the uncertainty of fertility rate development in order to better understanding fertility trends.

The preparatory work for the 2010 Revision was conducted previously to the Sixth Population Census, so the degree to which it fits the Population Census data can be seen as the first test of whether this revision is reasonable or not. Although the Sixth Population Census and is similar to any census or survey in that there may be issues such as omissions or duplicate reporting, National Bureau of Statistics Deputy Director Zhang Weimin stated when answering questions about the quality of data at an April 28, 2011 press conference announcing the findings of the Sixth Population Census, that the quality is high because quality checks after the census found an extremely low omission rate, and because of the continuity between the Sixth Population Census data and related administrative records, such as household registration management data, educational statistical data, population family planning birth data and Ministry of Civil Affairs funeral data. According to Sixth Population Census data released by the National Bureau of Statistics, China's population was 1.339 billion as of November 1, 2010. This number is very close to the estimate from the UN's 2010 Revision, with a gap of only 5 million people. But the difference between the numbers from the UN's 2010 Revision was 20 million people less than the 2008 edition. Therefore, the 2010 Revision is closer to the actual situation in China than the 2008 Revision, and its estimates are clearly more rational. It is an important correction of the errors in the 2008 Revision.

II   Changes to the Fertility Rate Decide the Future of the Chinese Population

The Sixth National Census once again confirmed the judgment of domestic and foreign population scholars of China's fertility situation: after falling below the replacement rate in the early 1990s, the fertility rate continued to decline rapidly, reaching 1.5 to 1.6 in the early 2000s. The under-reporting and omissions that the National Population and Family Planning Commission publicized over the years did not appear in the Sixth Population Census. On the contrary, the results of the Sixth Population Census have good continuity with previous population surveys (Guo Zhigang 2011; Zhao and Chen 2011). The Sixth Population Census counted 222.5 million Chinese between the ages of 0 and 14. On average each year was comprised of less than 15 million people. In accordance with the women's fertility patterns by age calculations obtained from surveys in recent years, if taking into account omissions, in the past 15 years, China's fertility rate has fallen below 1.4. Using the estimated value of 1.5 to 1.6 already leaves 10% to 15% room for omissions. Thus, in reality China's fertility rate may be below 1.5.

Although China's total population in the 2010 Revision is not too different from the result of China's Sixth Population Census, the 2010 Revision still lags behind changes to China's population in terms of the specific population age structure. Table 1.1 compares the Sixth Population Census data according to three age groups with the estimates in the 2010 Revision. For ease of

TABLE 1.1   *Comparison of Age Structures in the UN World Population Prospects*
2010 Revision and the Sixth National Population Census
Unit: 100 million, %

Age Group	Sixth Census		UN 2010 Revision	
0–14 years	2.225	(16.)	2.587	(19.2)
15–59 years	9.396	(70.1)	9.169	(68.2)
60 and older	1.776	(13.3)	1.694	(12.6)
Total	13.397	(100)	13.450	(100.0)

comparison, the 2010 Revision estimates have been adjusted with interpolation to November 1, 2010 so that there is a consistent, standard time between the two data sets. Compared to the Sixth Population Census, the total number and proportion of the juvenile population are higher in the UN estimates. The UN estimates that the population of 0 to 14 year olds to be 258.7 million, 19.2% of the population. But the Sixth Population Census found 222.5 million people in that age group, only 16.6% of the total population, making for a difference of 36.2 million people between the two data sets. At the same time, the Sixth Population Census found more in age groups 15 years and above than the UN estimates: 22.7 million more 15 to 59 year olds, and 8.2 million more of those 60 years of age and above. In other words, the 2010 Revision not only overestimated China's recent fertility rate, but also underestimated China's aging trend. One can expect that when the 2012 Revision is released, further adjustments will be to population projections for China.

Although the 2010 Revision overestimates China's current fertility rate and underestimated the rate of aging of China's population, the timely adjustments to the UN population projections have important reference significance for understanding the future development of China's population. In particular, the key to making successful population projections for a country in a population development stage such as China lies in properly judging the fertility rate. The new Bayesian model adopted by the UN provides a tool for measuring and assessing fertility rate uncertainty. Thus, the fertility rate projections for China in the 2010 Revision have important significance for understanding the trends in China's fertility rate changes. To this end, we will make a brief introduction to the methods and data used to make the UN population projections.

UN population projections use the most common method: the "queue component method." Simply put, this breaks causes of demographic changes into fertility, mortality, and international migration. Population is broken down by age and sex, and each age group's births, deaths, and international migration rules are measured separately. Because there are regularities in three factors—birth, death, and international migration—if a rational judgment can be made as to each, including its future trends, population projections can help us understand future population changes. For example, if we know the number of 20-year-old women this year, based on the annual mortality rate, we can work out the number of 30-year-old women in ten years. According to the rules of marriage and births, we can make projections of the number of children these women will give birth to in each of the next ten years. The same method is applied to each age group. With the current population situation, judgments as to these three factors, and assumptions regarding future trends, not only can we project the total future population, but we can know the specific age structure of the future population.

For most countries in the world today, the most important of the three factors determining population changes is fertility rate. With the exception of a few countries, international migration accounts for an extremely small proportion of the total population and thus has little effect. The experience of the past decade shows that declines in mortality rate have very strong regularity. Those in population studies have relatively consistent views on the direction and rate of changes to mortality rate, to the point where now the UN population projections only provide one mortality rate plan. Relative to migration and death, making a correct judgment of the fertility rate is much more challenging. This is not only because there is a high degree of uncertainty after the fertility rate falls below replacement level. There are also a variety of views on future trends in the population studies community. In addition, because of the "multiplier effect" of the fertility rate in population projections, that is, a generation of births 20-some years later gives birth to another generation, there may be a large bias in long-term projections if the wrong assumptions are made. The revision process between the 2008 Revision and the 2010 Revision described previously is a good example in which we can see the importance of the fertility rate in population projections. Therefore, the key to population projections lies in the quality of the judgment of the current population and the understanding of the rules of population change. If we are not more discriminating about the data, it can easily be abused and misused.

Although most demographers agree that the long-term population trend is that fertility rates must rise to the vicinity of replacement level. Otherwise would mean the demise of a country or nation. But there are large disagreements regarding the recovery process and speed, mainly because there is a high degree of diversity in countries whose fertility rates fall below replacement level. Some, like the US, Norway, and Ireland, fluctuate gently just below the replacement rate. Others, like Germany, Romania, and Japan have seen fertility rates continue to decline after falling below the replacement level, to around 1.3, where they remain. Others, like South Korea, Singapore, and Taiwan, have continued to fall to near 1.0 or even lower. And countries like The Netherlands, Denmark, and France have begun to rebound from their lows. It is difficult to derive a general rule from these numerous changes like we have done for changes in mortality rates. As the UN's World Population Prospects points out, "The future of population growth depends largely on future fertility changes."

Because of the uncertainty and importance of fertility rates, the UN provides high, medium, and low-fertility rate scenarios for each country. Prior to the 2010 Revision, the UN generally arrived at the medium fertility rate scenario by reviewing and commenting on the process of changes to a country's fertility rate and then forming an "expert judgment" by referencing the experience of other countries. This method is a bit arbitrary, but as experienced judgment it still has reference value. The so-called high fertility rate scenario and low fertility rate scenario simply add or subtract 0.5 children from the medium scenario, respectively. Therefore, the high and low scenarios are not upper and lower limits, nor can they tell us the possibility of the fertility rate hitting the high or low scenarios. In other words, the practical significance of these scenarios is difficult to explain.

The Bayesian projection technique employed by the UN for fertility rates in the 2010 Revision makes it more convenient for us to understand the statistical significance of the UN population projections. The Bayesian fertility prediction model is a stochastic model, which uses Markov chain Monte Carlo to simulate the process of changes to the fertility rate. The UN's medium fertility rate scenario is a median assumption generated from tens of thousands of stochastic simulations. On the basis of a large number of computer simulations, the Bayesian fertility rate projection model can not only provide a judgment on the fertility rate trends in the medium-term future, but can also be used to calculate the possible future range of fertility rates and the probability of different situations occurring.

Figure 1.3 is a comparison of the UN's high, medium, and low fertility estimates with the range of estimates from the Alkema Bayesian model. The thick, solid line in Figure 1.3 is the UN's 2010 medium fertility rate estimate, and the two dotted lines are the high and low fertility rate estimates. Gray areas are the possible range of future fertility rate projections. The dark gray area is the 80% projection range, that is, there is a 10% possibility that China's future fertility rate is above the dark gray level and a 10% possibility that it is below the dark gray area. The light gray area is the 95% projection range, that is, there is a 2.5% possibility that China's future fertility rate is 2.5% above the light gray

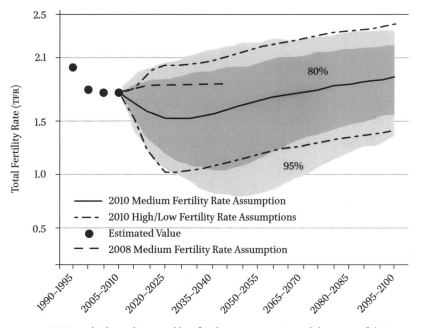

FIGURE 1.3   *2010 UN high, medium, and low fertility rate scenarios and the range of the Bayesian model*[1]

level and a 2.5% possibility that is below the light gray level. From Figure 1.3 we can see that China's future fertility rate trend projected by the Bayesian model is not symmetric with the high and low fertility rate scenarios. The depth of fertility rate drop exceeds the height of fertility rate rise. Before 2065–2070, the UN's high fertility rate scenario is basically within the 80% and 95% possibility ranges, but thereafter it moves outside of the 95% projection range. The UN's low fertility rate scenario is mostly between the 80% and 95% projection ranges, but in between, there are nearly 20 years where it falls within the 80% projection range. Therefore, the UN's high fertility rate scenario is basically the upper limit of Chinese population growth, while the low fertility rate scenario is not necessarily the lower limit for China's population.

According to the envelope range displayed by the high and low fertility rate scenarios by the UN, the greatest likelihood for China's population change in the 21st century is negative growth. After determining that the UN's high and low fertility rate scenarios basically encompass the possible range of future changes in Chinese population, we can compare their corresponding population projections to observe the trend of future changes during the remainder

---

1   This figure comes from Alkema et al. 2011 (p. 830, Figure 7).

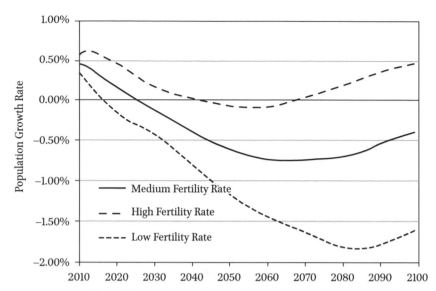

FIGURE 1.4   *The effects of the UN's high, medium, and low fertility rate scenarios on China's population growth*

of this century. Figure 1.4 shows a comparison of the population growth rates corresponding to the high, medium, and low fertility rate scenarios laid out by the UN from 2010 to 2100. According to the medium scenario, China's population will continue to grow until 2026, after which it will experience negative growth, the rate of which will accelerate until it stabilizes after reaching approximately -0.7% in 2060. After 2080, the negative growth rate will slow, but population shrinkage will continue to the end of the century, at which point China's population will be 400 million fewer than in 2010, approximately 941 million, and equivalent to the level in 1977. In the low birth rate scenario, China's population growth will only continue for six years, reaching a peak of 1.36 billion in 2017 before falling rapidly. After that, negative population growth will accelerate, reaching a loss of 1% per year in 2046 and stabilizing at a loss of 1.8% per year in 2080. According to this scenario, China's population is expected to fall to 510 million by the end of the century, a reduction of 62% from 2010 and smaller than in 1950. According to the high fertility rate scenario, China's population change over the next 90 years is basically a story of slow growth. Only in the middle of the century will there be a brief period of negative growth. The growth rate will basically be below 0.5%, with average annual growth over the next 90 years of 0.18%. In 2100, China's population will be 1.59 billion under this scenario. In Figure 1.3, we can see that after 2070,

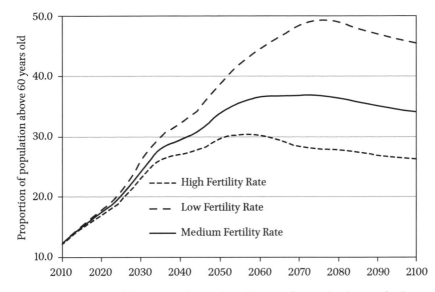

FIGURE 1.5 *Proportion of Chinese population above 60 years of age under three UN fertility rate projections form 2010*

the high fertility rate scenario falls outside of the 95% projection range, so the possibility of reaching the extent indicated by the high fertility rate plan after 2070 is small. In summary, the vast majority of the possible range of the future Chinese population growth rate shown in Figure 1.4 is in the negative growth area below zero.

The main concern of the previous analysis is the trend of the total population. For the many who are still subject to the effects of the so-called "moderate population theory," the rapid decrease in the total population may be something to be sought after and worked toward. But the goal of population policy should be to improve society and the welfare of citizens, not to reach a certain number for the total population. This is because in addition to the total population, the age structure of the population has a major effect on the socio-economic welfare of a nation. With the accelerating aging of the Chinese population in recent years, more and more people are realizing that in terms of the smooth development of society and the happiness of individuals and families, the age structure often plays a more direct and more important role than the total population.

Population projections can not only provide the direction of development for the total population. They also allow us to better understand the trend of changes to the population structure. No matter which fertility rate scenario,

China's level of aging will rise rapidly over the coming decades, reaching a level of 30% or more. According to the UN's high, medium, and low fertility rate scenarios, we can clearly see China's future aging trends in Figure 1.5. Under the medium fertility rate scenario, the proportion of those over 60 in China's population will increase rapidly to more than 30% in the coming decades and remain at around 35% until the end of the century. Under the low fertility rate scenario, the proportion of those over 60 will rise for 70 years, reaching 50% in 2075, meaning that nearly half of society will be made up of those over 60 years of age. Even under the high fertility rate scenario, the proportion of those over 60 will rise to around 30% by 2050. Although this proportion will fall somewhat over the following 50 years, it will remain above 26%, nearly twice the current level.

China's trend towards an aging society has been set and cannot be reversed. Even under the high fertility rate scenario, where China's fertility rate recovers rapidly and continues to climb gradually, the degree of aging can be mitigated, but cannot alter the fact that 21st century China will be an aging society. All we can do is delay as much as possible the rate of aging. But conversely, if the fertility rate continues its downward tendency, even after it recovers a bit, it will be recovering from a low of around 1.5, and the degree of aging may reach alarming levels. From the previous discussion, we can reach several clear conclusions: 1) The fertility rate will determine the future of the Chinese population; 2) China's main problem is that of a low fertility rate; 3) If China's fertility rate does not achieve a recovery in the short-term as projected by the UN, China's rapidly aging population will place unprecedented pressure on society and the economy.

III   The Role of Population Projections in Population Policy: Number-Oriented or People-Oriented?

Population projections are continuously improved with changes to reality and methods. This is normal. But if forecast assumptions, methods, and results are not further examined and adjusted, using these projections to decide the fate of the families and people of a country would be reckless and dangerous. Examples abound in history. By quickly adjusting the goals of population projections for each country based on new situations and new methods, the UN Population Division provides a reliable basis for the countries of the world to make scientifically based decisions for socio-economic development. This is in sharp contrast to a recent projection in China. In 2007, some 300 experts, including more than a dozen from the Chinese Academy of Sciences and Chinese Academy of Engineering, completed the "Research Report on National Population Development Strategy." The assumption used in the report's judgment and projection of Chinese population changes was that China's fertility rate was at "around 1.8" and would remain there for 30 years. The report thus came to the conclusion that China's population would peak in 2033 at "around 1.5 billion." It is not difficult to find that the population projections in this report are similar to the UN's 2008 Revision. However, this report, out of date on arrival, has not been amended, and it is still the foundation on which China formulates its socio-economic plans. For example, the 12th Five-year Plan still assumes that China's population will grow by 0.7% per year, adding between 8 million and 10 million citizens per year, when in fact, the population growth rate during the 12th Five-year Plan will not exceed 0.5%, adding an average of less than 7 million people per year to the population.

Inadequate understanding of and blind trust in population projections have created the unhealthy policy-making atmosphere in which concern with numbers takes precedence over concern with people's welfare. Population projections should be understood as a computational tool obtaining results under certain assumptions. They can be used as a reference, but should not be mechanically taken as principle by which to formulate social and economic policy. But combined with the simple pursuit of GDP per capita, the tragedy created by blind faith in population projections is still on-going. The aforementioned "National Population Development Strategy Report," which misjudged China's near-term population changes, put forward the new goal of a stable fertility rate of 1.8 under this "numbers-oriented," "GDP-dominated" logic. This report came to the following conclusion: "Based on the proposal from the 16th People's Congress to quadruple 2000 GDP by 2020 to a per capita rate of US$ 3,000, working backward, China's population in 2020 must be kept under 1.46 billion, and average total fertility must be maintained at around 1.8 to ensure the implementation of the goal of building a moderately prosperous society." If economic goals are truly to decide population policy, China's target fertility rate should long ago have been set much higher than 1.8, because China's population will never reach 1.46 billion by 2020. Moreover, per capita income levels have already exceeded the set target.

There is precedent for such reverse engineering of coercive population targets from projected economic goals further imposed on the people and society, is the one-child policy still practiced today. Behind this 30-year-old policy is a population target reverse engineered from economic goals: the erroneous belief that in order to achieve the quadrupling of per capita GDP, China's population must be kept under 1.2 billion by the end of the 20th century. We now know that the basic reason for China achieving the rapid development of its national economy is that reform and opening-up brought into play enormous enthusiasm and creativity among the Chinese people. Relaxing the social policy environment created space for individuals and families to develop. This did not happen because China implemented the "one child" family planning policy. Nor has any country ever achieved soaring economic growth by managing its population. In fact, if we are to assess China's "one child policy" as an instrument for population management, then it has been a failed policy. In 2000, China's population reached 1.27 billion, far exceeding the goal of 1.2 billion at the time the policy was introduced. But this did nothing to prevent China from reaching its goal of quadrupling GDP per capita.

Similarly, the most fundamental reason for the decline in the China's fertility rate is not the one-child policy. The most rapid decline in the fertility rate occurred in the 1970s before the introduction of the one-child policy. At the time, the fertility rate decreased from 5.8 children per woman in 1970 to 2.7 children in 1978. In the first decade of the implementation of the one-child policy, China's fertility rate did not decline significantly, but instead fluctuated around 2.5. The fertility rate fell further in the 1990s. At the time there was the role of the one-child policy as well as the "one ballot veto." But more important was that after the beginning of reform and opening-up, a fundamental change in people's views occurred due to a series of changes including industrialization, urbanization, and increasing education attainment. The failure of the one-child policy lies in the fact that when the government wanted it to have an effect, it did not. And when China no longer needed this policy, it undermined the stable development of the population. The continued existence of the one-child policy is accelerating the aging of the Chinese population, bringing a premature end to China's demographic dividend.

The failure of the "one-child policy" does not lie only in its erroneous economic assumptions, but also in its erroneous population assumptions. The argument for the introduction of the one-child policy was that according to population projections at the time, the only way to keep the Chinese population within 1.2 billion by the end of the 20th century was to allow each woman to give birth to one child only. But in reality, later marriage and larger spacing between births would achieve the same goal. Chinese population scholars represented by Liang Zhongtang vigorously called for such a plan (Liang Zhongtang 1985). Today, three decades later, the pilot he launched in Yicheng, Shanxi province, has fully proven this point (Wang Feng and Gu Baochang 2009). Five years after implementation of the one-child policy began, American scholars

Bongaarts and Greenhalgh (1985) used population projections to show that if China had begun implementing a late-birth, two-child, large-spacing policy in 1985, China could still have achieved the goal of keeping the population under 1.2 billion by 2000. If it were to implement a two-child, large-spacing policy, China could have not only avoided the kind of tension between government officials and the general public that has marred the enforcement of the one-child policy, but also greatly mitigated future pressure generated by population aging.

Although the one-child policy has not brought many benefits to China's economic development, Chinese society has also paid a steep price for them. The price is not only economic. More important is the social level. In order to enforce a rigid family planning policy, China established a family planning system with an immense organizational structure. From the central government to local governments, family planning agencies have employed some 500,000 people. Adding to that number the more than a million workers who work in various capacities relating to policy enforcement, state and local governments must invest heavily towards maintaining this massive institution. But a greater cost is the sacrifices that individuals and families have had to make. China now has more than 150 million families with only one child, and the number continues to increase each year. From a microscopic perspective, these families will face greater risks as they move into old age and look for support from the younger generations. The unfortunate experiences of many single-child families in the wake of the Wenchuan earthquake shows the vulnerability of one-child families.

From a macroscopic perspective, the profound impact of long-term low fertility is difficult to assess. At present, for each 60-year-old citizen, there are 4.7 20–59 year old workers working and paying taxes. But by 2030, each 60-year-old citizen will be supported by only two workers aged between 20 and 59. It is not difficult to imagine the pressure Chinese society will be under at that time. Unfortunately, this trend of rapid aging can no longer be changed as those who will be older than 20 years old in 2030 have already been born. The size of this group will not grow, but it will drop as those in the group die. Moreover, the changing of the population structure will have a huge impact on issues such as labor supply, consumption, and savings. In recent years, the public burden has increased due to pension and medical benefits expenses associated with aging populations, leading to economic and social crisis. This has sounded the alarm for China's future. Given the demographic situation, all the government and society can do is use the next one to two decades to establish a complete set of facilities to prepare for entering an aging society. More important is taking a longer-term view on population policy, placing the focus of policy on social stability and family wellbeing and being people-oriented rather than fixating on a few likely unreliable figures.

Population projections are an important tool for population policy and socio-economic decision-making. By understanding the rules of demographic changes, we can project the numbers and structure of changes to the population decades into the future. From the comparison between the two recent revisions to UN's World Population Prospects, we can see that the key to population projections is a proper understanding of fertility levels. This also reminds us that a long-term vision and a precautionary attitude are key to achieving stable development of the Chinese population and society. Given that China's fertility rate has been below the replacement level for some two decades, and is now below 1.5, if we don't adjust policies now, we are likely to fall into a "low fertility rate trap."

(This article was originally published in Chinese in 2012.)

References

Alkema, Leontine, Adrian E. Raftery, Patrick Gerland, Samuel J. Clark, François Pelletier, Thomas Buettnerand, Gerhard K. Heilig. 2011. "Probabilistic Projections of the Total Fertility Rate for All Countries." *Demography*, 48(3): 815–839.

Bongaarts, John and Susan Greenhalgh. 1985. "An Alternative to the One-Child Policy in China." *Population and Development Review*, 11(4): 585–617.

Cai Yong. 2008. "An assessment of China's fertility level using the variable-r method." *Demography*, 45(2), pp. 271–281.

———. 2009. "Are Educational Statistics Truly the Gold Standard for Estimating Fertility Levels?" *Population Studies*, 33(4): 22–33.

———. 2010. "China's Below-Replacement Fertility: Government Policy or Socioeconomic Development?" *Population and Development Review*, 36(3): 419–440.

Chen Jiajian, Robert D. Retherford, Minja Kim Choe, Li Xiru, and Cui Hongyan. 2010. "Effects of population policy and economic reform on the trend in fertility in Guangdong province, China, 1975–2005." *Population Studies: A Journal of Demography.* 64(1): 43.

China National Bureau of Statistics, United States East-West Center, ed. 2007. *Fertility Rate Estimates for China's Provinces:* 1975–2000, China Statistical Press.

China National Bureau of Statistics. 2007. *China Population 2005*, China Statistical Press.

Goodkind, Daniel. 2011. "Child Underreporting, Fertility, and Sex Ratio Imbalance in China." *Demography*, 48(1): 291–316.

Gu Baochang and Wang Feng, *The Experience of 800 Million People: Research Report from Two-Child-Policy Areas*, Social Sciences Academic Press, 2009.

Gu Baochang and Yong Cai. 2011. "Fertility Prospects in China." Expert Paper No. 2011/14. United Nations Department of Economic and Social Affairs Population Division.

Guo Zhigang, "Looking at Lifetime Fertility from Period Reproductive Behavior in Recent Years." *Population Studies*, 2000, Vol. 1.

———. "The Reason for the 'Rebound' in the Fertility Rate in Recent Years – Evaluation of the 2006 National Population and Family Planning Survey." *Chinese Journal of Population Science*, 2009, Vol. 2.

———. "China's Low Fertility Rate and Overlooked Demographic Risks." *International Economic Review*, 2020, Vol. 6

———. "Results of the Sixth National Population Census Show Serious Errors in Past Population Estimates." *Chinese Journal of Population Science*, 2011, Vol. 6.

Liang Zhongtang. *On China's Population Development Strategy*, Shanxi People's Publishing House. 1985.

Morgan, S. Philip, Zhigang Guo, and Sarah R. Hayford. 2009. "China's Below-Replacement Fertility: Recent Trends and Future Prospects." *Population and Development Review*, 35(3): 605–629.

Retherford, Robert D, Minja Kim Choe, Jiajian Chen, Li Xiru, and Cui Hongyan. 2005. "How Far Has Fertility in China Really Declined?" *Population and Development Review* 31(1): 57–84.

Wang Feng. "The World Population in a Global Environment and China's Choice." *International Economic Review*, 2010, Vol. 6.

Zhang Guangyu and Zhao Zhongwei. 2006. "Reexamining China's Fertility Puzzle: Data Collection and Quality over the Last Two Decades." *Population and Development Review*, 3(2): 293–321.

Zhao Zhongwei and Wei Chen. 2011. "China's far below replacement fertility and its long-term impact: Comments on the preliminary results of the 2010 census." *Demographic Research*, No. 25: 819–836.

Zheng Zhenzhen, Yong Cai, Feng Wang, and Baochang Gu. 2009. "Below-replacement fertility and childbearing intention in Jiangsu Province, China." *Asian Population Studies*, 5(3): 329–347.

CHAPTER 2

Provincial Disparities in Changes in Fertility and Related Implications

Niu Jianlin

China has witnessed rapid changes in fertility since the 1970s. The national total fertility rate (TFR) declined from around 6 in the early 1970s to below-replacement levels by the mid-1990s. Two factors—strict birth control policies and rapid socioeconomic development—have been suggested as the predominant forces driving fertility decline in China. Since its implementation in the 1970s, birth control policy in China has proven to be the most successful family-planning policy in the world. Meanwhile, along with urbanization and modernization, China's nearly four decades of rapid social and economic growth has contributed significantly to socio-cultural changes in marital and reproductive customs and practices. Couples in younger generations increasingly prefer to have smaller families.

Nevertheless, China is a highly heterogeneous society, and substantial fertility differences persist at regional levels in China both historically and at present. According to the 2000 Census, the TFR at provincial level in 2000 ranges from 0.67 (in Beijing) to 2.19 (in Guizhou) (National Bureau of Statistics of China, 2003). This variation is partly attributable to the significant regional disparities in culture, socioeconomic development, and institutional arrangements (Cai, 2010; Chen, 2005; Chen, et al. 2010; Li, 2004; Zheng & Wu, 2005). For instance, provinces in China differ substantially in their detailed fertility regulations and the implementation of policy, even though these institutional arrangements are all included under the umbrella term of "family planning programs." As such, in order to better understand historical and contemporary factors affecting China's changing fertility rates, it is necessary to systematically investigate regional differences in fertility transition. This study uses published data on provincial fertility and existing socioeconomic statistics, specifically the provincial-level socioeconomic statistics and fertility rates from 1975 to 2000, to examine the process of fertility changes and to explore related socio-demographic impacts. The fertility rates are indirect estimates based on the period parity progression ratios, with data from the 1990 and 2000 Censuses (National Bureau of Statistics of China & East-West Center, 2007). The indirect fertility estimates are employed in order to remove the influence of short-term

© KONINKLIJKE BRILL NV, LEIDEN, 2014 | DOI 10.1163/9789004273184_003

fluctuations from overall period fertility rates, and make it possible to reflect genuine trends of over-time fertility decline more closely. By examining provincial fertility transition trajectories, this paper also investigates the contribution of different driving forces in bringing down fertility and its dynamics over time. Finally, the study explores important socio-demographic impacts resulting from different fertility transition processes.

1   An Overview of Changes in Provincial Fertility

The time series data of provincial TFRs show that provinces in China have been quite different in their onset timing and the progression of fertility changes, despite the fact that significant declines in fertility rates have been observed from the early 1970s at the national level. Big municipalities and more developed provinces started fertility decline earliest. Figure 2.1 displays the distribution of provinces as indicated by TFRs in 1975 and 1990. In the mid-1970s, Beijing and Shanghai were the only two areas which had already achieved below-replacement fertility rates. The TFRs in other relatively developed areas, such as Tianjin, Jiangsu, Zhejiang, Shandong, Hebei, Liaoning, and Jilin, are around 3 in 1975. These provincial units are second only to Beijing and Shanghai for lowest fertility rates. By 1990, most of these provinces had reached a below-replacement fertility rate, and some of them reach a very low fertility. For instance, provinces such as Liaoning and Zhejiang have reached a TFR below 1.5, similar to the three municipalities, Beijing, Shanghai and Tianjin.

Table 2.1 presents the order by which all provinces achieved a replacement-level or lower fertility. As mentioned above, Shanghai and Beijing achieved a below replacement fertility before 1975, and they rank the first two (provincial units) throughout the country in completing fertility transition. Following these two municipalities, relatively more developed and urbanized areas achieved a replacement fertility rate no later than early 1980s, despite the fact that these provincial units employed quite different fertility regulations. For instance, according to the birth control policy, rural couples in Liaoning, Jilin, Heilongjiang, and Zhejiang are allowed to have a second birth if their first child is female, which is to say, rural areas in these provinces apply "one-and-a-half-birth" policies. In contrast, the other two provincial units of the same tier, Tianjin and Jiangsu, apply a strict one-child policy. In light of these policy differences, the temporal coincidence of fertility transition in these relatively developed areas suggests that socioeconomic factors have played a significant role in driving fertility transition net of, and possibly independent of, the strict birth control policy even in early stages of national fertility transition.

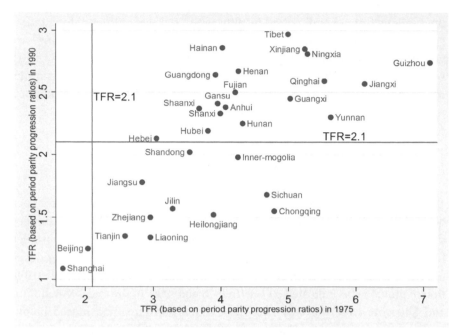

FIGURE 2.1 *Distribution of provinces classified by TFRs in 1975 and 1990*
DATA SOURCE: NATIONAL BUREAU OF STATISTICS OF CHINA AND EAST-WEST CENTER, 2007. *FERTILITY ESTIMATES FOR PROVINCES OF CHINA, 1975–2000.* BEIJING: CHINA STATISTICS PRESS. 2007.

Fertility rates in most of the remaining provinces declined to a replacement or lower level in the 1990s. As shown in Table 2.1, all the provincial units, with the exception to Guizhou, had completed their transition to a replacement-level fertility rate before 2000, while Guizhou's 2000 total fertility rate is also very close to the replacement level (Figure 2.2). Figure 2.2 displays the distribution of provinces in terms of their fertility rates in 1975 and 2000. In combination with the fertility decline shown in Figure 2.1, the fertility decline reflected in Figure 2.2 suggests that, in a certain sense, fertility transition processes may be self-sustaining once under way. The provincial units which initiated fertility transition earlier continued their declines in fertility rates to below replacement levels; for instance, most of the provinces which achieved replacement-level fertility rates before 1990 had a total fertility rate below 1.5 by 2000 (Figure 2.2).

The fertility transition trajectories, as shown in Figures 2.1 and 2.2, also suggest that the transition process is highly path-dependent. Those provinces with a later onset of fertility transition usually had higher fertility rates at the

TABLE 2.1   *A comparison by province of fertility rate policies, the year achieving replacement-level fertility, and the year of achieving policy fertility rates*

Province	Policy TFR #	I: Year arriving at replacement-level TFR	II: Year arriving at policy TFR	Province	Policy TFR #	I: Year arriving at replacement-level TFR	II: Year arriving at policy TFR
Beijing	1.086	1975	1992	Henan	1.505	1991	1994
Tianjin	1.167	1980	1993	Hubei	1.466	1991	1995
Hebei	1.592	1991	1994	Hunan	1.479	1991	1993
Shanxi	1.487	1991	>2000	Guangdong	1.413	1996	>2000
Inner-Mongolia	1.602	1988	1992	Guangxi	1.527	1993	1999*
Liaoning	1.383	1981	1989	Hainan	2.137	1997	1997
Jilin	1.450	1982	1991	Chongqing	1.273	1988	1999
Heilongjiang	1.392	1983	1991	Sichuan	1.188	1988	>2000
Shanghai	1.060	<1975	1984*	Guizhou	1.667	>2000	>2000
Jiangsu	1.060	1981	>2000	Yunnan	2.006	1991	1991
Zhejiang	1.467	1984	1991	Shaanxi	1.514	1991	1997
Anhui	1.480	1991	1997	Gansu	1.559	1991	1999*
Fujian	1.481	1992	1997	Qinghai	2.104	1993	1993
Jiangxi	1.464	1992	>2000	Ningxia	2.116	1996	1996
Shandong	1.453	1989	1992	Xinjiang	2.366	1993	1991

Data source: Guo et al. 2003 "Diversity of China's Fertility Policy by Policy Fertility" Population Research 5:1–10; Column I & II: National Bureau of Statistics of China and the East-West Center, 2007. *Fertility Estimates for Provinces of China, 1975–2000.* Beijing: China Statistics Press. 2007.
* Year in which fertility rate first declined to the policy fertility rate; fertility rate may fluctuate around the policy fertility rate after that.

beginning of transition, and their paces of transition proved to be relatively sluggish partly because of their relative underdevelopment (or lack of "readiness" in Coale's terminology, ref. to Coale and Treadway [1986]). This gives further evidence to the importance of socioeconomic development in promoting and speeding up a fertility transition.

Nevertheless, the differences in onset timing and pace of a transition at provincial level also highlight the relevance of fertility policy and detailed regulations and implementation, especially for those late-transiting provinces.

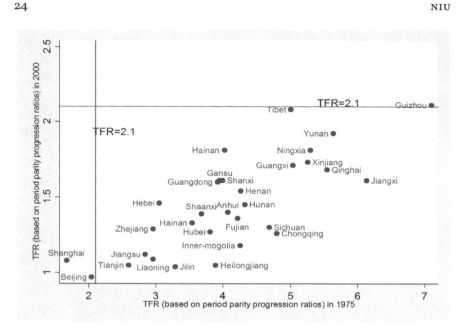

FIGURE 2.2 *Distribution of provinces classified by TFRs in 1975 and 2000*
DATA SOURCE: SEE FIGURE 2.1.

For instance, although the fertility rates in Sichuan and Chongqing were higher than many other provinces in 1975, they achieved much lower fertility rates by 1990 and 2000 partly because of their strict one-child policy. In contrast, by applying a more moderate birth control (two children allowed in its rural area) policy, Hainan has experienced a much slower fertility transition even though its initial fertility rate was not higher than Sichuan or Chongqing (as shown in Figure 2.1).

2   Factors Affecting the Fertility Transition Process

As discussed in earlier research (Chen, 2005; Gu, 1987; Li, 2004; etc.), the trajectories of provincial fertility transition suggest that both socioeconomic development and birth control policy have played important roles in bringing about rapid fertility transition in China during the past few decades. Early studies show that socioeconomic factors and national fertility policy have independent impacts on fertility transition, and they also interact with each other in determining a transition trajectory (Gu, 1987; Poston and Gu, 1987).

The dynamics of regional disparity in fertility transition have attracted continuing concerns, however, on the specific role and relative importance of
these factors at various stages of fertility transition. Recent empirical studies
suggest that the transition progress made before the 1990s resulted mainly
from birth control policies, while the progress afterwards is more attributable
to socioeconomic development (Chen, 2005; Li, 2004). The factors examined
in these recent studies include regional economic condition, living standard
of residents, women's social status, and policy implementation (such as preva-
lence of contraceptive use, unplanned births, and so on).

The existing literature is insightful in interpreting the forces driving fertility transition. Nevertheless, they are also limited in the following aspects.
First, using cross-sectional data measured at limited time periods, some of the
previous studies fail to examine the temporal order of the observed fertility
and its proposed "determinants." Second, the fertility measures used in most
of the previous studies contain temporal random fluctuations and therefore
a comparison between those measurements does not necessarily reflect the
overall trend of fertility change. In this study, the TFRs calculated are based
on the period parity progression ratio to minimize the disturbances of random fluctuations in period fertility rate, and a longer period of time series data
(1975–2000) for socioeconomic and demographic indicators at the provincial
level.[1] Employing time series data analysis methods, this study compares the
most important determinants of fertility decline before and after 1990.

Table 2.2 presents the time series model results for the provincial TFRs from
1975 to 1998, from 1975 to 1990, and from 1990 to 1998, respectively. Due to the
fact that the sample size is relatively small at provincial level and the covariates are correlated with each other to various degrees, this study fit models
separately for each covariate to make the results robust. These model results

---

1   Data sources for the provincial socioeconomic statistics include: a) Population Census
    Office under the State Council & Department of Population, Social, Science and Technology
    Statistics, National Bureau of Statistics of China, 2005, *National Key Project Report Using
    the 2000 Census*, Beijing: China Statistics Press, 2005: pp. 2142–2143; b) Department of
    Population, Social, Science and Technology Statistics, National Bureau of Statistics of China,
    Data Collection of 2005 China 1% *Population Sample Survey-National*, China Statistics
    Press, 2007; c) Comprehensive Department, National Bureau of Statistics of China, 1999,
    Comprehensive Statistical Data and Materials on 50 Years of New China, Beijing: China
    Statistics Press, 1999; d) Department of Population, Social Science and Technology Statistics,
    National Bureau of Statistics of China, 2004, *China Population Statistics Yearbook 2004*,
    Beijing: China Statistics Press, 2004.

TABLE 2.2   *Times series model estimates for each covariate by time periods (DV=TFR)*

	I (1975–1998)	II (1975–1990)	III (1990–1998)
Variance components of TFR (null model)			
σ_u / σ_e	0.51 / 0.63	0.63 / 0.47	0.40 / 0.25
ρ	0.40	0.64	0.72
Simple Time Series Models on TFR:			
Policy Fertility Rate (ref.:<1.3)			
1.3~1.5	0.63***	0.81***	0.35*
1.5~2	0.97***	1.22***	0.61***
2+	1.39***	1.75***	0.95***
σ_u / σ_e	0.24 / 0.63	0.32 / 0.47	0.26 / 0.25
GDP (In Thousand Yuan)per Capita	−0.12***	−0.49***	−0.05***
σ_u / σ_e	0.38 / 0.54	0.48 / 0.38	0.33 / 0.21
% Non-Agriculture Employees	−0.05***	−0.04***	−0.03***
σ_u / σ_e	0.49 / 0.44	0.60 / 0.37	0.37 / 0.18
Urbanization Rate	−0.05***	−0.04***	−0.04***
σ_u / σ_e	0.38 / 0.35	0.46 / 0.25	0.32 / 0.17
% Agricultural Hukou Holders	0.06***	0.05***	0.03***
σ_u / σ_e	0.49 / 0.47	0.60 / 0.37	0.36 / 0.20
% Women Aged 15–64 having at least a High School Education	−0.11***	−0.08***	−0.07***
σ_u / σ_e	0.40 / 0.35	0.50 / 0.27	0.32 / 0.17
Life Expectancy	−0.24***	−0.22***	−0.16***
σ_u / σ_e	0.43 / 0.32	0.55 / 0.26	0.31 / 0.16

Note: The model is fit with xtreg in STATA, where the panel variable is "province" and time variable is "year." Policy fertility rate levels <1.3, 1.3~1.5, 1.5~2, and >=2 correspond to one-child policy dominated area, area mixed with one-child policy and 1.5-child policy (second birth allowed only for rural residents with their first birth being a girl), area mixed with 1.5-child policy and 2-children policy, and a two-child or lax policy area respectively.

make it possible to compare the significance of the socioeconomic and policy-related factors underlying the dynamics of TFR.

As shown in Table 2.2, the unconditional model parameters, σ_u and σ_e, give the variance components of TFRs between provinces and over time respectively. We see that the share of between-province variation (i.e., the intra-cluster correlation ρ) is substantial. Despite this, the variations of TFR both between province and over time decline as fertility transition progresses nationally (e.g., post-1990 as compared with pre-1990). This signifies that the fertility transition process is converging over time. As an increasing number of provinces move towards the end of transition, absolute fertility difference declines substantially across provinces.

The model coefficients for each covariate verify that both policy-related factors and socioeconomic covariates are highly relevant to the provincial fertility variation in the studied period. On average, the stricter a fertility policy is applied in any given province, the lower fertility rate it will achieve. By the same token, the higher economic development or urbanization level in a province, the lower fertility rate it will have. Similarly, the developments of population health and education in a province also show prohibitive impacts on its fertility.

Partly for the reason of declined variation in TFR in late transitional stage (i.e., the floor effect), impacts of both the policy-related and socioeconomic factors examined in this study decline after 1990 (with the exception to one variable "% of non-agriculture employees"), as telling from the estimated model parameters. The declining impacts of socioeconomic and policy-related forces suggest that the fertility transition process could be self-sustaining and diffusive. As Caldwell and Caldwell (2001) have demonstrated, once fertility transition is under way in a society (indicated by fertility rate declining by 10% or more), it will continue regardless of the economic, cultural, or political conditions until the transition is accomplished. The converging trends in provincial fertility changes and the declining role of the initial driving forces since 1990 give support to the conclusion that fertility transition is diffusive. This is evident in the society's changing attitudes towards traditional reproductive norms. Changing family reproductive attitudes and practices are central to the transition process and its diffusion, and they are themselves endogenous to the initial socioeconomic development status, ongoing developments and fertility policy (Gu, 1987).

3   Social Effects of Rapid Fertility Transition

3.1   *Changes in the Age Structure of the Population*

The provincial differences in the fertility transition progress have manifested in many demographic and social aspects. During the past few decades, the transitional differences across provinces have led to substantial variation in provincial age structures. Figure 2.3 presents the correlation between provincial implementation of fertility policies and the median age of population in 2000. On average, the lower a provincial policy fertility rate (in other words, the stricter the birth control policy) is in a province, the older the population will be. For example, the median age of the officially registered (with *hukou*) population of Shanghai was above 40 in 2000, and the median age of current residents (resided w/o a local *hukou*) in Shanghai was close to 40 as well. Although net in-migration of young people has alleviated the population aging process in Shanghai to some extent, more than half of its residents were above 37 in 2000.

Similarly, the median ages of the population officially registered in Beijing and Tianjin in 2000 were 36.8 and 36 respectively, although the median ages of the residents in those two cities were slightly younger, at 34.2 and 35, respectively. Other regions which started fertility transition earlier and have made rapid transitions, such as Liaoning, Jilin, Heilongjiang, Shandong, Jiangsu, Zhejiang, Sichuan, and Chongqing, all had a median age above 30 by 2000.

Compared with these earlier transitional areas, the provinces with moderate birth control policies started fertility transition later on average, and as a result they have much younger population age structures. For instance, the population median age was around 27 in provinces such as Hainan, Yunnan, Qinghai, Ningxia, Xinjiang, and Guizhou in 2000, while Tibet (not shown in Figure 2.3) had an even younger population age structure, with a median age of around 23 in 2000. It is noteworthy that Guangdong has a quite young age structure for its de facto residents, with the median age resting at around 27 in 2000. This is largely attributable to the great influx of young migrants and its relatively slow fertility transition during the past few decades.

3.2   *Changes to the Sex Ratio in Younger Generations*

Coinciding with the rapid fertility transition in many provinces of China, large amounts of data and empirical studies have revealed an outstandingly imbalanced sex ratio at birth, which has been increasing since the 1980s. This has aroused heated debate on the genuine relationship between fertility decline and the imbalanced sex ratio at birth (Editorial Board of Population Research, 2008; 2009; et al.). Figure 2.4 displays the provincial sex ratios of the population

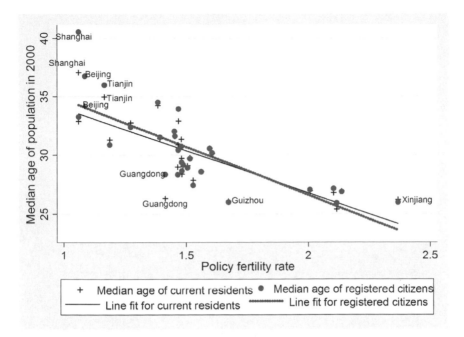

FIGURE 2.3 *Distribution of provinces classified by policy fertility rate and population median age in 2000*
DATA SOURCE: ORIGINAL MICRO-DATA FROM THE 2000 CENSUS.

aged 0 to 30 in 2005 by policy fertility rate.[2] Except for a few "outliers," the scatter plot seems to suggest an inverse U-shaped curvilinear relationship between policy fertility rate and sex ratio of the population aged 0–30 at the provincial level. For instance, the provinces having a policy fertility rate of around 1.5 (having applied a mixed birth control policy with one-child policy and two-children policy, e.g., 2nd birth is permitted for rural couples whose first birth is a girl) have a relatively higher population sex imbalance. In contrast, provinces applying either a strict one-child policy (e.g., Sichuan, Jiangsu, Shanghai, Tianjin) or a lax birth control policy (such as Qinghai, Ningxia, Xinjiang) have relatively lower sex ratios (100~105 in 2005).

There is no denying that regional culture bears great relevance to fertility behaviors and sex preference. Partly for the reason of traditional or regional reproductive norms, people in some provinces (such as Henan and Hainan) have a strong preference for sons and, as a result, are more likely to practice prenatal sex selection. As such, the population in these areas, especially

---

2   The population aged 0–30 in 2005 corresponds to the surviving population of birth cohorts after 1975 when migration effect is not considered.

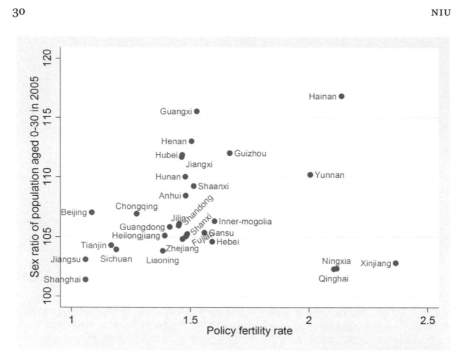

FIGURE 2.4 *Distribution of provinces classified by policy fertility rate and sex ratio of population aged 0–30 in 2005*

DATA SOURCE: DEPARTMENT OF POPULATION, SOCIAL SCIENCE, AND TECHNOLOGY STATISTICS, NATIONAL BUREAU OF STATISTICS OF CHINA, DATA COLLECTION OF 2005 CHINA 1% *POPULATION SAMPLE SURVEY-NATIONAL*, CHINA STATISTICS PRESS, 2007.

among newborns, has an abnormally higher sex ratio. In addition to the cultural and policy factors, migration (interprovincial or cross-board) can also affect the population sex ratio, the detailed impacts of which may be left for further studies.

3.3 *Changes in the Family Structure and Family Life Cycle*

China's rapid fertility transition has also induced great changes in the structure of families, the most significant of which is the emergence of vast numbers of only-child families. Figure 2.5 displays the proportion of only-child among those aged 0 to 30 in 2005, as classified by provincial fertility policies. Overall, the lower the policy fertility rate in a province, the higher the proportion of only-child (in the younger generations) will be. For instance, the share of only-child in age group 0–30 was close to 60% in Shanghai in 2005, and similarly, it is above 50% in Beijing, Tianjin, and Liaoning province. The provinces that initiated fertility transition earlier all have more than a third of the population aged 0–30 living in only-child families.

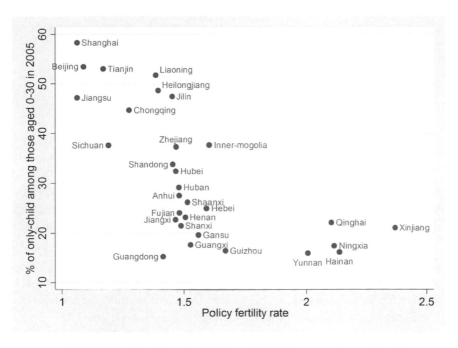

FIGURE 2.5 *Distribution of provinces classified by policy fertility rate and proportion of only-child individuals aged 0–30 in 2005*
DATA SOURCE: SEE FIGURE 2.4.

In addition to the great increase of only-child families, an increasing number of families experience empty-nest stage earlier. According to the 2000 census, the share of empty-nested families is higher in the provinces with stricter birth control policies. This is especially true for the middle-aged population (for instance, those with a head-of-household aged below 60). The proportion of empty-nested families in a province increases significantly as the policy fertility rate decreases. For instance, in the provinces applying a strict one-child policy, the proportion of empty-nested families for the household heads aged 40–44 was close to or above 10% in 2000, and the corresponding proportion was as high as 26% in Shanghai. In contrast, in the provinces applying a moderate birth control policy (mixed with one-child and two-children when the first is a girl in rural areas), the proportion is below 10%. The proportion is below 8% in the provinces with laxer birth control policy. For the families in which the head-of-household's age is between 50 and 54, the proportion of empty-nested families is close to or above 30% (40.7% in Chongqing) in the areas applying strict one-child policy, while it is below 13% in the areas applying lax fertility policies (where 2 or more children are allowed). The substantial variation in family structure and important family life events reflects the significance of rapid fertility transition in family and social life.

4   Conclusion & Discussion

All provinces in China have undergone rapid fertility transition since the 1960s and 1970s. Municipalities such as Shanghai and Beijing first accomplished their fertility transitions and achieved below replacement-level fertility by the mid-1970s. Following these pioneers, highly urbanized provinces and municipalities with early development accomplished their fertility transition no later than the mid-1980s. These areas form the second tier of accomplishing their fertility transition, and provinces such as Liaoning, Jilin, Heilongjiang, Jiangsu, Zhejiang, and Tianjin belong to this group. By the early 2000s, all provinces and municipalities in China were characterized with below replacement-level fertility. Those areas which accomplished fertility transition earlier have very low fertility rates now, and quite a few of them have rates below 1.3.

The trajectories of provincial fertility transition show that both socioeconomic and fertility-policy-related factors have been central to drive the decline in fertility. Yet, it is important to note that fertility transition is diffusive across regions. The transition of earlier transitional provinces and areas is instrumental to changing fertility norms and practices in late transitional areas, through mass media, population migration, or interregional cultural exchanges. As such, the decline in fertility rates has continued since the 1990s, even though the driving forces of socioeconomic and policy-related factors have declined. In many provinces, the fertility rate has continued to decline even after that province attained the official fertility rate.

The rapid fertility transition occurring during the past three to four decades has greatly benefited the socioeconomic development of China, but it has also brought about significant challenges to socio-demographic and family structures. This study examined the provincial disparities in changing population and family structures, which are directly related to the country's rapid fertility transition. In general, the provinces which experienced fertility transition earlier have quickly-aging populations. Due to rapid and early fertility transition, municipalities such as Shanghai and Beijing have the oldest population age structures, even though their increasing in-migration has alleviated the aging process to some extent. In addition to the rapidly-aging population, rapid fertility transition also induces a rising sex ratio imbalance at birth, especially in the regions with strong son-preference customs. The rising sex ratio imbalance at birth during the past two to three decades has had significant impacts on social harmony and the happiness of individuals and families. Moreover, with the rapid decline in fertility, family size has shrunk substantially in the younger generations, and only-child families have become prevalent in society. The empty-nest stage has become significantly prolonged for many families. The difference in fertility transition across provinces gives rise to the important disparities in the socio-demographic sphere. As a result, it is important to understand these disparities in order to respond to new sustainable demographic and socioeconomic challenges.

(This article was originally published in Chinese in 2012.)

References

Cai Yong. 2010. "China's Below-Replacement Fertility: Government Policy or Socioeconomic Development?" *Population and Development Review* 36(3): 419–440.

Caldwell, John C. and Pat Caldwell. 2001. "Regional Paths to Fertility transition." *Journal of Population Research* 18(2): 91–117.

Chen Jiajian, Robert D. Retherford, Minja Kim Choe, Xiru Li and Hongyan Cui. 2010. "Effects of Population Policy and Economic Reform on the Trend in Fertility in Guangdong Province, China, 1975–2005." *Population Studies* 46(1): 43–60.

Chen Wei. 2005. "The Development-Family Planning-Fertility Relationship in China: A Reexamination Using Provincial Level Data." *Population Research* 1: 2–10.

Coale, Ansley J., and Roy Treadway. "A Summary of the Changing Distribution of Overall Fertility, Marital Fertility, and the Proportion Married in the Provinces of Europe," in *The Decline of Fertility in Europe*, ed. Ansley J. Coale and Susan Cotts Watkins (Princeton, NJ: Princeton University Press, 1986): 31–181.

Department of Population, Social, Science and Technology Statistics, National Bureau of Statistics of China, *Data Collection of 2005 China 1% Population Sample Survey-National*, China Statistics Press, 2007.

Editorial Board of Population Research. 2008. "Fertility Practices and Implication in Two-Child-Policy Regions." *Population Research* 4: 33–49.

———. 2009. "Is fertility Policy Relevant to the Imbalance of Sex ratio at Birth." *Population Research* 3: 32–52.

Gu Baochang. 1987. "The Impact of Socioeconomic Development and Family Planning on the Decline of Fertility Rates in China." *Population Science of China* 2: 1–11.

Guo et al. 2003. "Diversity of China's Fertility Policy by Policy Fertility." *Population Research* 5: 1–10.

Li Jianmin. 2004. "Fertility Rationale, Fertility Decision-Making, and Transition of Mechanisms in Stabilizing Low Fertility in China." *Population Research* 6: 2–18.

National Bureau of Statistics of China, *County-level Statistics from China's 2000 Census.* Beijing: China Statistics Press, 2003.

National Bureau of Statistics of China, and the East-West Center, *Fertility Estimates for Provinces of China, 1975–2000.* Beijing: China Statistics Press, 2007.

Poston Jr., D.L. and Gu Baochang. 1987. "Socioeconomic Development, Family Planning, and Fertility in China." *Demography*, 24(4): 531–551.

Zheng Zhenzhen and Wu Yaowu. 2005. "Population Change and Its Impact on Education Development." *Peking University Education Review*, 2: 84–89, 107.

CHAPTER 3

Intergenerational Effects on Fertility and Intended Family Size: Implications for Future Fertility Change in China

Zheng Zhenzhen

1 Background

China's fertility rate has been below replacement level since the early 1990s, and China entered the list of low-fertility countries in the 21st century. The fertility transition of over three decades in China has been a result of the combined effect of family planning programs, birth policy, and socioeconomic development. While China's birth policy largely changed childbearing behavior nationwide, the sustained and rapid social development and economic growth since China's reform and opening-up (改革开放) facilitated the diffusion of new concepts of marriage and childbearing, and changed both macro- and micro-circumstances of family decision making regarding childbearing.

The demographic consequences of long-lasting low fertility will be advanced population aging, a reduction in population size after reaching a peak, and negative growth momentum. Due to the ever-decreasing number of women of reproductive age, the amount of newborns will further decrease. Given the shrinking number of women who are able to reproduce, the number of newborns would not increase easily even if there were a rebound in fertility. There is a lack of awareness of possible challenges brought about by the demographic situation. Although there have been quite a few researches into and discussion on fertility change in China in the last decade as well as on possible causes, different judgments and estimates still vary; some even believe that the low fertility rate will be difficult to maintain. A careful review and discussion of the historical trajectory of fertility rates in China would help in the evaluation of stable low fertility rates and their future trend.

Studies have found different intergenerational effects on childbearing preferences and behavior. For example, a regional study in Europe found that older generations' childbearing behavior has a strong influence on the fertility preferences of young people aged 20–39 (Testa and Grilli, 2006); another study found that individuals' childbearing preference is influenced by the childbearing behavior and preferences of family members. The mother's influence is

© KONINKLIJKE BRILL NV, LEIDEN, 2014 | DOI 10.1163/9789004273184_004

most significant, with the next most important influence coming from siblings (Axinn, Clarkberg, and Thornton, 1994), nevertheless, this influence may be altered by different events in one's life course (Régnier-Loilier, 2006). A study utilizing the Jiangsu Fertility Intention and Behavior Study (JFIBS) data found that parental preferences, if women are willing to seriously consider older generations' advice, can play a role in raising fertility intentions (Chen, et al., 2011).

This paper intends to analyze the intergenerational effect on fertility and intended family size in China from the macro- and micro-level, to infer fertility changes in China over the next decade, and to discuss the policy implication. Provincial fertility since 1975 will be used to analyze fertility level correlation of different time periods in different regions, and the JFIBS 2010 follow-up survey will be used to analyze intergenerational effects on fertility intentions at the individual level.

2   A Study on Provincial Fertility over Time

The national average fertility level in China has decreased since the 1970s, but with different paces in different regions. Three municipalities (Beijing, Shanghai, and Tianjin), three east coastal provinces (Jiangsu, Zhejiang, and Shandong), and three north-eastern provinces (Liaoning, Jilin, and Heilongjiang) were the first to drop to below-replacement level, followed by Sichuan and Inner-Mongolia. Provincial fertility converged in the 21st century, and variances continue to decline (Chen, 2011). The narrowed provincial gaps in fertility are largely due to the reductions in developmental differences among provinces. A multi-factor analysis on Provincial total fertility rates in 2000 found that, in addition to birth control policies, the GDP per capita and Human Development Index (HDI) are significant variables related to total fertility, and the effect of birth control policies is largely reduced after controlling for development variables (Chen, et al., 2009).

Assuming a generational interval of 25–30 years, a correlation test between two sets of fertility rates at two time points is able to represent the intergenerational relationship of provincial fertility. Figure 3.1 shows the relationship between 1975 and 2000 provincial fertility rates, using period parity progression total fertility rates estimated from 1990 and 2000 population census data by the National Bureau of Statistics of China and the East-West Center (2007). The two groups show a positive linear correlation, with a Pearson correlate of 0.78. The figure also shows that as a result of simple linear regression, the provincial fertility of 1975 explains 60% of the variation in 2000. Furthermore, the fertilities of almost all provinces were steadily decreasing during this period.

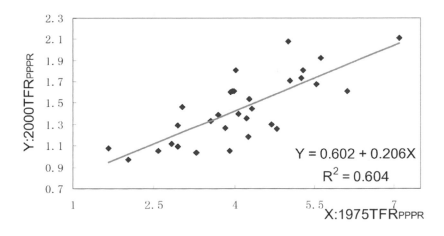

FIGURE 3.1 *Relationship between 1975 and 2000 provincial fertility levels*
SOURCE: NATIONAL BUREAU OF STATISTICS OF CHINA AND THE EAST-WEST CENTER
(2007).

Further using Provincial total fertility rates from 2005 one percent population survey of China, Figure 3.2 compares provincial fertility change in 1975–2005 (the total fertility in this figure is estimated from age-specific fertility). Hardly any of the provinces had a total fertility reach two in 2005, although the decline in fertility slowed down during the 1995 to 2005 time period. Most provincial fertilities continued to show a downward trend or remained stable, with the exception of some fluctuations for Hunan, Anhui, Shandong, and Hebei (an analysis of whether such changes should be considered fluctuations or an increase in fertility needs to wait for a longer period, such as include the provincial fertility rates from the 2010 census). The Pearson correlates between 2005 and two other time points are still quite high, 0.63 (for 1995) and 0.76 (for 1975) respectively. Although almost all provincial fertilities converge to below replacement level, there is still a clear correlated relationship.

3   Intergenerational Effects on Intended Family Size:
     A Case of Six Counties in Jiangsu

*An Introduction to Jiangsu Fertility Intention and Behavior Study
(JFIBS)*
In areas of early declines in fertility rates in China, the first generation born after significant fertility decline has reached the age of marriage and

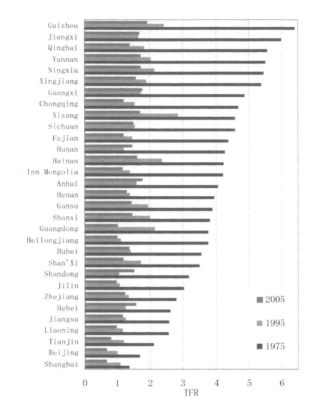

FIGURE 3.2 *Provincial fertility ranked by 1975 levels, 1975, 1995, and 2005*
SOURCE: SAME AS IN FIGURE 1 FOR YEARS OF 1975 AND 1995; FOR 2005: POPULATION
AND SOCIAL-SCIENCE-TECHNOLOGY DEPARTMENT. SUMMARY TABLES OF NATIONAL
1% POPULATION SAMPLING SURVEY, 2005. BEIJING, STATISTICS PRESS OF CHINA,
2007.

childbearing. It is possible to study the effect of parental influence on their attitudes towards childbearing and behaviors at the micro level. According to the Miller and Pasta (1995) framework of childbearing motivation and behavior pathways, childbearing motivation has both biological and experiential origins. Childbearing behavior and the opinion of parents are important factors in shaping and changing children's childbearing motivation. The Jiangsu Fertility Intention and Behavior Study (JFIBS) considered parental factors to be an essential component of the childbearing decision-making and reproductive behaviors of women, and designed related items in the survey questionnaire.

JFIBS is a collaborative longitudinal research designed to investigate childbearing desire, reproductive intention, and behavior. The first wave of data collection took place in early 2007 and the second in early 2010, in six selected counties along the east coast of Jiangsu Province, with two counties each representing different economic levels (south, middle, and north, with the northern part being the least developed among the three). The six counties differ in population dynamics and economic development, but they have converged towards current low fertility and share many similarities.

The JFIBS was proposed to address topics such as: (1) fertility desire, opinions, intention, and planning about childbearing among young couples, especially couples have more choice; (2) the relationship between birth policy and ideal family size, childbearing attitude and intention, and childbearing practice; and (3) the role of policy, cultural, social-economic, familial and individual factors in childbearing decisions. The study population covers women aged 18–40 and their household members in the six counties, utilized a two-stage cluster sampling design. In the first stage, a village in rural areas or a neighborhood in urban areas was used as the primary sampling unit. A weighted sampling scheme was used to randomly select 49 primary sampling units. In the second stage, an attempt was made to interview every woman age 18 to 40 in each of the selected units. Trained interviewers (mainly community staff) carried out face-to-face interviews using a standardized survey questionnaire. The 2007 baseline survey has a sample of 18,513 women and the follow-up in 2010 has 20,827 with 76% had the baseline survey (with a follow-up rate of 86%). Individual interviews were also used to collect information after each survey.

The survey asked questions about reproductive preferences and intentions, including a question on what the respondent's ideal family size would be in the absence of the one-child policy. To some respondents, these questions are hypothetical. To others, they are real, as some of the young respondents are eligible to have two children under the current policy. The survey also included questions aimed at collecting individual, household, and community data on economic changes, such as non-farming activities, migration, income, and the cost of children's education.

The baseline survey found that there is a considerable gap between ideal family size and reality regarding having one or two children. Although almost all women agreed that to have children is necessary for personal satisfaction and family happiness, a large majority also agree that "one is good enough." Among couples who are eligible under the current policy to have two children (about 1/3 of the surveyed sample), the majority said that they have voluntarily chosen to have only one child. About 10% already had two children; that proportion is less than 30% of women age 35–39. They cite economic considerations as the primary reasons for this choice (Zheng, et al., 2009). Individual interviews at survey sites found that although parents seldom interfered with the young couples' childbearing decisions, the presence of intergenerational

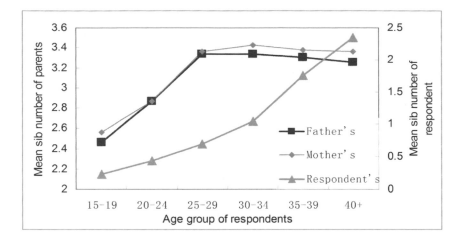

FIGURE 3.3 *Mean number of siblings of respondents and parents*
          SOURCE: JFIBS FOLLOW-UP SURVEY, 2010.

influence was still evident. A multi-level multivariate analysis revealed that the number of siblings the husband had, as well as the expectation of parents and in-laws to have both a son and daughter, was significantly related to the willingness of women to have a second child (Chen, et al., 2011).

The follow-up survey in 2010 found that ideal family size, intended family size, and actual childbearing plan are related to each other, but closer to reality gradually. Ideal family size is a ceiling which significantly larger than the intended family size, while the latter is more closely related to practice. The childbearing plan, which includes a clearly-set number of children and timing are much more likely to translate into reproductive behavior (Zheng, 2013).

Intergenerational Relationship of Number of Siblings
To further investigate parental influence, the 2010 follow-up survey collected information about the number of siblings of respondents' parents and parents-in-law, in additional to the number of siblings of respondents and their husbands. There are clear correlations between the number of siblings of the two generations, while a clear intergenerational gap is also observed (see Figure 3.3).

Note that for parents of women age 25 and above, the average number of siblings is about 3.4, but it drops to about 2.5 for the youngest age group, implying a significant change in childbearing behavior in the late 1960s and early 1970s. The decreasing in number of siblings by age of women shows the effect of family planning programs in the 1970s and 1980s. The average number of siblings is less than 1.5 among the respondents, and a large proportion of younger women have no siblings.

There are differences among six counties, with respondents having fewer siblings in the south and more siblings in the north. Differences were also observed between age groups of parents, as well as among age groups of respondents. The pattern of change in number of siblings is the same between the two generations, that is, the number of siblings decreases in younger age groups. The intergenerational association is observable for each county and among all age groups.

The Impact of Parents' Reproduction Behavior on Their Children's Intended Family Size

To reduce the confusion between ideal family size and intended family size, the follow-up survey questionnaire included two separate questions about ideal family size and personal preferred number of children: (1) What is considered as the ideal number of children for a general family, not considering the government's birth policy and other constraints? (2) How many children would you like to have? The first question emphasized "family" in general and "ideal" rather than reality; it measures common public opinion. The second question emphasized a more practical consideration, which is much closer to the "desire" of an individual or family. In this paper, "ideal number of children" is hereafter used for the first measurement, and "intended number of children" for the second measurement.

The survey results show that both the ideal and intended number of children of respondents is highly correlated to the number of siblings of her parents as well as to her own. Table 3.1 lists the average sibling size of family members and women's own grouped by women's ideal and intended number of children. Since very few respondents reported an ideal or intended number of children other than one or two, there are only two groups to compare. A t-test is used to exam whether the difference is statistically significant between the two groups.

Table 3.1 shows that women who reported an ideal of two children per family were statistically more likely to have parents with more siblings, and the number of siblings of those women were also significantly more. The results are similar for women's intended number of children, the difference is that only the mother-in-law's number of siblings is significantly related to it. It seems that the women's own parents play a relatively more important role in forming an opinion on childbearing; the influence of the mother-in-law

TABLE 3.1   *Ideal and intended number of children and average number of siblings*

Number of children \ Number of siblings		Father's	Mother's	Woman's	Father-in-law's	Mother-in-law's	Husband's
Ideal							
	1	3.31	3.39	1.26	3.61	3.73	1.37
	2	3.42***	3.51***	1.37***	3.66	3.82*	1.41*
Sample size		17,195	18,380	20,570	13,148	13,547	16,769
Intended							
	1	3.33	3.41	1.30	3.63	3.73	1.41
	2	3.46***	3.56***	1.37***	3.66	3.88***	1.38
Sample size		17,261	18,459	20,652	14,213	14,607	16,842

Note: *p*-value from *t*-test: *<.05, ** <.01, ***<.001.
Source: JFIBS follow-up survey, 2010.

and husband is relatively weak, and the role of father-in-law is insignificant. The same significant correlation can also be observed between the average number of siblings of parents and the intended family size of women at the county level.

According to the analytical results from the first and follow-up surveys, for women who are eligible to have two children by provincial birth regulation, the average ideal number of children is 1.7, the intended number of children is 1.5. On average, they give birth to 1.1 children, and the expected total number of children would be 1.3 if adding the number of children they plan to have (for details of the analysis, please refer to Zheng, 2011, or Zheng, 2013). From the summary above and results of Table 3.1, it is reasonable to expect that the total fertility of this generation would not exceed 1.5.

Regarding the motivation for having a second child, the JFIBS follow-up survey included the following options: one child is lonely, the couple wishes to have both a son and a daughter, necessary for satisfaction in family life, to lower the risk of elderly care, education of one child is difficult, remarriage, to satisfy parents, more children are easier to raise, to increase family labor, birth policy allows, contraception failure, or the first child is unhealthy or disabled. The most commonly selected responses concerned children's development:

52.4% selected "one child is lonely," followed by "birth policy allows" (51.8%), but still nearly 23% selected "to satisfy parents" as one of the major motivations for having a second child. However, among women who already had a child and were eligible to have a second one, only 5.3% of them believed that parents and in-laws have an "important role" in their second child decision, and 24.6% thought that they have "some influence." From interviews with women in the field, parental influence is often indirect or through supportive action, such as taking an active role in childcare responsibilities.

4   Summary

A better understanding of the intergenerational transfer of childbearing intention and behavior is helpful to understanding current demographic status and to make a knowledgeable judgment about future trends.

Evidence from the macro level shows an indisputable and stable low fertility trend, regardless of decades-long debates on actual total fertility. Years earlier, Li (2009) already concluded that fertility transition in China had already been completed, that childbearing behavior had experienced a revolutionary change over three decades, and that current low fertility rates are mainly constrained by the cost of having more children. Note that the observed intergenerational transfer of fertility is a one-way change, that is, it is always lower for the younger generations. The drop in fertility seems constant across regions, with the only difference being timing and pace of change. The areas that were first to achieve a decline in fertility rates to below replacement level are unable to further decrease their fertility rates, and also show no sign of increasing. The central and western provinces, which experienced a somewhat later decline in fertility, still have some leeway to further decrease their fertility rates through ongoing social-economic development and an increase in GDP per capita or improvement in the human development index.

Evidence from the micro level indicates that new concepts about childbearing have been exist across two generations in the areas of earliest fertility decline. Small families have become the norm among young people, and they no longer believe "more children, more happiness." Given their parents mostly had two children, it is unlikely that their own fertility rate would be higher. In a highly competitive society, the social policy and employment situation is not conducive to young people having both career and family, and as such, the fertility intentions of young people are more likely to be repressed than encouraged.

It is reasonable to expect that, if there is still an absence of family/childcare-supportive social policy and inadequate social welfare and public service, the total fertility in China would not exceed two even in the most developed cities in the future. On the other hand, certain areas still indicate the possibility of further decline in fertility, if the intergenerational effect we have observed in Jiangsu are applicable elsewhere. To conclude, there is little possibility for fertility rebound in the lowest low fertility areas, and the possibility for further fertility decline remains in other areas. For the national average fertility trend in China in the coming decade, it is possible to drop further. With regards to demographic trajectories and the current status of neighboring countries or regions, fertility in China probably has not yet declined to its lowest level.

(This article was originally published in Chinese in 2012.)

References

Axinn, William G., Marin E. Clarkberg, and Arland Thornton. 1994. "Family Influences on Family Size Preferences." *Demography*, 31(1): 65–79.

Chen Feinian, Yingchun Ji, Yong Cai, Zhenzhen Zheng. 2011. "Do Parents Matter?" *Intergenerational Ties and Fertility Preferences in a Low Fertility Context.* Paper presented at Population Annual Meeting of America, Washington D.C.

Chen Jiajian, Robert D. Retherford, Minja Kim Choe, Li Xiru and Hu Ying. 2009. "Province-level variation in the achievement of below-replacement fertility in China." *Asian Population Studies*, Vol. 5(3): 309–328.

Chen Youhua. 2010. From divergence to convergence: global fertility transition and implication to China. *Academia Bimestrie*, 1: 26–34. (in Chinese)

Li Jianmin. 2009. "Fertility Revolution in China." *Population Research*, 33(1): 1–9. (in Chinese)

Miller, W. and Pasta, D. 1995. "Behavioral Intentions: Which Ones Predict Fertility Behavior in Married Couples?" *Journal of Applied Social Psychology*, 25(6): 530–555.

National Bureau of Statistics of China and East-West Center of USA. "Fertility Estimates for Provinces of China: 1975~2000." Beijing, Statistics Press of China, 2007.

Régnier-Loilier, Arnaud. 2006. "Influence of Own Sibship Size on the Number of Children Desired at Various Times of Life: the Case of France." *Population-E*, 61(3): 165–194.

Testa, Maria Rita and Leonardo Grilli. 2006. "The Influence of Childbearing Regional Contexts on Ideal Family Size in Europe." *Population-E*, 61(1–2): 109–138.

Zheng Zhenzhen, et al. 2009. "Below-Replacement Fertility and Childbearing Intention in Jiangsu Province, China." *Asian Population Studies*, 5: 3, 329–347.

———. 2011. "Studies of Childbearing Intention and Implication." *Academia Bimestrie*, 2: 10–18. (in Chinese)

———. 2013. "The Choice of Having a Second Child and its Implication for Future Family Structure in China." In *Fertility Rates and Population Decline: no time for children?* edited by Buchanan and Rotkirch. Palgrave Macmillan.

CHAPTER 4

When Demographic Dividends Disappear: Growth Sustainability in China

Cai Fang and Zhao Wen

I   Introduction

Since the introduction of gradualist economic reform and opening-up (改革开放) in the late 1970s, as well as through its relentless efforts to join and operate within the World Trade Organization in 2001, China has increased both its participation in economic globalization and engagement in the market-based allocation of resources. The reformation of the Chinese economy has so far achieved considerable success, as it has fulfilled its original policy design, leading to significant improvements in economic growth and people's income level. In 2010, China replaced Japan as the world's second largest economy, with its per capita GDP hitting $4,300—according to the World Bank's estimate—and has become a middle-income economy.

As the country's economic growth achievement has been globally recognized, there have been many optimistic forecasts regarding future economic development. The IMF, for example, forecast that China's PPP-based GDP will hit $19 trillion in 2016, up from $11.2 trillion in 2011, accounting for 18 percent of global total GDP. Meanwhile, the US GDP will increase to $18.8 trillion from $15.2 trillion during the same period, but its proportion in the global economy will drop to 17.7 percent. Some economists are also optimistic toward China's per capita GDP growth. For example, Nobel laureate Robert Fogel forecasts that by 2040, China's GDP in terms of PPP will reach $123.7 trillion, accounting for 40 percent of the global total, and that with its population rising to 1.46 billion, its per capita GDP will amount to $85,000, 2.4 times the global average and 80 percent of the US level (Fogel, 2007).

China is now transitioning from a middle-income country to a high-income country. If it can maintain an average annual GDP growth of 8.8 percent—the rate over the past 32 years, when it adopted the reform and opening up policy—then, based on constant prices, in 2014, China's per capita GDP will exceed $6,000 and reach $12,000 in 2022. However, the crux of the issue is whether China will be able to maintain a steady growth rate in the coming decade or over a longer period of time. Recently, researchers have conducted a series of comparative studies targeted at China's predicted economic slow-down, discussing when, under what conditions, and how China's economic growth will slow down. For example, Wang et al. (2010) find that if history is any guide, the growth of an economy is set to decelerate after it experiences a high rate of expansion. The turning point that serves as the watershed comes when PPP-based per capita GDP reaches $7,000, according to their studies. Eichengreen et al. (2011) also find from international comparisons that, when a country's per capita GDP reaches $17,000 in 2005 US dollars, its high-rate growth normally encounters a slow-down. Based on the per capita GDP criterion used in these studies, China is undoubtedly coming closer to the point of a possible slowdown of economic growth.

The Chinese economy is facing two crucial turning points of development, which herald a fundamental change in its development phase. First, in 2004 along its coastal regions, labor shortages featuring a shortage of migrant farmers-turned workers, loomed large and will soon spread nationwide. In the meantime, the wages of ordinary workers have consistently risen, and there has been a recent trend toward convergence in the wages of skilled and unskilled workers. According to the dual economy theory, this phenomenon indicates that China is embracing the Lewis Turning Point, where unlimited labor supply is beginning to disappear (Lewis, 1972; Ranis and Fei, 1961; Minami, 2009). Secondly, according to various forecasts, in 2015, China's working-age population (those aged 15–64) will stop increasing and start to decline. Accordingly, the dependency ratio will then drop to its lowest point and rise again afterward. According to studies on the impact of the demographic dividend on economic growth in various countries (e.g. Williamson, 1997, Cai and Wang, 2005), this turnabout in the dependency ratio means the disappearance of the demographic dividend that has thus far contributed to economic growth. Therefore, the Chinese economy is losing one of its traditional sources of growth, and if it cannot shift to a new growth pattern, then it is set to suffer an economic slowdown. Worse, based on previous international experiences, such an unexpected economic slow-down could transform into long-term stagnation.

Following its passage through the Lewis Turning Point and with the loss of its demographic dividend nearing, China's economy is gradually stepping out of the dual economy pattern and assuming more and more neoclassical characteristics, i.e., given the constraint of the labor supply, the continued accumulation of physical capital will entail diminishing returns. If Total Factor Productivity (TFP) cannot be raised to compensate for this, then economic growth will no longer be sustained. Japan reached the Lewis Turning Point in the early 1960s (Minami, 1968), and its dependency ratio bottomed out by 1970 before starting to rise in the early 1990s, due to the population aging after two decades of standstill. During that period, the country's overall human resource bottleneck (Godo 2001) and insufficient protection of inefficient enterprises led to an underperforming TFP and the ensuing "lost two decades." For example, during the 1955–1975 period, when the dependency ratio was dropping to its lowest level, Japan's annual GDP growth was 9.2 percent on average; during the 1975–1990 period, when its dependency ratio remained low, its economic growth slowed to 3.8 percent; during the 1990–2010 period, when its dependency ratio rose rapidly, its economic growth only averaged 0.85 percent (UN, 2009; Hoshi and Kashyap, 2011; Aoki 2012).

In recent years, there have been heated debates as to whether China's demographic dividend has come to an end. However, some unusual phenomena have affected the quality of discussion. First, although there have been repeated voices denying that China has lost its demographic dividend, such opinions are seldom seen in formal academic papers; instead, such voices, expressed mainly in newspapers, the Internet, conferences, or media interviews, are often not backed up by solid arguments for further academic debates. Second, some participants in the discussion even deny the necessity of using the concept of demographic dividends, or simply call it a "pseudo hypothesis" (Liu, 2011). Therefore, the best way to respond to these opinions is further empirical studies and to provide more evidence for the declining role of demographic dividends. Moreover, it is also necessary to conduct further fundamental discussions as to why theory is necessary for understanding the phenomenon and its practical implications.

Economists generally hold that the value of theory lies in abstraction, i.e., summarization and abstraction of various phenomena, which are then put into a framework for standardizing the laws behind the phenomena. In other words, such abstraction is analogous to geographical theory and maps for grasping the world without personally traveling to every corner of the globe. Furthermore, economists are interested in using theory to forecast what has not yet happened. Therefore, the more applicable a theory is in making forecasts, the better it is (Friedman, 1953). A good theory relates a series of stylized facts or experiences in order to go beyond superficial and false appearances and grasp the essential trend or nature of things free from false conventional wisdom.

In this sense the concept of a demographic dividend is meaningful and valuable, i.e., it helps us to understand the nature of changes in the phase of economic development in China so that we can tell such changes are different from those of a structural, cyclical, or accidental kind. Since population dynamics are relatively slow and gradual, it is the most predictable factor among those affecting economic growth. Therefore, grasping the trend of change in population size and composition will help us to understand the challenges and opportunities facing a country's economic growth. In fact, when we judge that the demographic dividend is disappearing, our main concern is how to extend the role of the first demographic dividend to boosting economic growth and how to fully tap the benefits of the second demographic dividend in line with changes in population and economic development laws. What we are proposing is that the transition from a dual economy pattern to a neoclassical growth pattern rely more on TFP.

This paper, by estimating the production function to examine the contribution of demographic transition to China's economic growth, reveals the challenges posed by the disappearance of demographic dividends and puts forward policy suggestions regarding how to maintain and accelerate the growth of TFP to ensure the sustainable growth of the Chinese economy.

II   China's Demographic Transition and Economic Growth

So far, China's economic growth has followed a fairly typical Lewisian model of a dual economy. The formation of the dual economic structure is closely related to the specific phase of the demographic transition. Therefore, changes in the development process and phase of the dual economy are to be influenced by changes in the phase of demographic transition. During the reform and opening-up initiated in the early 1980s, China's high rate of economic growth has been accompanied by a rapid demographic transition, with the total fertility rate declining, which rendered China one of the countries with the lowest rates of fertility in the world (Figure 4.1). Thanks to the decline in fertility and, accordingly, the formation of a favorable population structure in terms of relative increases in the working-age population and lowered dependency ratio, surplus labor has moved from agriculture to non-agricultural sectors and from rural to urban areas to provide an unlimited labor supply for accelerating industrialization and urbanization. Thus, the Chinese economy, like other East Asian economies, was able to benefit from the rapidly-changing population structure (Williamson, 1997, Cai and Wang, 2005).

The significance of the demographic transition in contributing to economic growth manifests in various ways. First of all, the continual decline in the dependency ratio helps the national economy maintain a high rate of savings, which lays the foundation for capital formation that is crucial for high-rate economic growth. Second, the continual increase of the working-age population ensures an ample labor supply, and as the level of education of laborers improves, China is able to maintain a low-cost labor advantage as it

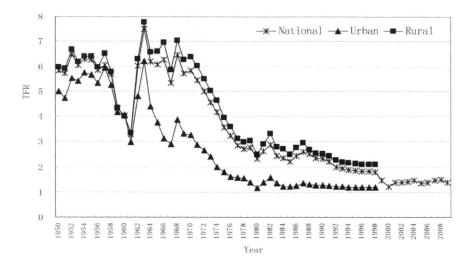

FIGURE 4.1 *Decline of total fertility rates in rural and urban China*
SOURCES: DATA ON TFR BY REGION BEFORE 1998 IS CALCULATED BASED ON THE
DATABASE OF THE CHINESE CENTER FOR POPULATION INFORMATION; DATA ON
NATIONAL TFR AFTER 1998 IS CALCULATED BASED ON VARIOUS POPULATION
SURVEYS OR CENSUSES.

participates in economic globalization. Third, rural areas have lagged behind
the urban areas in terms of demographic transition, and—as rural surplus
labor, accumulated in the planned economy period, moves out of the countryside after the country started the period of reform and opening-up—efficiency
of resource reallocation has improved, which is becoming the main source of
TFP (Cai and Wang, 1999). Fourth, other intangible changes in the population
yield demographic dividends, such as the fact that younger generations exhibit
more creativity, thus promoting technological progress. In fact, if the population dependency ratio is seen as a proxy variable of the demographic dividend,
then it can be interpreted as a contribution to further economic growth.

We may measure the contribution of the dependency ratio to economic
growth as a proxy for demographic dividends as follows. We start from the
Cobb-Douglas (CD) production function:

$$Y = AK^{\alpha} (LH)^{1-\alpha} \qquad \ldots\ldots\ldots\ldots (1)$$

where Y is output, K is capital stock, L is the number of employment, and H
refers to the labor force's (average) years of schooling. If we assume that labor
participation and employment are both 1, which means that all working-age
people are employed, then L can be expressed as function of dependency ratio:

$L = POP/(1 + DR)$, where POP refers to the total number of the population and DR denotes the dependency ratio. In reality, however, there is a difference between the size of the working-age population and the amount of employment. Taking into account the unemployment and labor participation rate, we convert the equation (1) into:

$$Y = AK^\alpha (POP \times H)^{1-\alpha} \left[\frac{1}{1 + DR}\right]^{1-\alpha} EP^{1-\alpha} \quad \dots\dots\dots\dots (2)$$

where EP refers to the labor participation ratio times the employment rate.

To estimate the output elasticity of capital α, we use data from 31 provinces, autonomous regions, and municipalities from 1982 to 2010: provincial GDP at 1952 price as Y, and total number of employed people in each province as L. H (years of schooling of laborers) is measured by the educational level of the employed (*China Population Statistics Yearbook* and *China Labor Statistics Yearbook* provide data on education attainments of those employed).[1]

K (capital stock) is calculated as the perpetual inventory stock. The capital depreciation rate is fixed at 9.6 percent, assuming that the average life of capital is 30 years, and the capital stock of the base year 1982 is assumed to be ten times the gross capital formation in 1952. Annual investment is represented by the gross fixed capital formation minus depreciation at constant prices, or inferred by using "Total Investment in Fixed Assets in the Whole Country" in the case of data unavailability in some provinces. We use "Price Index for Investment in Fixed Assets" to deflate capital stock data. In most cases, we use data from the *China Statistical Yearbook* and *Historical Statistical Materials for China's GDP Estimation*.

Using this data, we estimated the equation (2) and derived the output elasticity of capital α to be 0.638 (T test = 118.8 and R^2 = 0.94) while that of population, labor, and education is 0.362. Then, we can derive the relative contributions of different factors to GDP growth by multiplying their growth rates by relevant elasticity. The results are reported in Table 4.1.

During the entire period from 1982–2010, the relative contribution of capital to GDP growth is 73.7 percent, while that of labor is 7.1 percent, that of education is 4.2 percent, and TFP (residual) contributes to 15 percent of GDP growth. By breaking down the contribution of labor further, the relative contribution of the increase in population is 3.5 percent, and that of improvement in employment and of labor participation rates is 1.1 percent. The total

---

1   When data are lacking for some provinces, we made heuristic assumptions on comparative bases. The same applies to the investment price index introduced below.

TABLE 4.1   *Relative factor contributions to GDP growth by period (%)*

| | TFP | H | K | K through | | L through | | | Demographic Dividend |
				(1+DR)$_K$	L	POP	(1+DR)$_L$	EP	
1982–1990	21.7	5.6	60.7	6.1	12.0	5.5	3.4	3.0	9.5
1991–1996	23.4	2.4	69.9	1.4	4.3	3.2	0.8	0.3	2.2
1997–2003	3.3	7.0	88.4	5.6	1.3	3.1	3.2	−5.0	8.9
2004–2010	10.1	1.6	80.4	4.7	7.9	1.7	2.7	3.6	7.3
1982–2010	15.0	4.2	73.7	4.3	7.1	3.5	2.4	1.1	6.7

contribution of decline in the dependency rate identifiable as demographic dividend is 6.7%, which is broken down into those through capital and labor as shown in Table 4.2, using the respective elasticity of output.[2]

The demographic dividend was nearly 10 percent during the 1982–1990 period. During the 1991–1996 period, however, due to policies restraining the flow of key factors and resources, demographic dividends were not fully exploited in urban regions, manifesting in the fact that the contributions of labor, education, and the decline in dependency ratio were all smaller than during the preceding 1982–1990 period. Since the mid-1990s, migrant workers from rural areas flew into cities, injecting vitality into economic growth. Although the contribution of demographic dividends reached 8.9 percent during 1997–2003, the layoffs resulting from the state-owned enterprise reform at that time drove the contributions of the employment rate and labor participation ratio into the negative. During the 2004–2010 period, as the process of rural surplus labor moving to urban areas began to approach an end, we see the labor market maturing and the contribution of demographic dividend to economic growth decreasing while that of employment and labor participation increases.

The patterns in each factor's contribution to GDP growth over time are presented on an annual basis in Figure 4.2. To exhibit independent patterns free from short-term fluctuations, here we use one year's data to estimate the relative contributions for 1983, two years of data for 1984, and so on, culminating

---

2   This is done by taking into account the following relationship. Denoting y as a unit of labor output and k as the capital intensity of labor, we have:

$$Y = AK^\alpha \left[\frac{1}{1+DR} \right]^\alpha H^{1-\alpha} \left[\frac{1}{1+DR} \right] \times POP \times EP$$

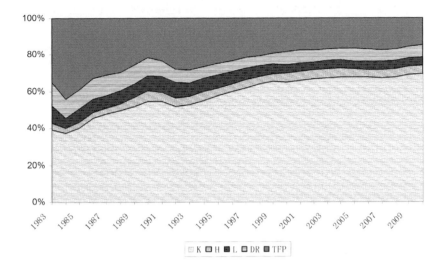

FIGURE 4.2 *Relative factor contributions to GDP growth over time*

in 28 years of data for 2010. The following patterns can be observed: (1) the relative contributions of capital dominate other factors and increase over time, (2) the relative contributions of labor and the demographic dividend decline as the population structure changes; (3) the relative contribution of human capital is comparatively small and stagnant, and (4) the relative contribution of TFP as the most important source of economic growth tends to decline over time. These general trends are consistent with Aoki's breakdown of contributions to per capita GDP into demographic factors, structural change due to domestic migration out of the agriculture sector, and change in labor productivity in the nonagricultural sector comprising the effect of the increasing capital-labor ratio and TFP to overall GDP.

III   Disappearance of the Demographic Dividend

The demographic transition has so far made contributions to China's high rate of economic growth and provided demographic dividends for the country. However, the country's low fertility rate, which has lasted for some time, has pushed China to face a new phase of demographic transition. As this demographic dividend is set to disappear, economic growth will be affected accordingly. The population dependency ratio, which is an indicator of demographic dividends, and various forecasts all point to a deceleration of the downward

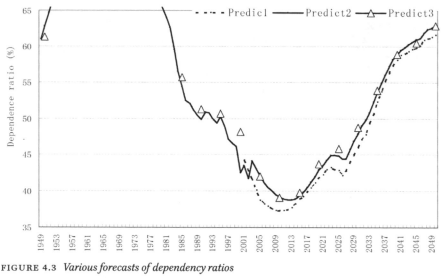

FIGURE 4.3 *Various forecasts of dependency ratios*
SOURCE: FORECAST 1 AND 2 ARE MADE BY HU YING AND WANG GUANGZHOU,
RESPECTIVELY, AT THE REQUEST OF THE AUTHORS; FORECAST 3 IS MADE BY THE
UNITED NATIONS (2009).

trend of past years, with the ratio dropping to its lowest point around 2013
(Figure 4.3). There are, however, arguments opposing such a conclusion.
According to those arguments, the ratio was already at a low level in the mid-
1990s and will remain below that level for another 20 years or so, thereby
continuing to benefit the Chinese economy. If the criteria can be further loos-
ened—for example, if we take the dependency ratio around 1999 as the one
that can produce the most demographic dividends—then China can benefit
from demographic dividends even after 2030 (Zhou, 2010).

Although there are various explanations of the demographic dividend that
have been quantified by using certain indicators, there is yet to be a clear
explanation so far as to what the nature of the demographic dividend is, or in
other words, why an increase in the working-age population can provide an
extra source of growth for the economy. However, one thing is certain, this is
not just a demographic issue, and should be tackled from the perspective of
economic growth theory.

The neoclassical growth theory assumes that with a fixed labor supply, the
continual accumulation of physical capital will diminish. There can be two
ways out of this. One is technological advancement, through which the continual improvement of TFP can sustain economic growth. The other is getting rid of the constraint of the labor shortage. The latter is just what the dual
economy inherently provides for. As far as an unlimited supply of labor can

be mobilized for productive uses, the demographic dividend will be realized. Thus, to understand the workings of the demographic dividend, it should be put within the framework of the dual economy development and related to the capital accumulation process. When elaborating on his dual economy theory, Arthur Lewis himself repeatedly emphasized that the utilization of an unlimited labor supply should be always understood together with capital accumulation. For example, in his *Economic Development with Unlimited Supplies of Labor*, he points out:

> *The key to the process is the use which is made of the capitalist surplus. In so far as this is reinvested in creating new capital, the capitalist sector expands, taking more people into capitalist employment out of the subsistence sector. The surplus is then larger still, capital formation is still greater, and so the process continues until the labor surplus disappears* (Lewis, 1954).

A key to understanding the mechanism by which the demographic dividend is brought about is to understand how the declining dependency ratio can offset the law of diminishing capital returns. From equation (2), marginal returns of capital can be written as:

$$MPK = A\alpha \left[\frac{K(1 + DR)}{(POP \times II)} \right]^{\alpha-1} \quad \ldots\ldots\ldots\ldots (3)$$

From equation (3), we can expect that as capital accumulates, the marginal product of capital tend to diminish, while population growth, improved educational levels, and decline in the dependency ratio offset the diminishing returns to capital. In particular, when capital output elasticity, capital stock, population, and education level are fixed, the decline in the dependency ratio will bring about an improvement in the marginal product of capital. Therefore, even if physical and human capital stocks are the same, different economies can have different economic growth rates depending on the difference in their dependency ratios. As indicated by Figure 4.4, during the period in which the dependency ratio declines, it can accelerate improvement in the marginal capital returns, but once the dependency ratio falls below a certain threshold point and bounces back (as is expected soon in China), then the marginal capital returns will drop.

Indeed, China has enjoyed a demographic dividend prior to the 2010–2015 period (Figure 4.3), or more precisely, during the period before the dependency ratio drops to 37–39 percent. Since the 2010–2015 period, the role of the changing population structure in preventing diminishing return to capital will

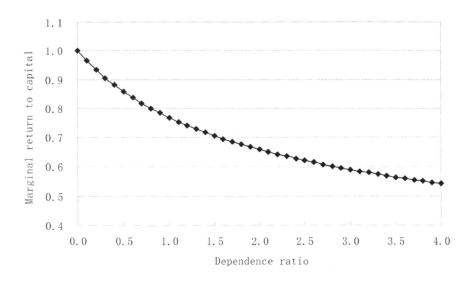

FIGURE 4.4 *Effect of the dependency ratio on marginal capital returns (theoretical)*
NOTE: WE ASSUME THE OUTPUT ELASTICITY OF CAPITAL (α) USED HERE IS 0.638.

quickly disappear. As indicated by Figure 4.5, the capital-labor ratio has risen rapidly in the last fifteen years, and there has been a clear trend of diminishing marginal returns to capital. In the figure, capital refers to capital stock at 1952's constant prices, and labor refers to the number of total employment. Marginal capital returns are calculated by average capital productivity multiplied by the output elasticity of capital. In the case of MPK (a variable), we take the share of capital income of GDP as the output elasticity of capital, and in the case of MPK (0.55) we take the constant ratio of 0.55 as the output elasticity of capital.

In order to examine more directly the effect of an unlimited supply of labor, consider the following functional form:

$$MPK = f(K, POP, DR, H, AG) \quad \ldots\ldots\ldots (4)$$

where AG refers to the share of agriculture in GDP. Before an economy reaches the Lewis Turning Point, the higher the ratio of the agricultural share to GDP, the higher the number of rural surplus laborers. Therefore, a relatively high ratio of this variable represents a relatively large number of available laborers and thus the effect of AG on MPK is negative. If we use the generalized least squares method to estimate the log-linear form of equation (4), then we can get the results indicated by Table 4.2.

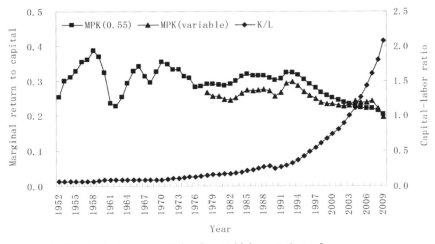

FIGURE 4.5 *Marginal return on capital and capital-labor ratio (actual)*
SOURCE: AUTHORS' CALCULATION.

TABLE 4.2 *Estimated results of equations on the marginal product of capital*

		C	LnK	LnPOP	LnDR	LnH	LnAG	R²
Equation (4)	Coefficient	−4.09	−0.474	0.351	−0.452	1.023	−0.341	0.926
	T test		−8.4	−26.7	5.5	−6.1	7.7	−8.65

The results are in line with our anticipations. The dependency ratio and capital stock are negatively correlated with MPK, while population and education are positively correlated with MPK, i.e., the greater the population, the more competent laborers are available and the higher the marginal capital output is. The share of agriculture in GDP (AG) also passes the test, indicating that given the existence of surplus labor, the law of capital's diminishing marginal product may be mitigated.

IV Policy Options for Sustainable Growth

What substantive impact will the disappearance of the demographic dividend on the Chinese economy be? Are there any methods to prevent the slow-down of growth? For economists across different periods, an enduring issue has been the exploration of decisive and sustainable sources of economic growth. While redundant labor can postpone the premature emergence of diminishing returns on capital, the demographic dividend is nevertheless limited in its duration and will ultimately disappear as the population's age structure changes. Ultimately, only an improvement in labor productivity will prove to be a sustainable source of economic growth.

In many cases, raising the capital-labor ratio could easily be taken as a way to improve labor productivity. In reality, this is reflected by the fact that as labor costs rise, enterprises buy more machines to replace labor. However, there is a limit to the improvement of the capital-labor ratio, and there would also be a limit to curbing the phenomenon of diminishing returns on capital in this way. That is to say, with labor skills and technological level unchanged, an excessive increase in the capital equipment ratio tends to reduce the efficiency of industrial production and coordination between workers and equipment.

The most fundamental way to improve labor productivity is to enhance TFP. Improvements in TFP can offset the adverse impact of the diminishing marginal product of capital within labor constraints and it can sustain economic growth in the long run. It can serve as a unfailing engine for economic growth. With the disappearance of the demographic dividend or labor surplus, it's necessary for further capital input to be technologically more advanced and for the quality of workers to be further improved; TFP growth also requires corresponding reforms in economic mechanisms and systems for the improvement of operational efficiency. On the other hand, those factors can play a role only if there is a competitive environment for enterprises and industrial restructuring continues.

It is very difficult for a country to make the transition from mainly relying on capital and labor inputs to an improvement in TFP to achieve economic growth. For an economy that has experienced demographic dividend gains, the prospect that the dependency ratio will stop declining means the disappearance of a demographic dividend. If the contribution of TFP to economic growth cannot compensate for that loss, then the economy will be set to slow down or even stagnate.

In recent years, factors that have driven improvements in China's labor productivity have significantly changed. According to an estimate by a World Bank economist (Kuijs, 2010), the relative contribution of TFP to labor productivity improvement dropped from 46.9 percent during the 1978–1994 period to 31.8 percent during the 2005–2009 period and is expected to further drop to 28.0 percent during the 2010–2015 period. Meanwhile, the improvements in labor productivity are primarily a result of the rising capital-labor ratio due to tremendous investment increases. In the above-mentioned three periods, the contribution of the capital-labor ratio to improvements in labor productivity rose from 45.3 percent to 64.7 percent and is expected to further rise to 65.9 percent. It indicates that from the supply side, heavy reliance on physical capital investment will not sustain economic growth in the long run. Moreover, the current investment growth in China is driven by government forces and features a high dependence on labor. It could easily go against the comparative advantage of China, and thus harm the allocative efficiency of resources. Therefore, it is highly essential to find a sound method of maintaining sustainable economic growth in the future.

TFP is composed of resource reallocation efficiency and technical efficiency. Resource reallocation efficiency is gained through industrial restructuring and upgrading. For example, labor and other factors moving from low-productivity sectors to high-productivity sectors is a typical form of resource reallocation. Additionally, the reallocation of resources can also be realized within a specific sector. It is mainly induced by the relative (not necessarily absolute) expansion of the highest-productivity enterprises. Studies show that a significant part of an improvement in TFP comes from such a reallocation process (for example, Foster et al., 2008).

As a part of China's rapid economic growth, resource reallocation among sectors has made a significant contribution. An early study finds that the transfer of rural surplus labor to non-agricultural sectors comprises about 22 percent of the country's economic growth (Cai and Wang, 1999. See also Aoki 2012). There have been recent signs of change on this front: the number of migrant rural workers who work outside their home township for over 6 months increased at an annual rate of 6.0 percent during the 2002–2006 period, while it only increased at 3.7 percent annually during the 2006–2010 period, even though the policy climate for rural immigration improves and the wage rate continues to increase significantly.

Ostensibly, the emergence of a migrant rural worker shortage and the rapid rise in wages of non-skilled workers may appear to herald an end of China's comparative advantage in labor-intensive sectors. However, such a conclusion is short-sighted. Because there is always room for the outbound transfer of rural labor until the marginal productivity of agricultural and non-agricultural labor are equalized, i.e., when the commercial point is reached (Ranis and Fei, 1961), the resource reallocation can therefore continue to drive economic growth. To that end, it is of high importance to reform the *hukou* household registration system to further eliminate the institutional obstacles blocking the flow of labor.

The technical efficiency of TFP can generally be achieved through economic system reform, improvements in incentive mechanisms, managerial innovation, and technological innovation. What the government can do is not to make concrete decisions for enterprises regarding what fields in which to invest, but to create an appropriate policy environment so that the most efficient enterprises can survive and develop while those that are not efficient enough will shrink and exit. To this end, what could and should governments do?

First, the government should be willing to have those inefficient enterprises that are unable to follow an efficient growth path eliminated from the market. The Chinese government, especially local governments, have long played the role of the developmental state and taken pains to help enterprises survive market competition. Therefore, when enterprises encounter difficulties, the governments—taking into consideration either emotional bonds or their potential contribution to GDP, taxation, and employment—are often reluctant to let them go. However, it is a necessary price to pay for some enterprises to go bankrupt during the transition of the economic development phase and industrial restructuring so that the overall efficiency can be improved.

Secondly, the function of the governments lies in strengthening human capital accumulation and accelerating the social security system so that laborers can gain skills that cater to the requirement of industrial structure upgrading and have an access to a social security network if they suffer from labor market shocks. After the Lewis Turning Point is reached, there remains the phenomenon of a non-skilled labor shortage, with non-skilled laborers facing a golden era in which job opportunities increase and wage rises rapidly. However, such a golden period will not last long. If at this time, an incentive mechanism that is unfavorable to human capital formation comes into play on the labor market—for example, if more jobs and ever-rising wages are so attractive that young students opt for dropping out of schooling and entering the job market prematurely—then this generation of laborers are set to encounter shocks in the future as a result of further industrial upgrading.

Third, a social security network that can effectively protect laborers temporarily squeezed out of the market should be a systemic guarantee for creative destruction to be effective. The purpose of creative destruction is not just to destruct, nor to ignore the needs of vulnerable groups on the labor market, but to improve the overall health of the economy through restructuring. Therefore, the time is ripe for China to improve its social security regime and expand social protection to cover areas such as education assistance, medical assistance, and to support disadvantaged families.

Last but not least, the government should properly handle macroeconomic policies to create an environment that allows for creative destruction. Overly-restrictive macroeconomic policies are no good for new enterprises that are building their competitiveness upon innovation, nor for those dynamic small- and medium-sized enterprises that are eager to get loans. It is equally unfavorable for the Chinese economy to adopt overly-loose macroeconomic policies, since it will be easy for those inefficient enterprises to survive and cause misallocated investments. Mishandling of macroeconomic policies, on either end of the spectrum, makes it difficult for the creative destruction mechanism to play its screening role. In essence, prudent and proper macroeconomic policies provide the best environment for the market to carry out the principle of "survival of the fittest."

(This article was originally published in Chinese in 2012.)

References

Aoki, M. 2012. "The Five-Phases of Economic Development and Institutional Evolution in China, Japan, and Korea." Chapter 1 of Volume I: M. Aoki et al., eds. Houndmills: Palgrave and Macmillan.

Cai, F. and D. Wang. 1999. "China's Economic Growth Sustainability and Labor Contribution." *Economic Research Journal*, issue X: 62–68.

———. 2005. "China's Demographic Transition: Implications for Growth" in *The China Boom and Its Discontents*, Garnaut and Song, eds. Canberra: Asia Pacific Press, 34–52.

Eichengreen, B., D. Park, and K. Shin. 2011. "When Fast-Growing Economies Slow Down: International Evidence and Implications for China," *NBER Working Paper* No. 16919, Cambridge, Mass: NBER.

Fogel, R.W. 2007. "Capitalism and Democracy in 2040: Forecasts and Speculations." *NBER Working Paper*, No. 13184, Cambridge, Mass: NBER.

Foster, L., J. Haltiwanger, and C. Syverson. 2008. "Reallocation, Firm Turnover, and Efficiency: Selection on Productivity or Profitability?" *American Economic Review*, 98: 394–425.

Friedman, M. 1953. "The Methodology of Positive Economics," in *Essays in Positive Economics*. Chicago: University of Chicago Press, 3–43.

Godo, Y. 2001. "Estimation of Average Years of Schooling by Levels of Education for Japan and the United States, 1890–1990," memo. Tokyo: Meiji Gakuin University.

Hayashi, F. and E.C. Prescott. 2002. "The 1990s in Japan: A Lost Decade." *Review of Economic Dynamics*, 5: 206–35.

Kuijs, L. 2010. "China through 2020—A Macroeconomic Scenario." *World Bank China Research Working Paper* No. 9. Washington, DC: World Bank.

Lewis, A. 1954. "Economic Development with Unlimited Supply of Labor." *The Manchester School*, 22: 139–191.

———. 1972. "Reflections on Unlimited Labour Supply," in L. Di Marco, ed., *International Economics and Development* (New York: Academic Press), 75–96.

Liu, F. 2011. "The Demographic Dividend is a Pseudo Hypothesis." *China Human Resources Development*, VI: 5–7.

Minami, R., and X. Ma. 2009. "The Turning Point of the Chinese Economy: Compared with Japanese Experience." *Asian Economics*, 50: 2–20 (in Japanese).

Minami, R. 1968. "The Turning Point in the Japanese Economy." *The Quarterly Journal of Economics*, 82: 380–402.

Ranis, G. and J.C.H. Fei. 1961. "A Theory of Economic Development." *The American Economic Review*, 51: 533–565.

Hoshi, T., and A. Kashyap. 2011. "Why did Japan stop growing?" *National Institute for Research Advancement (NIRA) Working Paper*. Cited October 2011. http://www.nira .or.jp/pdf/1002english_report.pdf.

Wang, Q., S. Zhang, and E. Ho. 2010. "The Chinese Economy through 2020." *The China Files*, Morgan Stanley Research, Asia/Pacific.

Williamson, J. 1997. "Growth, Distribution, and Demography: Some Lessons from History." *NBER Working Paper*, No. 6244. Cambridge, Mass: NBER.

Zhou, T. 2010. "China's Dependency Ratio will Reach a Turning Point in 2013, with still another 25 Years of Demographic Dividends." http://news.xinhuanet.com/ politics/2010-05/18/c_12115988.htm.

CHAPTER 5

Accumulating Human Capital for China's Sustainable Growth

Cai Fang and Wang Meiyan

After China has passed the Lewisian turning point and gradually loses its demographic dividend, not only will the traditional factors promoting economic growth need to be recomposed, but those long-term input factors that do not produce diminishing returns will also become more important. This places new requirements on improving the overall quality of China's human capital. At the same time, this particular stage of economic development transformation will form incentives that are not conducive to the accumulation of human capital because of strong demand for low-skilled labor in the labor market in the near term. If we cannot respond to this effectively, China will face a problem of unsustainable accumulation of human capital. Namely, in the near future, this will be exhibited in a quality of labor that does not fit the industrial demands of an improved value chain, a lack of high-end talent required to support an innovative nation, as well as a portion of the labor force becoming a vulnerable group in the market.

China is bound to pass through the upgrading of the industrial structure, which is something developed countries have experienced. Thus, it would be worthwhile for China to draw lessons from developed countries regarding the accumulation of human capital. This article discusses the transformation of the economic growth model, particularly the demands that the upgrading of the industrial structure places on labor skills. It explores how to learn from the international experience, avoid negative incentives caused by declining educational returns, and create new sources of human capital through the appropriate role of education at all levels.

1   Industrial Upgrading and Skills Requirements

Following the general laws of economic development, after passing the Lewisian turning point and the disappearance of the first demographic dividend, China will inevitably undergo industrial restructuring and the rapid upgrading of the technological structure. A series of changes accelerating the transformation of the methods of economic development will ultimately be exhibited in the upgrading and optimization of the industrial structure, demanding the furtwher upgrading of product quality and added value. Although the core of industrial upgrading is total factor productivity increasingly becoming the main source of economic growth, the process and results of upgrading will inevitably be reflected in a shift from labor-intensive industry to capital- and technology-intensive industry, mainly from manufacturing to service. Since the purpose of industrial upgrading is to increase labor productivity, particularly total factor productivity, so the direction of evolution reflects a higher demand for human capital of workers.

First, China's manufacturing industry itself will climb toward the higher end of the value chain. This process may first start in coastal developed regions, ultimately extending to central and western regions until a comprehensive upgrade of industry is achieved. Although the Chinese manufacturing industry is already the world's largest, the added value of the manufacturing industry is only 26%. This value is 23 percentage points lower than the United States, 22 lower than Japan, and 11 lower than Japan. In terms of the intermediate input contribution coefficient, in developed countries, the new value created by one unit value of intermediate input is generally one unit or more. But China only produces 0.56 units of new value (Ouyang Junshan, 2011). The position of a country's industry in the value chain is decided by a number of factors, including technology, management, and skills, which are ultimately closely correlated with the human capital of workers. Thus, a prerequisite for industrial upgrading is skills upgrading.

Second, China's industrial upgrading is also reflected in a move from the manufacturing sector to segments before and after the direct production process, including research and development, innovation, and marketing, leading to a substantial increase in the proportion of producer services. Because these sectors require the input of knowledge-intensive factors like information, technology, branding, management, and talent, they place higher requirements on the skills and creativity of workers.

By observing the educational level of workers in different industries, we can see the lowest human capital requirements of the reallocation among industries, as well as the alternation of labor-intensive, capital-intensive, and technology-intensive industry in the secondary and tertiary industries. In Table 5.1, in secondary industry, the labor force in capital-intensive industry has a higher level of educational achievement than labor in labor-intensive industry. In the tertiary industry, the labor force in technology-intensive industry has a higher level of educational achievement than labor in labor-intensive industry. The labor force in labor-intensive industries in the secondary industry has the lowest level of educational achievement. The labor force in

TABLE 5.1   *Composition of urban educational achievement by industry*

	Secondary Industry		Tertiary Industry	
	Labor-intensive	Capital-intensive	Labor-intensive	Technology-intensive
Education (%)				
Primary and below	17.1	9.4	15.6	1.7
Junior middle	63.7	46.9	50.2	11.9
High school	16.4	30.3	26.4	29.0
Three-year college and above	2.9	13.4	7.9	57.4
Average years of education	9.1	10.4	9.6	13.3

Source: Calculated based on a 20% microdata sample of the 2005 1-percent Population Survey.

technology-intensive industries in the tertiary industry has the highest level of educational achievement.

From this information one can see that a laborer wanting to move from labor-intensive employment in the secondary industry to capital-intensive employment in the secondary industry would need to increase his educational achievement by 1.3 years. Moving to technology-intensive employment in the tertiary industry would require 4.2 more years of education. Only moving to labor-intensive employment in the tertiary industry would require 0.5 more years of education.

The educational requirements this industrial conversion places on workers are not insignificant, because raising the level of education requires long-term accumulation and cannot be done overnight. For example, based on the census and 1-percent Population Survey, even with the increasing penetration of compulsory education and expanded recruitment for higher education, from 1990 to 2000, the average education of those over 16 years of age only increased from 6.24 years to 7.56 years, a total increase of only 1.32 years. By 2005, this had increased to 7.88 years, growth of only 0.32 years over five years.

2   Human Capital for the Future

The Human Development Index (HDI) led by the United Nations Development Program (UNDP) is an indicator reflecting the overall level of economic and social development based on per capita GDP, health levels (expressed by life expectancy), and educational levels (expressed by adult literacy and total

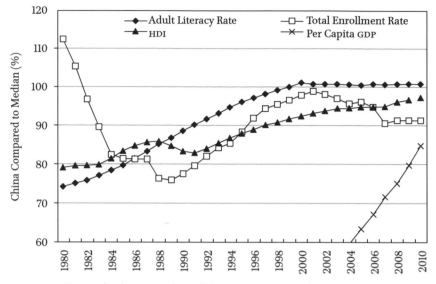

FIGURE 5.1 *Human development index and the relative increases of its components*
SOURCE: UNITED NATIONS DEVELOPMENT PLANNING OFFICE WEBSITE, HTTP://
WWW.BETA.UNDP.ORG/CONTENT/UNDP/EN/HOME.HTML.

enrollment in the three levels of education) calculated based on purchasing power parity. In Figure 5.1, we use China's level as a percentage of the median of 135 countries for this indicator, showing the relationship between educational development and per capita income growth and increases to the HDI. In the two decades since the 1990s, the HDI has increased steadily. In the first decade, the contribution of educational development to the level of human development was significant. But in the second decade, the contribution of educational development fell, while per capita GDP rose, undoubtedly making a prominent contribution to the HDI.

At the same time, the rising educational level of workers has been displayed in the human capital input variable in the economic growth process, becoming a positive contribution factor to rapid economic growth during reform and opening. The majority of the various studies using growth accounts or the production function to analyze the various factors contributing to China's economic growth use years of education as an explanatory variable, obtaining statistically significant results that are consistent with expectations. However, because the studies employ different methods, there are large variations in the contribution rate of human capital to economic growth.

For example, Gao Luyi uses potential growth and its elements and concludes that of growth sources including total factor productivity, the human capital-labor ratio, the capital-labor ratio, and employment growth, the contribution of human capital (the human capital-labor ratio) as 5.2% between 1978 and 1994 and 3.2% between 1995 and 2009 (Kuijs, 2010). This contribution is similar to that calculated by Cai Fang and Zhao Wen using the production function, that is, of factors including capital inputs, labor inputs, laborer years of education, the population dependency ratio, and total factor productivity, from 1982 to 2009, the contribution rate of human capital (years of education) was 4.3% (Cai and Zhao, 2012).

The human capital contribution rate calculated by John Worley et al. is much higher. From 1978 to 2008, using the neoclassical growth accounting method, among numerous factors including physical capital stock, the labor force, the human capital stock measured by years of education, and the total factor productivity rate, the contribution rate of human capital was 11.7%. And considering the different productivity of different levels of education, they estimated that the contribution rate of human capital is 38% (Whalley and Zhao, 2010).

The significant contribution of human capital to economic growth undoubtedly requires the development of education and the effective allocation of human capital as prerequisites. Thus, when there is a problem with the accumulation of human capital or its allocation, its ability to drive sustained economic growth is out of the question. Although years of education cannot perfectly express the human capital of laborers, it is still a quantitative indicator that is fairly easy to calculate, measure, and obtain.

So, how can years of education be increased? In the lower stages of economic and social development, universal basic education undoubtedly has the most obvious effect. But once compulsory education is implemented, universality approaches 100%, and continuing to increase the years of education must be achieved by popularizing higher education. According to statistics from the Ministry of Education (Ministry of Education, 2010), the 2009 gross enrollment rate was 105% for primary school, 99% for junior high school, 79% for high school, and 24% for higher education. From this, one can see that the effective path to increasing years of education in the future on the one hand will rely on consolidating the high enrollment rate of compulsory education and on the other hand on substantially increasing high school and university enrollment rates.

China is fixated on catching up to the educational level of developed countries and has made great achievements, especially in the popularization of compulsory education and higher education. However, in recent years, many factors unfavorable to the sustainable development of education have emerged, not only including traditional supply-side constraints, but also demand-side constraints, as well as some misleading factors of knowledge. Let us first look at misconceptions unfavorable to using the development of higher education to increase years of education in society and training productive and innovative professionals.

With the prominence of youth employment difficulties, represented by college graduates, as well as the decline in quality of higher education, some have begun to express doubt about expanding enrollment in higher education. Some have even called for putting a halt to expanding enrollment. We agree with any warnings about the declining quality of higher education but reject any policy implications for giving up because of these obstacles. In this respect, the lessons of Japanese education are worth thinking about and learning from.

Throughout the process of rapid economic growth in Japan, the country made great achievements in catching up to developed countries. For example, calculated based on per capita years of education for the working-age population, Japan's level compared to America's was 19.7% in 1890, increasing to 71.2% in 1947, 80% in 1966, and 84.8% in 1990 (Godo, 2001). But Japan's educational catch-up with the US slowed markedly after the mid-1970s. However, research into changes to the educational gap between Japan and the US at different levels of education is not without benefit to China. We will now examine the changes to the gap in years of education between Japan and the US at the various levels of education period from 1947 to 1990 (Figure 5.2).

After the 1950s, the pace of Japan's educational catch-up began to waver. In fact, due to fears of a declining quality of higher education, the Japanese Ministry of Education also intended to stop the expansion of higher education. After the mid-1970s, while Japan continued to narrow the gap with the US in primary and secondary education, the gap continued to widen in higher education. In terms of per capita years of higher education of the working age population, Japan fell from 45.3% in 1976 to 40.4% in 1990 compared to the US, returning to the 1965 level.

These different manifestations in different stages of education not only reduced the proportion of high-level talent among Japanese workers but also meant that Japan could not further close the gap with the US in terms of overall years of education in the workforce. In fact, when discussing the slowing Japanese economy after the mid-1970s and economic stagnation after 1990, the question we pose is: why did Japan not maintain modest economic growth on the forefront of technological innovation like the US and Europe? Obviously, slow development of education was a very important factor.

That Japanese education was unable to catch up to that of the US is related both to the economic model that relied on rapid growth, as well as the inability to achieve a transformation in the economic growth model after reaching

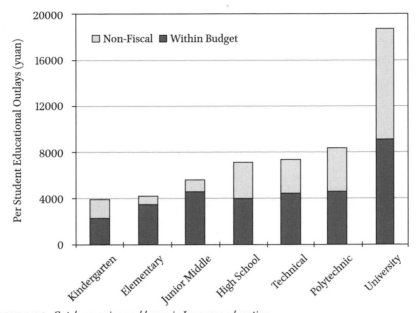

FIGURE 5.2 *Catch-up gains and losses in Japanese education*
NOTE: PRIMARY EDUCATION IN THIS FIGURE REFERS TO GRADES ONE THROUGH
EIGHT, SECONDARY EDUCATION REFERS TO GRADES NINE THROUGH TWELVE, AND
HIGHER EDUCATION REFERS TO THE EDUCATIONAL STAGE AFTER GRADE TWELVE.
SOURCE: GODO (2001).

the Lewisian turning point. In catching up with the US economy, Japan mostly relied on borrowing from and imitating European and US manufacturing technologies. Thus, secondary education among the large, young labor force met the demands of economic growth and indeed had a positive and significant effect. In a particular stage of development, namely the dual economic development period of ample labor and continued movement from agricultural to non-agricultural industry, this sort of economic development model fully utilizes the advantages of being a latecomer to economic development and is an effective development strategy.

The Japanese economy reached the Lewisian turning point around 1960, and subsequent economic growth increasingly relied on improving labor productivity. Starting in the 1960s, Japan invested in increasing the proportion of heavy industry in its economy, leading to a significant increase in the overall capital-labor ratio. At the same time, because Japan could not make constant breakthroughs on the forefront of technological innovation like Europe and the US, the country inevitably encountered diminishing returns on capital, stagnating growth in total factor productivity, and a decreasing contribution to economic growth. Thus, Japan failed to achieve a transformation of the economic growth model, and the country fell into a "lost decade" after 1990. Mistakes in the development of education are not without blame, and provide many lessons to be learned.

3   Educational Incentives in the Labor Market

In addition to estimating the contribution of human capital to economic growth on a macro level, economists have done a lot of research into the private rate of return on human capital on a micro level. Some studies have focused on the significance of increases to educational levels, in particular increasing high school and university enrollment rates, especially gains for individual workers and employment units. These studies undoubtedly have real relevance to the problems facing China.

One study focused on educational returns for households and individuals (Wang Meiyan, 2009). If starting from the current years of education in the rural workforce, that is, 9.4 per capita years of education for the urban workforce and 6.8 years for the rural workforce, and increasing this to 12 years, that is, completing high school, gains from urban labor force education could increase 17%, and the rate of return from rural labor force education could increase 21.1%. If years of education were further increased to 14 years, that is, adding two years of higher education, the returns from education from the urban labor force would increase 41.2%, and returns from the rural labor force would increase 43.3%.

Another study was aimed at the rate of return on education at businesses (Qu Wan, 2009). Simulations show that for every year added to the years of education, labor productivity will increase by 17%. Converting years of education to graduation from formal schooling, if a company's employees, all of whom have a primary school education and below, all graduate to a high school education, the company's labor productivity will increase 24%. If employee education is further improved to a three-year college degree, the company's labor productivity will increase a further 66%.With the development of the labor market, the market mechanism has played a more and more important role in the allocation of labor resources. Therefore, the higher requirements that economic growth places on human capital and the private and societal returns on human capital overall will be expressed as a labor market signal leading businesses, individuals, and households to invest in human capital. However, like other market sectors, market failures related to returns on capital will appear in the allocation of laborresources.

The sign of the arrival of the Lewisian turning point is widespread shortage of unskilled labor and increases in the wages of common workers. Corresponding to this is a trend toward uniformity in the wages of skilled and unskilled labor manifested in shrinking income gaps between university graduates and common workers and among common laborers of different levels of educational attainment. This phenomenon is by its nature a relative decline in the return on human capital. Estimates on the relative educational gains of migrant workers show that from 2001 to 2010, the educational yields of migrant workers with high school educations and above fell from 80.4% to 57.1% compared to those with junior middle school educations. The relative educational yields of migrant workers with high school educations fell from 25.9% to only 16.9% compared to junior middle school graduates (Cai Fang, Du Yang, 2011).

From 2001 to 2010, the relative educational yields of migrant workers with high school educations and above fell from 80.4% to 57.1%. The extent of the decline far exceeded the decline in the rate of return on junior middle school in the same period (from 25.9% to 16.9%). Correspondingly, the relative educational yields of migrant workers with high school educations fell from 25.9% in 2001 compared to junior middle school graduates to 16.9% in 2010 (Cai and Du, 2011).

Converting the findings of these econometrics into directly observed phenomena in real life would mean that families do not want their children to continue schooling. In particular, aspirations for attending high school and higher education are falling, to the point where students drop out of junior middle school in the compulsory education stage. Especially in poor, rural households, increasing migrant worker wages have significantly increased the opportunity cost of completing compulsory education, leading to more dropouts. A survey in poor rural areas found that in the year from September 2009 to October 2010, the dropout rate was 5.1% for first grade, 9% for second grade, and around 10% for third grade, making the total junior middle schooldropout rate as high as 25% (Zhang Linxiu, et al., 2011). With free, compulsory education like this, the opportunity cost and direct costs of the expensive high school state is even more unattractive to rural households.

This article has demonstrated, through the case of Japan, that the slowing development of higher education, or even stagnation, poses a threat to the sustainability of future economic growth. Here, we might as well look at the example of the US and what labor market result would occur if the next generation of laborers do not complete high school education or even do not complete compulsory education. Let us start with the current jobless or even the job-losing recovery. After the economic recession of 1991 and the financial crisis of 2008, there was a phenomenon where jobs did not return with economic recovery. There are many explanations for the jobless recovery, of which the decline of the US real economy is one. However, the inability of the skills of workers to adapt to changes in the industrial structure is another important reason.

In the accelerated development of the knowledge economy, computers have replaced some jobs requiring mid-level skills. The US labor market has exhibited a trend of polarization, namely that high-skill jobs and low-end, unskilled jobs are growing quickly, while mid-level jobs are decreasing relatively (Autor et al., 2006). The concurrent economic globalization, that is, the reallocation of jobs on a global scope, has not caused low-end employees and high-end employees to profit to the same extent. In fact, globalization will harm the latter (Samuelson, 2004). And these harmed workers employed in low-skill jobs are immigrants with low levels of education or those who "directly entered the middle class from middle school." In short, American workers at this level do not have human capital adapted to the requirements produced by structural upgrading. Consequently, within fluctuations in the economic cycle, they not only face the employment effects brought on by recession, but will endure a more long-term, jobless recovery.

The polarization of the US labor market and thus the widening income gap and employment vulnerability are to a certain extent a result of the failures of human capital policies in the US. For some time, the US has been a world leader in the development of education and the target model of late-developing countries attempting to catch up. Today, although the US still has the world's highest level of university education, many young people do not attend university, and even the high-school enrollment rate is falling significantly, causing a drop in the overall level of human capital. For example, the average years of education of the US population 25 years and older fell from 13.22 years in 2000 to 12.45 years in 2010. The ratio of this educational level to the median of 173 countries for the same indicator also fell correspondingly (Figure 5.3). This human capital situation will inevitably lead to an accumulation of low-end labor, and the global division of labor will harm a large number of laborers.

Since the arrival of the Lewisian turning point in China, there has been a shortage of unskilled workers, who are facing a period of more employment opportunities and rapidly rising wages. However, these "good days" will not last too long. If at this time an incentive mechanism not conducive to the formation of human capital is formed in the labor market, such as additional employment opportunities and continually increasing compensation causing young people being unwilling to go through additional schooling or dropping out of school to enter the labor market, the upgrading of the industrial structure will

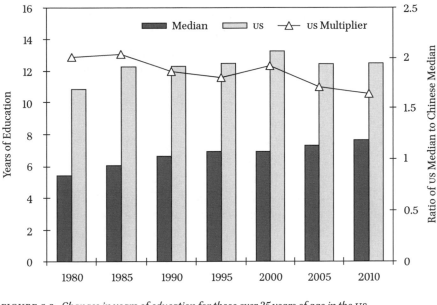

FIGURE 5.3 *Changes in years of education for those over 25 years of age in the US*
SOURCE: UNDP WEBSITE, HTTP://WWW.BETA.UNDP.ORG/CONTENT/UNDP/EN/HOME
.HTML.

affect this generation of workers, who will become a vulnerable group in the
labor market of the future.

4   The Governmental Responsibility to Supply Education

In the period of reform and opening, the Chinese government made continuous
efforts in the development of education. The most important breakthroughs in
terms of policy promoting the development of education mainly came in two
areas. The first breakthrough was the rapid popularization of compulsory education after the introduction of the *Compulsory Education Law*. In particular,
the cancellation of tuition and miscellaneous fees for compulsory education in
2007 markedly increased the enrollment rate in nine-year compulsory education. The second breakthrough was significantly expanded university recruitment in 1999, which not only improved university enrollment rates, but also
served as impetus to further improve high school enrollment rates.

Needless to say, these two breakthroughs in educational development provided a strong protection for the accumulation of human capital during the
period of rapid economic growth in China, promoting the development of

the demographic dividend. However, in the new stage of economic development, not only do long-standing, traditional supply factors still constrain the
development of education, but many new circumstances have emerged, as
well as changes to the demand side, erecting obstacles to achieving new breakthroughs in human capital accumulation.

For some time, Chinese society has placed responsibility for the undertak-
ing of educational development on the government expenditure guarantee,
calling for increasing the ratio of education expenditure to GDP. Insufficient
spending on public education is indeed an important constraint facing the
development of education. In 2008, the proportion of fiscal expenditures on
education to GDP was 2.87%, only 53.4% of the 5.37% ratio in the US. In addition, the overall size of educational investment is associated with a country's
population age structure. When a country's education-aged population makes
up a high proportion of the total population, more resources need to be used
on education.

Standardizing educational investment according to the proportion of the
education-aged population and then making international comparisons can
more scientifically reflect national differences in the level of investment in
education. On the basis of the proportion of the 6 to 24-year-old population in
the US, comparing the proportions of state investment in public education to
GDP, we find that because the education-age population still makes up a high
proportion of the total population in China, the actual public investment after
standardization is 2.4% of GDP, only 50% of the ratio of public expenditures
on education to GDP in the US (Cai Fang et al., 2009).

One can see that setting a goal of increasing public expenditures on education is a highly operative measure. "National Middle and Long-term Education
Reform and Development Plan (2010–2020)" proposed increasing the ratio of
fiscal expenditures on education to GDP to 4% in 2012. As a binding requirement on government, this is conducive to significantly increasing public
investment in education. However, simply focusing on increasing the proportion of public investment has the limitation of looking only at material factors.
In other words, even if public investment in education increases significantly,
the difficulty of allocating resources in accordance with the rules of education
itself is no less than the mobilization of resources.Education is both an investment in human capital that can receive private returns, reflected in a higher
private rate of return, and a public field in which in which private investment
incentives are not enough to reach an appropriate scale, reflected in a higher
social rate of return. For public expenditures on education to achieve appropriate allocation and use, they should be consistent with the laws of education's
external distribution. Studies show that the social rate of return on education

is highest in the preschool stage, as well as vocational education and training (Heckman and Carneiro, 2003).

However, in China's educational expenditures, the proportion of household spending is too high, significantly higher than in other countries, including developed countries. For example, in 2005, the proportion of private spending on education was 54.1%, 45 percentage points higher than the average of 19 European countries, 35.6 percentage points higher than Mexico, and 13.8 percentage points higher than South Korea (Cai Fang et al., 2009).

We divide education spending as in-budget spending and funds from other sources. From per student expenditures from other funding sources at different levels of education, that is, the proportion of individual and social expenditures on running schools and tuition and miscellaneous fees, we can observe the household burden for education (Figure 5.4). First, even in the compulsory education stage, the proportion of expenditures coming from other sources is high—17.9% of total expenditures in primary school, and 18.5% in junior middle school. Second, the proportions of educational expenditures from other sources for kindergarten and ordinary high school are abnormally high at 42.6% and 44.6%, respectively, which is unfitting for the high social returns of these two stages of education. Third, although related to vocational education, in the stages of secondary education and higher education, there is some rationality to higher proportions of expenditures from other sources in these areas. Still, the absolute burden is relatively heavy.

This condition where the majority of household spending goes toward education causes an excessive educational burden on households, not only suppressing consumer demand, but also creating negative educational incentives. Especially for low-income households, the relative burden of educational expenditures is high. This means that the government has failed at its function of equal provision of public goods in education as well as at carrying out necessary redistribution functions, causing a regressive distribution pattern. Human capital decides the degree to which households participate in the labor market and thereby enjoy the fruits of economic development. Educational inequality implies unequal opportunities for participation and sharing. If it continues, the poor will become richer, and the poor will become poorer due to intergenerational inheritance of inequality.

People have generally observed the unequal distribution of educational resources, especially public educational resources, between cities and the country, developed regions and poor regions, and between compulsory education and higher education, affecting the effectiveness of educational development. Many researchers have noted that gap between urban and rural educational development is several times that between urban and rural

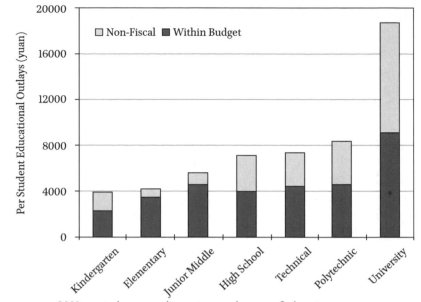

FIGURE 5.4 *2009 per student expenditure structure by stage of education*
SOURCE: MINISTRY OF EDUCATION, NATIONAL BUREAU OF STATISTICS SOCIAL AND
SCIENCE AND TECHNOLOGY STATISTICS DEPARTMENT, "CHINA EDUCATIONAL
EXPENDITURES STATISTICAL YEARBOOK (2010)," CHINA STATISTICS PRESS.

incomes. Therefore, truly to grasp the bottlenecks constraining educational
development and the key areas of inequality in the distribution of educational
resources, not only must we begin with backward rural education, but we must
also specifically observe the educational problems of relevant groups in accordance with the order of the life cycle.

Rural children fall behind at the earliest stages of education. In 2006, among
twenty-eight OECD countries, the average gross enrollment rate of preschool-
age children was 83.9%. Among these, nine countries including Spain have
enrollment rates of 100%. But in China, the gross enrollment rate for preschool
was only 50.9% (Xu Zhuoting, 2010). The low-penetration areas for preschool
education are mainly in the countryside.

Demand-side incentives and supply-side resource allocation factors have
had detrimental effects on human capital accumulation. This can be seen
prominently in the education of migrant children and those that stay behind
in the countryside. In addition to parental neglect of these children, serious
mental and physical health problems during growth, and significant pressure
to drop out to work, in terms of education, children who stay behind in the
countryside encounter poor rural education, while those who move to the
cities have difficulty enrolling in school, especially in public school. The results
of these problems are manifested in two ways.

The first is that this creates a significant gap in the rates of enrollment in secondary education for these two categories of children and urban resident children. While there is little difference in the enrollment rates in primary education among left-behind children, children who follow their parents to the cities, and children with urban permanent residency status, after completing primary education, the dropout rate of the first two groups begins to exceed that of urban children. And the higher the stage of education, the lower the enrollment rate. For example, for migrant children between 15 and 17 years old, the enrollment rate for boys is only 56.3% of urban resident children. For girls, the enrollment rate is only 44.2% of their urban counterparts (Gao, 2010).

Second is the greatly reduced opportunity that these two categories of children have to enter into university education. For migrant children, parents work in the city but have no urban residency, meaning they must return to their hometowns to take university entrance exams. In rural areas, not only are levels of education lower, but because there are fewer spots for admissions, opportunities for attending university are much fewer than in the city. For the migrant children of migrant workers and the left-behind children, the opportunities are few and far between. In higher education, and particularly among key universities, the proportion of students coming from the countryside is declining. In the 1980s, students from rural areas made up 30% of college and university students. Today, they make up 17.7%. In thirty years, the proportion of rural college students has been cut almost in half (Li Long, 2009).

The proportion of rural students among freshman enrollments at key universities has also been on a downward trend. From 1978 to 1998, 30% of freshmen at Peking University came from rural areas. From 2000 to now, this has fallen to only around 10%. Students from rural areas made up only 17% of the Tsinghua University class of 2010. The falling proportion of rural population to the overall population is of course one reason for the falling proportion of students from rural areas, but this cannot fully explain the change. In 2010, rural students made up 62% of examination candidates (Pan Xiaoling et al., 2011). Clearly, poor quality education in rural areas caused by unequal education resources and other reasons, as well as low enrollment quotas, are more important reasons.

Although there are many problems, educational development is undoubtedly improving the amount of human capital increase of new, maturing laborers. However, China's particularity lies in less educated, older workers—the older the worker, the lower the level of education. Among the working-age population, the average years of schooling of the 40-year-old population is 1.12 years lower than the 24-year-old population, the 50-year-old population is 1.11 years lower than the 40-year-old population, and the 60-year-old population is 1.44 years less than the 50-year-old population (Wang Guangzhou and Niu Jianlin, 2009).

Looking at migrant workers, the main source of China's labor supply now and in the future, older workers are also significantly less educated than younger workers. For example, in 2010, of the new generation of 16 to 30-year-old migrant workers, 27.4% had a high school education, while only 19.9% of 31 to 40-year-olds and 18% of 41 to 50-year-olds had reached the same level of educational achievement. Among 16 to 30-year-old migrant workers, 14.9% have graduated from a three-year college or above. For the latter two age groups, this proportion falls to 5.4% and 2.1%, respectively (Cai Fang, Wang Meiyan, 2010).

The relatively low existing stock of human capital means that with industrial upgrading, older workers will be more and more unsuited to the skills requirements of the labor market, and they will face frictional and structural unemployment, becoming a disadvantage group. Migrant workers and other urban workers with employment difficulties often concentrate in informal sectors of employment, the employment instability of which increases the difficulty of learning skills on the job. Thus, increasing the educational level and skills of the existing labor force through rational institutional arrangements to strengthen training is not only to mine the need for labor supply potential in future economic growth, but is also to strengthen the ability of these people to resist the lashing of the labor market and therefore reduce the need for social risk.

5   Conclusions and Policy Recommendations

Although education is not a purely public good, because there is a difference between its private and societal returns, even most economists who highly praise the market mechanism admit that government involvement in this area is necessary and essential. For China, which has just passed the Lewisian turning point, a particular failure is emerging in the market mechanism, namely, the reduction of the relative returns on education in the current labor market, which will inevitably harm the accumulation of human capital necessary for the future.

Education not only promotes sustainable economic growth, but is also the foundation of overall human development, improvement of income distribution, and social stability, so it is an externalized field with broader significance. Especially in China's current stage of transition, the government has an extra-onerous function to carry out. On the other hand, the development of education also relies on the incentives produced by returns on human capital, driven by the needs of society, households, and individuals. The micro incentives to strengthen the acceptance of more education and expand the overall demand for expanded human capital accumulation not only require education authorities to make additional efforts, but also require a broader perspective.

First, we must extend compulsory education to preschool and high school and maintain the pace of expansion of higher education. The focal point of preschool education is in rural areas, and significantly increasing the coverage of preschool education through three public supply can markedly reduce the gap between urban and rural education. Through means of compulsory education, reducing and eliminating private expenditures on high-school education is the only way to truly improve the high school penetration rate and thereby markedly increase the average years of schooling in the working-age population. And more opportunities to attend university and thereby the popularization of higher education are not only requirements for future economic growth relying on technological innovation and productivity improvements. It is also the only way to improve the distribution of income and achieve inclusive growth.

Second, beginning with the construction of the labor market system, we should strengthen various job training and improve the stock of human capital among laborers. With a weak correlation between job training and the labor market, the labor force that comes out of training cannot sufficiently satisfy the requirements of the labor market. This is an important issue in China's training system. In this situation, training has no significance and will ultimately reduce the willingness to undergo training. The irregular household registration system and employment have reduced the enthusiasm among businesses to provide training and have reduced the relevance and effectiveness of public training. Stable and normal employment can correct distortions in the returns on human capital, and supply and demand of training can improve its efficiency.

Third, we should further expand the scale of education and improve the quality of education through reform of the educational system. Continuing to expand higher education does not mean that there is no need to carry out reform of the educational system, the layout of disciplines, the setting up of majors, and teaching methods to guide institutions of higher educations to adapt to the needs of the labor market and economic and social development. At the core of urgent, thoroughly remolding reform of the education system is changing over-management by government and its approach of running all levels and all types of education, that is, the government should focus on management, standardization, and the fair distribution of educational resources while giving education more room to realize independent development. After graduating from higher education, students should place more value on matching their specialized knowledge with their jobs. Coupled with the industrial restructuring China currently faces, matching the major they studied with a job will be increasingly difficult. Thus, studying general knowledge and cultivating skills in higher education becomes more and more important. We should therefore reduce the proportion of specialized knowledge content to ensure that university graduates are able to adapt to many different types of jobs.

(This article was originally published in Chinese in 2012.)

Reference Literature

Cai Fang, Du Yang, Wang Dewen. 2009. "Research into Issues with China's Education Reform and Development Strategy," in *China's Population and Labor Green Paper No. 9* edited by Cai Fang, Beijing, Social Sciences Academic Press.

References

Autor, H. David, Lawrence F. Katz and Melissa S. Kearney. 2006. "The Polarization of the U.S. Labor Market." NBER Working Paper No. 11986.

Cai Fang, Du Yang. 2011. "Wage Growth, Wage Convergence, and the Lewisian Turning Point." *Economic Perspectives*, Vol. 9.

Cai Fang, Wang Meiyan. 2010. "When China's Manufacturing Encountered the Lewisian Turning Point." *Manager*, November Edition, 66th Issue.

Cai, Fang and Zhao Wen. 2012. "When Demographic Dividend Disappears: Growth Sustainability of China." Forthcoming.

Gao, Wenshu. 2010. "Providing an Education for Left-behind and Migrant Children", in Cai Fang (eds). *The China Population and Labor Yearbook No. 2: The Sustainability of Economic Growth from the Perspective of Human Resources*. Leiden & Boston: Brill, pp. 75–91.

Godo, Yoshihisa. 2001. "Estimation of Average Years of Schooling by Levels of Education for Japan and the United States, 1890–1990." Meiji Gakuin University.

Heckman, James and Pedro Carneiro. 2003. "Human Capital Policy." NBER Working Paper No. 9495.

Kuijs, Louis. 2010. "China through 2020—A Macroeconomic Scenario." World Bank China Research Working Paper No. 9, World Bank, Washington, D.C.

Li Long. 2009. "Why Do Rural Students Make up Less Than Half of University Students?" Guangzhou Daily, January 24.

Ministry of Education Website: http://www.moe.edu.cn/publicfiles/business/htmlfiles/moe/s4959/201012/113470.html.

Ouyang Junshan. 2011. "Manufacturing is the Foundation of a Powerful Nation." China Business Times, September 7.

Pan Xiaoling, Shen Qianrong, Xia Qian, Liu Xing, He Qian. 2011. "No Spring for Poor Children? Why Poor Families Are Further and Further from Tier 1 Universities," Southern Weekend, August 24, http://cul.sohu.com/20110824/n317222450_3.shtml.

Qu Wan. 2009. "Demographic Dividend: Continuing or Replacing." In China's Population and Labor Green Paper No. 9 edited by Cai Fang. Beijing: Social Sciences Academic Press.

Samuelson, Paul. 2004. "Where Ricardo and Mill Rebut and Confirm Arguments of Mainstream Economists Supporting Globalization." Journal of Economic Perspectives, Vol. 18, No. 3, pp. 135–146.

Wang Guangzhou, Niu Jianlin. 2009. "Overall Structural Situation, Problems, and Development Forecast for Chinese Education." In China's Population and Labor Green Paper No. 9 edited by Cai Fang, Beijing, Social Sciences Academic Press.

Wang Meiyan. 2009. "Universal High School and Mass Higher Education." In China's Population and Labor Green Paper No. 9. Beijing: Social Sciences and Academic Press.

Whalley, John and Xiliang Zhao. 2010. "The Contribution of Human Capital to China's Economic Growth." NBER Working Paper, No. 16592.

Xu Zhuoting. 2010. "Research and Thoughts on China's Unviersal Preschool Education." Social Science Battle Line, Vol. 11.

Zhang Linxiu, Luo Renfu, Yi Hongmei, Huang Likun, Shi Huijiang. 2011. "The Dropout Problems of Rural Middle School Students in Poor Areas Is Worth Attention." Policy Research Bulletin, Vol. 1.

CHAPTER 6

Changes to the Employment Structure and Problems

Zhang Juwei

The changes to the job structure brought on by economic growth and structural change are the basic driving force of continuous social development and progress. Observing the course of development for the world's various economies, it is not difficult to see that in a country's process of moving from impoverished to prosperous, from backward to advanced, and from traditional to modern, the job structure will undergo two fundamental changes: first, from agriculture-led jobs to non-farm jobs; second, from mainly self-employment to mainly having employers.

If the two processes are synchronized, social development moves onto a healthy track. If the two are not synchronized, there will be problems with social development. Specifically, if workers cannot find formal employment in the process of moving away from agriculture, social development will be a problem. Some developing countries go through a long period of development but are unable to escape the middle-income trap to join the ranks of developed countries. There are of course many reasons, but one important reason is that the two changes to the job structure are out of sync, and the employment of workers lags behind the move to non-farm jobs. In this case, laborers transferring away from farms can only become self-employed in cities and towns in the informal sector, breeding serious social problems. Genuine social progress and development cannot be achieved.

I The Trend toward Non-farm Jobs in the Employment Structure

China was once a country whose jobs were dominated by agriculture, and manufacturing and lifestyle lagged behind. But the situation today has undergone fundamental change. With the declining proportion of agricultural jobs, the agriculture-led job structure has changed to a structure dominated by the non-farm sector. At the same time, employment has increased, many of the country's self-employed have become employed with companies, and wages

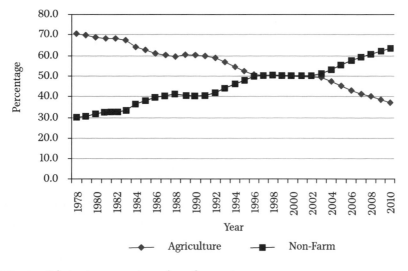

FIGURE 6.1 *Job structure moves toward non-farm sector*
SOURCE: *CHINA STATISTICAL YEARBOOK*, VARIOUS YEARS.[1]

for workers have risen. This indicates that China is on a track of healthy social and economic development.

One major change China's job structure is undergoing is the trend toward non-farm jobs. As the world's most populous nation, China of course also is the world's largest country by employment. As of the end of 2010, China had total employment of 761 million people, of which 279 million worked in the primary industry, 218 million in the secondary industry, and 263 million in the tertiary industry. The primary industry is still the country's largest sector by jobs. If we look at the primary industry as agriculture and the secondary and tertiary industries as non-farm industry, then we can see that China's job structure has already shifted from agriculture-led to non-farm-led. As of 2010, non-farm jobs accounted for 63.3% of total jobs, while agricultural employment had dropped to only 36.7%.

Of course, China was once an agricultural country with employment dominated by agriculture. In 1978, agriculture accounted for 70.5% of jobs, while non-farm jobs took up 29.5%. Rapid economic development has caused the agricultural proportion to decline. In 1997, non-farm jobs overtook agricultural jobs for the first time. In the half a decade afterward, agricultural and non-farm

---

1   If no source is given in the following figures, data comes from *China Statistical Yearbook* for the relevant years.

jobs were in roughly equal proportions. After 2003, the proportion of non-farm jobs grew quickly, and the move away from agricultural jobs accelerated. (See Figure 6.1)

Two aspects have driven the trend toward non-farm jobs: first, the transfer of rural labor to urban jobs; and second, the transitioning of rural labor to local, non-farm work.

The transfer of rural labor to urban areas has been the main driving force for the move toward non-farm jobs. With rapid urbanization, the rural population has transferred to cities, and China has transitioned from a country of mostly rural citizens to one of mostly urban citizens. However, in terms of employment, the jobs in rural areas still outnumber those in urban areas. As of 2010, total rural employment was 414 million jobs, or 54.4% of the nation's total, while urban employment was 347 million jobs, 45.6% of the total. With a majority of the population living in cities, how can there be more jobs in the countryside? The main reason is the difference in labor participation rates between the urban and rural population. Because the labor participation rate is higher in the countryside, rural employment is higher in aggregate than urban employment. For example, in 2009, the urban labor participation rate was 61.5%, while in the countryside the rate was 81%, a difference of nearly 20 percentage points, which determines the difference in population and employment distribution between urban and rural areas. Overall, with increasing urbanization, the proportion of urban employment is also increasing, and thus, the rate of non-agricultural employment has also risen (See Figure 6.2).

The transitioning of rural laborers into local, non-farm jobs is another important force driving the move toward non-farm jobs. We know that agricultural employment necessarily takes place in the countryside, but perhaps many do not realize that not all rural employment is agricultural employment. With rapid economic and social development, the structure of rural employment has divided. More and more non-farm jobs have been created, and even the countryside has shown a trend toward non-farm jobs.

According to data from the National Bureau of Statistics, jobs in rural areas are divided into several types: primary industry jobs (agricultural jobs), township enterprise jobs, private enterprise jobs, and self-employed individuals. Obviously, these divisions can be summarized as agricultural and non-farm jobs. Primary industry jobs are certainly agricultural jobs, while jobs with township enterprises, private companies, or self-employment are non-farm jobs. Thus, with data from the National Bureau of Statistics, it is easy to understand the changes and trends in the rural job structure.

Using rural employment data from the National Bureau of Statistics, we find that adding the various categories yields a number greater than the total.

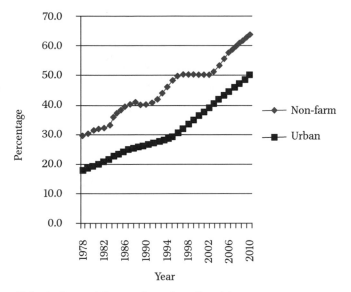

FIGURE 6.2 *Urbanization and the move toward non-farm jobs*

So, is this a statistical error or is there another reason? In fact, there is little possibility of this sort of error appearing in statistics because this difference has existed continuously since 1978. Moreover, it has widened. For example, in 1978, the difference between the two was 5.07 million; in 1990 it was more than 20 million; in 2000 it exceeded 4,000; and in 2010 it exceeded 80 million. If this were a statistical error, this sort of systemic growth should have been corrected long ago.

After ruling out statistical error, we can assume that the "total" and "broken-down" figures are both correct, but that each uses a different definition of rural jobs. The "total" job numbers reflect employment numbers calculated by number of people. The "broken-down" job numbers reflect employment calculated by job positions. As job positions often overlap, and one person may have multiple jobs, the number of jobs may exceed the number of employed persons. In fact, during the busy season, farmers engage in agriculture. During the slack season, many work in nearby mines or engage in self-employed activities. When calculating rural employment, this portion may be counted as rural agricultural jobs and also as rural non-farm jobs. The result is the difference between "total" jobs and jobs broken down by category. This seems like "erroneous" information, but it provides a possibility for us to understand changes to the rural employment situation. This is because the difference between "total" job figures and those broken down by category can be understood as the number of farmers simultaneously employed elsewhere, in other words, those we have

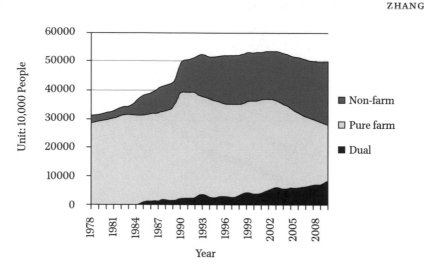

FIGURE 6.3 *Divergence of agricultural employment*

identified as being counted for both agricultural and non-farm jobs. Therefore, rural employment is not entirely agricultural employment. It not only includes agricultural and non-farm jobs, but a considerable portion of those holding jobs in multiple industries. In terms of trends, the proportion of agricultural employment in rural employment has fallen continuously, while non-farm jobs and dual employment have risen. Overall, rural employment is moving toward non-farm jobs (See Figure 6.3).

If we remove dual-employed workers from agricultural employment, the clear, steady, downward trend in the proportion of those fully engaged in agricultural jobs in the countryside is even clearer. In 1978, rural employment was almost entirely agricultural employment. Dual-employed farmers were basically non-existent, with the proportion of pure agricultural jobs at 91%. Later, this proportion declined continuously. By 2010, the proportion of rural agricultural employment had fallen to 47% (See Figure 6.4). From an absolute perspective, the number of those employed in agriculture in rural areas began to fall in 1990, when the total number of those employed in agriculture was 368 million. By 2010, this had fallen to 196 million, an average annual decline of 7.82 million people. In recent years in particular, the decline in the number of Chinese employed in agriculture has accelerated. In the six years from 2005 through 2010, the absolute number of those employed in agriculture fell by an average of 13.05 million annually. Whether in terms of relative proportions or absolute numbers, rural employment has transformed from an agriculture-led structure to an irreversible trend toward non-farm jobs.

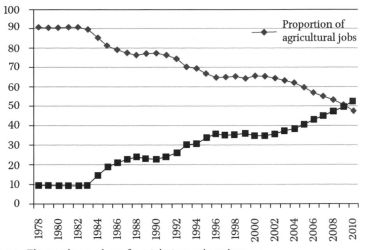

FIGURE 6.4 *The trend toward non-farm jobs in rural employment*

In summary, China's employment is now in a rapid process of moving toward non-farm jobs, which is driven both by rural labor moving to cities and by rural labor engaging in non-farm jobs. With rapid social and economic development, this movement toward non-farm jobs will continue. The proportion of agricultural employment in China is not only much higher than in developed countries, it is actually even higher than the world average. In 2008, the proportion of agricultural employment to total employment in developed countries was only 3.4%, and the world average was 34.5%. China's proportion was 39.6%. Agricultural employment as a proportion of overall employment is a fundamental indicator in weighing a country's level of development. No country can become a modern, rich country and still ahve a high percentage of agricultural employment. China is no exception.

II   The Trend toward Employment within Changes to the Employment Structure

Another trend within the changes to China's job structure is that employment is going from self-employment to being employed. "Self-employed" means simply a job in which there is no employer, where one pays oneself remuneration. Being employed means to work for someone else and be compensated by an employer. In general, mainly two types of activities are seen as self-employment. First is business activity at the household level in the countryside, where most business activity is at the household level. Families use their own labor and some capital goods as investment, and output and income are obtained from the land. The profit obtained is embodied in the difference between input and output. Another type private industry and commerce conducted in cities or the countryside, which is an individually owned business. It should be noted that the activities of individually owned business are undertaken by an individual or a family, its self-employed nature goes without saying. But under current laws and regulations, individually owned businesses can have employees. As long as the number of employees does not exceed a threshold, it is still seen as an individually owned business. In this situation, while someone pays the laborers employed by the individually owned business, they are still seen as self-employed.

Compared with the self-employed, the employed tend to have more stable employment, higher income levels, and a higher degree of security. Thus, for a country, the transition from self-employment to being employed symbolizes social development and progress. Overall, China while China's job structure is moving away from agricultural employment, more Chinese are also becoming employees. However, looking at cities and the countryside separately, there are differences in the progression of this trend.

China's urban employment is mainly made up of employees. Historically, urban employment has basically always been those who are employed, particularly in the planned economy, when urban employees all had formal work units with good social protections. In that time, urban employment was not only manifested as employee employment, but was also manifested as formal employment. After reform and opening, as labor market reforms deepened, the urban employment model underwent a trend of diversification. Besides employment with formal work units, self-employment, flexible-employment and other forms emerged, and urban employment showed a certain degree of movement away from employment.

In the *China Statistical Yearbook* published by the National Bureau of Statistics, urban employment is broken into the following categories: state-owned work units, collective work units, cooperative work units, associated work units, limited liability companies, joint-stock companies, Hong Kong, Macau, and Taiwan-invested work units, and foreign-invested work units, all of which can be referred to as work unit employment. Employment at private companies and individually owned companies can be called non-work-unit employment. Of course, work unit employment can be called formal employment, while employment outside of work units can be classified as informal employment.

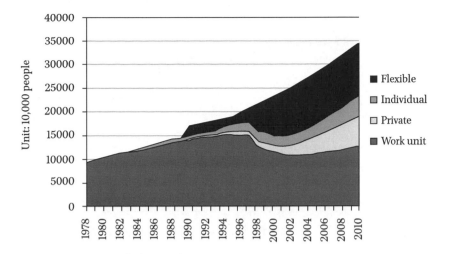

FIGURE 6.5 *Divergence of urban employment types*

The urban employment data from the National Bureau of Statistics has a problem exactly the opposite of rural employment data. In urban employment statistics, the "broken down" figures are less than the "total." Given that the urban employment statistics are also probably not in error, we can infer that the statistics broken down by category may be leaving out a certain type of employee, that is to say, some jobs may not be able to be included in any existing employment type and are therefore excluded. In fact, the jobs of many urban residents are relatively flexible, such as domestic service workers, freelancers, and those doing other odd jobs. These people's jobs are difficult to place into the aforementioned categories, and they are thus left out of the broken-down statistics. Here, we can classify some of the persons missing from the broken-down statistics as "flexible employees" or "other." Thus, urban employment can be roughly divided into several categories: urban work unit jobs, urban private company jobs, urban individually owned company jobs, and urban flexible jobs (See Figure 6.5).

The divergence of urban employment reflects changes to the urban job structure. In a planned economy, work unit employment made up almost 100% of total urban employment. After reform and opening, the job structure began to divide, with other job forms, like self-employment, private company employment, and flexible employment, emerging. Because of the stable work, high incomes, and good social protections, work unit employment can be referred to as formal employment. From this perspective, urban employment has gone through a process of in-formalization. The proportion of urban work

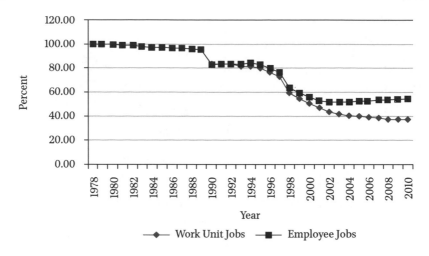

FIGURE 6.6 *Changes to the urban job structure*

unit employment fell from 99.84% in 1978 to 82.5% in 1995. From there the decline accelerated, but the proportion has remained stable at around 40% since 2005. In 2010, it fell further to 36.8%. That is to say, more than 60% of urban employment today is non-formal employment. The increasing proportion of informal employment means a decline in laborer income and social protection.

Changes to the urban job structure can also be reflected in the process of moving toward being employed. As work unit employment and private company employment both involve being employed by an employer, adding these two groups together yields the number of employed workers. Thus, from the perspective of the trend of changes to the proportion of urban employees, there has been an equally rapid decline since reform and opening. In 1978, employed workers made up nearly 100 percent of the working population. This fell to its lowest point in 2003 at 50.91%. The trend has reversed since, reaching 54.31% in 2010 (See Figure 6.6).

In contrast with the huge fluctuations in the urban employment trend, rural employment has undergone a relatively steady shift toward workers becoming employees. Traditionally, agriculture has a self-employed activity with the family as the basic unit. Jobs are of course dominated by the self-employed. But with the development of non-farm industry in the countryside, more and more rural laborers have transferred to non-farm activities. These laborers shift from being farmers to working in township enterprises or private companies, and their status shifts from family self-employed to employed by a firm. According

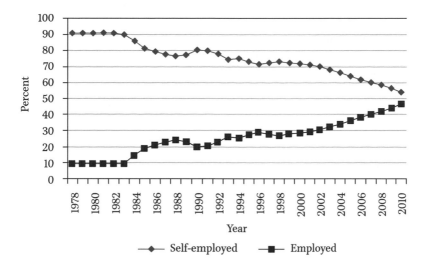

FIGURE 6.7 *The trend toward employment in rural areas*

to National Bureau of Statistics data, workers in jobs at township enterprises and private companies in the countryside are employees. Adding together these two types of jobs, we can arrive at the number of rural employees and thereby observe the trend toward employment in rural areas. In 1978, the proportion of the self-employed in rural jobs was 91% while those employed by firms made up only 9%. In 2010, the self-employed proportion had fallen to 54%, while the employed proportion had risen to 46%, making for almost equal numbers of employed and self-employed workers. (See Figure 6.7)

Putting urban and rural jobs together, we can observe the trend toward employment in the job structure. In Table 6.1, we arrange data from the National Bureau of Statistics to show changes to the jobs landscape. In theory, workers are either employed or self-employed, and there is little possibility of other states of employment. But undeniably, the flexible employment group in urban areas is a special group that is difficult to categorize as employed or self-employed. This is because flexible employees include both the self-employed such as freelancers as well as employees such as domestic service workers. Due to a lack of more detailed information, we can only list the list the urban flexible employment group independently from the self-employed and employed as "Other." Thus, the national job landscape includes three classes: the self-employed, employees, and other. Since 1978, the proportion of the self-employed has fallen, from 69% to 35% in 2010. The proportion of employee jobs has climbed steadily, from 30% in 1978 to 50% in 2010, and the

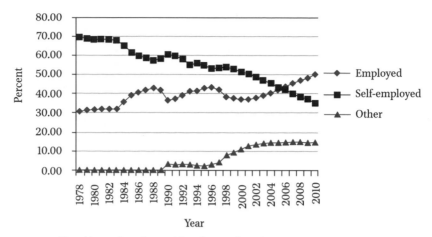

FIGURE 6.8 *Trend toward employment in urban and rural areas*

job structure thus exhibits a trend toward employment. Of course, "Other" jobs have grown out of nothing, and in 2010, this class of jobs had risen to 15% of total jobs (See Figure 6.8).

III   Problems within Changes to the Job Structure

In general, undeveloped countries have predominantly agricultural econo-mies, their jobs are mostly agricultural, and workers are predominantly self-employed. Looking at development from a jobs perspective, development is a process of moving toward non-farm jobs and employment and achieving employment within the process of moving toward non-farm jobs. Of course, movement toward employment has a prerequisite of movement toward non-farm jobs, because in order to become an employee, a worker must move to a non-farm industry. But the movement toward non-farm jobs does not nec-essarily lead to a movement toward employment because laborers moving out of agriculture can also become self-employed. When unable to find suit-able employment, laborers transferring out of agriculture have no choice but to engage in individual industrial and commercial activities in the city and become self-employed. Thus, by observing the process of moving toward non-farm jobs and moving toward employment, we can judge whether or not a country's development is healthy. If in the process of moving toward non-farm jobs the level of employment increases in concert, then healthy development is being achieved. If employment lags in the process of moving toward non-farm jobs, this means that good jobs are scarce, and social development is hindered.

TABLE 6.1   *Total nationwide jobs and changes to the jobs landscape*

| Year | Jobs | Proportion of Total (%) | | |
	(10,000 people)	Employee Jobs	Self-employed Jobs	Other Jobs
1978	40152	30.70	69.30	0.00
1979	41024	31.39	68.61	0.00
1980	42361	31.74	68.26	0.00
1981	43725	31.81	68.19	0.00
1982	45295	31.78	68.22	0.00
1983	46436	31.76	67.58	0.00
1984	48197	35.40	64.52	0.08
1985	49873	38.77	61.23	0.00
1986	51282	40.46	59.55	0.00
1987	52783	41.71	58.28	0.00
1988	54334	42.61	57.39	0.01
1989	55329	41.76	58.23	0.01
1990	64749	36.28	60.15	3.57
1991	65491	37.10	59.54	3.36
1992	66152	38.77	57.85	3.38
1993	66808	41.24	55.30	3.47
1994	67455	41.38	55.88	2.74
1995	68065	42.77	54.73	2.50
1996	68950	43.35	53.20	3.45
1997	69820	42.14	53.43	4.43
1998	70637	38.13	53.80	8.07
1999	71394	37.59	52.84	9.58
2000	72085	37.19	51.48	11.32
2001	72797	36.98	50.18	12.83
2002	73280	37.62	48.71	13.68
2003	73736	38.90	46.86	14.24
2004	74264	40.15	45.25	14.60
2005	74647	41.96	43.40	14.64
2006	74978	43.68	41.41	14.91
2007	75321	45.33	39.72	14.95
2008	75564	46.75	38.16	15.08
2009	75828	48.16	37.06	14.78
2010	76105	50.03	35.01	14.96

Source: China Statistical Yearbook from the relevant years.

Is China currently moving in-step toward non-farm jobs and employment? Comparing China's progress in moving toward non-farm jobs and employment, we find that from 1978 to 2010, jobs underwent a rapid movement toward the non-farm sector, with non-farm jobs more than doubling from around 30% of the total to 63%, an annual increase of more than a percentage point. Correspondingly, while growth in employees has been the trend, the rate of growth lags far behind the move toward non-farm jobs. The proportion of employed workers has increased only from 30% to around 50%, annual growth of 0.6 percentage points. Of particular note is that the trend toward employment has recently lagged further behind the trend toward non-farm work. Prior to 1990, movement toward non-farm work and movement toward employment advanced almost in sync with almost no difference in the proportions. But thereafter, the two diverged, with the gap widening suddenly in 1997 and 1998, from 7.9% to 12.07%. After 2000, the gap between the two remained steady at about 13%, hitting 13.27% in 2010 (See Figure 6.9). The consequence of employment lagging behind the move toward non-farm jobs is that although labor is transferring from agriculture to the non-farm sector, many workers have become self-employed or have flexible jobs and have not become employees. This shows a lack of good positions and a low quality of jobs.

At present, developed countries have already completed the process of moving toward employment, and employees count for a high proportion of job holders. According to the latest data from the International Labor Organization (ILO), the proportion of employees among all job holders in developed countries and the European Union was on average 86.2% (See Table 6.2), with some countries over 90%. Australia had a proportion of 88.2%, France 89.5%, Germany 88.4%, Japan 86.5%, Britain 86.6%, and the US 93%. In contrast, developing countries have a low proportion of employees. In Southeast Asian countries, the proportion is 36.4%. The average, for sub-Saharan African countries is 24.7% and only 21.5% for South Asian countries.

Generally, a country's level of development can be seen in its proportion of employees. Because developed countries have completed the urbanization and industrialization process, the economic structure is stable, and the level of employment is high and relatively stable. For example, over 90% of US workers have had employers since 1980. In the UK, 85–92% have had employers since 1980. In contrast, developing countries are still urbanizing and industrializing, and the proportion of workers with employers is lower. In Indonesia, it was 33.4% in 2008; in Vietnam, it was 25.6% in 2004; in India, it was 15.8% in 2005, a reflection of the relatively primitive form of these economies and their early stage of development.

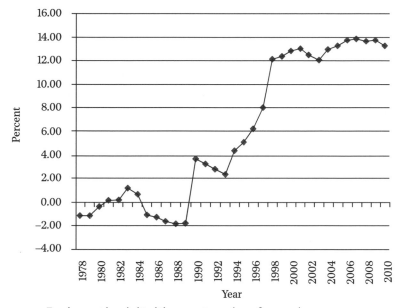

FIGURE 6.9 *Employment lags behind the move toward non-farm work*

Of course, the continuous improvement in the proportion of workers with employers is actually a process of healthy national development. The development of South Korea and Japan has confirmed such a development process. In 1980, 44.5% of South Korean workers had employers, a proportion that had grown to 70% by 2009. In Japan, 71.7% of workers had employers in 1980, which had risen to 86.9% by 2009, reaching the average level of developed countries (See Figure 6.3). In slower developing countries, growth in the proportion of workers with employers is also slower, and even stagnant in some countries. In Indonesia, this proportion was 35.5% in 1995, and this had actually fallen to 33.4% by 2009. In the Philippines, the proportion was 49.9% in 1995 and had only grown to 52.4% by 2008. This is a reflection of these countries falling into the middle-income trap.

In terms of the proportion of workers with employers, China is still a typical developing country. As of 2010, China's proportion was 50%, far from the average of around 86% in developed countries. In the nearly 20 years from 1985 to 2003, this proportion fluctuated around 38%. From 1985 to 1995, this proportion grew slowly, from 38.8% to 42.8%. But from 1995–2003, the proportion actually fell, from 42.8% to 38.9%, which is actually not uncommon for a developing country. China has its own reasons for this drop. At that time, urban labor market reforms aimed at increasing efficiency at SOEs caused several tens of millions of urban workers to be laid off, many of which could not find

TABLE 6.2   *Employment in different regions*

Year	Employee Proportion		Non-employee Proportion		Agricultural Jobs Proportion	
	1998	2008	1998	2008	1998	2008
World	44.0	48.0	56.0	52.0	41.6	34.5
Developed countries + EU	84.4	86.2	15.6	13.8	5.8	3.7
Central and southern Europe (non-EU)	76.6	78.4	23.4	21.6	27.3	18.5
East Asia	36.4	45.1	63.6	54.9	51.0	40.6
Southeast Asia + Pacific	33.0	36.4	67.0	63.6	50.2	42.5
South Asia	17.9	21.5	82.1	78.5	59.4	47.7
Latin America and Caribbean	61.8	63.5	38.2	36.5	22.1	17.4
Middle East	50.3	62.0	49.7	38.0	22.4	17.8
North Africa	45.6	54.1	54.4	45.9	36.9	33.2
Sahara and South Africa	18.1	24.7	81.9	75.3	66.7	61.0

Source: International Labor Organization, *The Key Indicators of the Labor Market*, Sixth Edition.

new jobs and became self-employed or simply left the labor market. Between 1995 and 2003, the number of workers at state-owned and collective work units fell from 144 million to 78.76 million, a reduction of 65.33 million workers. The percentage of urban workers with employers fell from 82.86% to 50.91%, losing more than 30 percentage points. After 2003, with urban labor market reforms basically complete, more workers again began to work for employers, and the proportion increased from 50.91% in 2003 to 54.31% in 2010.

It should be said that after 2003, the proportion of workers with employers grew quickly in China, advancing at an average rate of around 2 percentage points a year. This China's development has climbed onto a healthy track, exhibiting characteristics similar to the development of South Korea and Japan in their rapid development processes. Figure 6.10 compares the trends of the proportions of workers with employers in China and selected countries since 1982.

Although the proportion of Chinese workers with employers has growth rapidly, in absolute terms it is still significantly below the level of developed economies, not only below the 70% level of South Korea, but far lower than the levels of Japan, the UK, and US (See Table 6.3 and Figure 6.10). In 2008,

TABLE 6.3   *Level of employment by year in selected countries*
            unit: percent

Year	US	UK	Japan	South Korea	Mexico	Indonesia	Philippines	Thailand	China
1980	90.6	91.9	71.7	47.2	44.5	—	—	—	31.7
1985	90.9	88.5	74.3	54.1	—	—	—	—	38.8
1990	91.2	85.7	77.4	60.5	68.1	—	—	28.4	36.3
1995	91.5	86.2	81.5	62.6	58.4	35.5	49.9	35.7	42.8
2000	92.6	87.6	83.1	63.1	63.9	32.8	50.7	39.6	37.2
2001	92.6	87.6	83.7	63.3	63.4	33.3	49.5	40.4	37.0
2002	92.8	87.6	84.2	64.0	63.0	32.3	48.7	40.0	37.6
2003	92.4	87.1	84.5	65.1	63.2	31.0	50.1	40.5	38.9
2004	92.4	86.7	84.6	66.0	63.3	31.9	52.1	43.8	40.2
2005	92.5	86.8	84.8	66.4	64.3	33.6	50.5	43.7	42.0
2006	92.6	86.6	85.7	67.2	65.4	33.9	51.1	43.7	43.7
2007	92.8	86.4	86.1	68.2	65.5	34.0	52.2	43.6	45.3
2008	94.4	86.4	86.5	68.7	65.9	32.6	52.4	43.2	46.8
2009	—	86.2	86.9	70.0	66.1	33.4	—	44.6	48.2

Source: Chinese data comes from Table 6.1; data for other countries comes from the International Labor Organization, *The Key Indicators of the Labor Market*, Sixth Edition. *Note*: Indonesia's 1995 data is 1997. Philippines 1995 data is 1998.

developed countries had an average proportion of about 86% workers with employees. China had a proportion of around 46% that year, a difference of 40 percentage points.

If China wants to become an advanced, developed country, the most fundamental task is to continuously improve the proportion of workers with employers and bring the large number of self-employed and flexibly employed workers in low-level positions into high-quality, guaranteed positions at companies. Currently, although China's transfer of rural labor has made great achievements, agriculture is still the largest job sector. As of 2010, the proportion of jobs in agriculture was 36.7%, employing 279 million workers. This is the largest source of workers without employers. If the number of workers in the agricultural sector does not continue to fall, the number of workers with employees and the number of formal jobs will not continue to increase, and worker wages will lack an objective basis for improving. To this end, we must first persist in accelerating the unwavering transfer of rural labor and continue

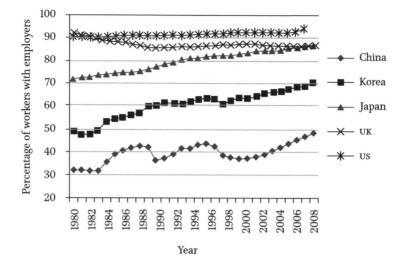

FIGURE 6.10 *Comparison of proportions of workers with employers*
SOURCE: INTERNATIONAL LABOR ORGANIZATION, *THE KEY INDICATORS OF THE LABOR MARKET*, SIXTH EDITION; CHINA DATA COMES FROM THE CHAPTER.

to increase the level of non-farm jobs. Of course, if laborers transferring out of the agricultural sector cannot find suitable work, they will have no choice but to become self-employed. This sort of transfer of rural labor will not bring about an increasing proportion of workers with employers, nor will it greatly improve wages. At present, rural labor transferring to the urban sector is to a certain degree informal, which is a key factor constraining China's economic and social development. Therefore, to accelerate the pace of development in China, at the same time as promoting the movement toward non-farm jobs, we must accelerate the pace of economic development and structural transformation, actively expand employment, create more high-quality positions, continuously increase the proportion of workers with employers and the level of formal work, and achieve the synchronized development of the movement toward non-farm work and employer-based jobs.

(This article was originally published in Chinese in 2012.)

CHAPTER 7

Labor Market Vulnerability in Urban China

Du Yang, Qu Yue and Cai Fang

I   Introduction

The Chinese labor market is facing a significant transition. As evidenced by frequent labor shortages and rising wages for migrant workers, it is believed that China has already passed through the Lewis Turning Point (LTP) (Cai, 2007). This labor market change affects the quality of jobs through several channels.

During the era of unlimited labor supply, the ceaseless exodus of surplus agricultural labor has weakened the bargaining power of labor. Due to the preeminent position of employers, employees are incapable of bargaining for salary level, working time, labor intensity, or quality of the working environment, so that they are always obliged to passively accept unfavorable conditions. In such a market environment, even if the laborers demand an increase wages and improvement in labor protection conditions, companies are unwilling to acquiesce to their demands and make the appropriate modifications. It is therefore difficult to address the vulnerability of jobs in such situations even the government wishes to do so.

After passing through the LTP, the increased scarcity of labor will force firms to compete for laborers. As a result, employers must improve wages and working conditions so as to attract labor, otherwise workers will "vote with their feet" by choosing other employment opportunities.

The current Chinese labor market indicates that, when faced with a labor shortage, enterprises that provide quality jobs actually have no trouble in recruiting enough migrant workers. As a result, enterprises facing a shortage in the labor supply must improve working conditions so as to reduce the difference in wages for those who were previously out of the labor market. The new changes in the supply and demand of the Chinese labor force is forcing more and more entrepreneurs to "shoulder social responsibilities."

Under the pressure of migrant workers "voting with their feet," the Chinese government has been promoting tripartite negotiation mechanisms for dealing with employment and wage decisions, which increases the opportunities for workers to express their salary, working condition, and related workplace requirements. In particular, the Employment Contract Law enacted in 2008

© KONINKLIJKE BRILL NV, LEIDEN, 2014 | DOI 10.1163/9789004273184_008

is widely considered to be a milestone marking the movement of the Chinese labor market towards employment protection.

As an important stakeholder in the labor market, local governments taking the responsibility for keeping economic development in local areas also find themselves responsible for social stability. When facing a labor shortage situation, attracting migrant workers is of the utmost importance in guaranteeing labor input and sustainable local economic growth. In such a situation, local governments tend to make policies that are amenable to migrants. For example, in recent years, some alterations to the social security system have been applied in coastal areas in order to extend coverage to migrant workers. In addition, local governments play an active role in the labor market by monitoring businesses to reduce the vulnerability of jobs, so as to mitigate the negative impacts of labor shortages on local economic development.

Despite these positive changes, if providing quality jobs is to be established as one of the developmental goals of the labor market, China still has a long way to go. In particular, significant disparities in the quality of jobs are found between migrant workers and those urban workers holding a local permanent residence permit, or *hukou*. In this respect, labor market policies aiming to reduce the overall level of job vulnerability also need to bridge the gap between groups of workers.

This paper is organized as follows: the following section (section II: Labor and Employment in China) introduces recent developments in China's labor market, including topics such as rural to urban migration, the trend of informality, social protection systems, and recent development in labor market institutions. Section three tries to assess the vulnerability of the urban labor market by introducing a new method for measuring social security and job security. Section four describes the vulnerability of jobs using the new tools we developed, and to observe variations in vulnerability across various groups of workers. A regression-based breakdown is applied to analyze the sources contributing to job vulnerability. The final section summarizes our conclusions.

II   Labor and Employment in China

Migration

China has witnessed the largest labor migration in the world since reform and opening-up (改革开放) policies were implemented. According to the most recent statistics, the total number of rural to urban migrant workers reached 159 million in 2011. This migration flow has, through an increase in labor productivity and social restructuring, propelled the economic and societal transition in China. Accordingly, the Chinese government has adapted its migration policies to the increase in migration flow and changes in the labor market.

Migrant workers have been stable sources of labor in the urban labor market over the past several decades. In recent years, in addition to increasing rates of employment, migrant workers' average monthly earnings have also increased. For instance, the annual growth rate of real monthly earnings (in 2001 prices) for migrant workers was 19.6% in 2008. In 2009, although suffering from the global financial crisis, we still see an increase in employment and wage growth for migrant workers. In 2010, as one of the outcomes of economic recovery, average real monthly earnings for migrant workers increased 15.5 percent. Currently, there are no nationally-representative sources of data measuring the overall number of migrant workers, but in this paper, we take advantage of the CASS Institute of Population and Labor Economics' three "urban labor market survey" data sets in order to observe trends in the urban labor market. Shown in the sample cities of Figure 7.1, the overall trend of migrant employment increasing and then decreasing is consistent with other sources of aggregated data.

During an era featuring a dual economic structure, the transferred labor forces from rural areas would enhance their marginal productivity no matter whether they work in manufacturing or service industries. Therefore, labor reallocation from low- to high-productivity sectors results in greater economic

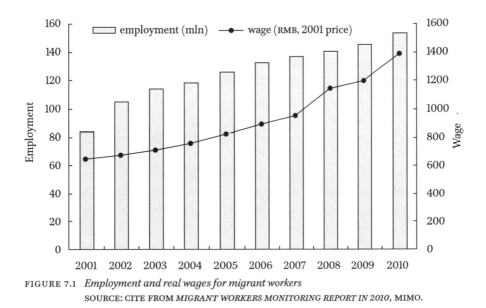

FIGURE 7.1 *Employment and real wages for migrant workers*
SOURCE: CITE FROM *MIGRANT WORKERS MONITORING REPORT IN 2010*, MIMO.

efficiency, which contributes to overall economic growth. Previous studies have demonstrated that labor mobility between rural and urban areas contributed 16%–20% to overall economic growth during the first two decades of the reforming period (Cai and Wang, 1999; the World Bank, 1998). While passing through the Lewis Turning Point, the contribution of labor migration to overall economic growth declines, even though it is still an important factor driving growth. From 2001 to 2009, the average contribution of labor migration to China's overall economic growth was 16.7% and has continued to decrease in recent years (Cai, et al., 2011).

The rural to urban migration has characterized the labor market over the past decades, along with rapid employment growth and economic transitioning. As an indispensable component in the urban labor market, the needs of migrant workers must be a central focus for policy makers aiming to improve the quality of jobs.

Informality

Informality is the one of the most significant features of the developing labor market. The trend of informality in China has been changing since China started its reform of economic markets, and it is widely believed that both the urban economic restructuring and the rural to urban migration have contributed to the subsequent informalization of the urban labor market. However, due to data limitations, it is difficult to measure the trend of informality using public data sources. As an alternative, Cai and Wang (2004) suggest that the difference between total employment and unit employment in data published by the National Bureau of Statistics (NBS) could be approximated as informal employment. If the "employment residual" approach is applied, the size of China's informal urban sector accounted for 31.5% of urban employment in 2008 and 36.1% in 2005. The informality characteristic of the urban labor market is mostly due to migrant workers. According to a report by NBS (2010), if self-employment and salaried employment without a contract are defined as informal, a full 60% of migrant workers worked informally in 2009.

However, as there is no micro-level national representative data to measure the overall size of informal employment in the urban labor market or to distinguish its components, the three waves of the China Urban Labor Survey are employed here in order to look at the changing trend of informality in urban China. As Figure 7.2 presents, the overall size of informal employment in sampled cities increased from 2001 to 2005 and decreased in 2010.

Figure 7.2 also characterizes the development of the labor market at different stages. For instance, between 2001 and 2005, the market's increased informality was mostly due to increases in the informal employment of local

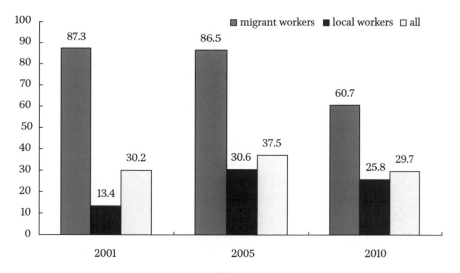

FIGURE 7.2 *The size and components of informal employment in the urban labor market*
SOURCE: AUTHORS' CALCULATIONS FROM CULS DATA.

urban workers due to SOEs restructuring. From 2005 to 2010, the decline in informality was mostly from an increase in the formal employment of migrant workers as a result of stricter labor market regulation. This trend also implies that employment quality might have been improved in past years, as this paper will demonstrate in the following section.

The Framework of Social Protection

Although we have used micro-data to analyze the vulnerability of jobs at the individual level, to a large extent, job quality and stability are determined by the social protection system. Given the fact that resources have increasingly been allocated towards social protection systems, in recent years the Chinese government has been able to implement new social programs so as to cover more vulnerable people. Figure 7.3 depicts the framework of the social protection system in China. This system mainly consists of social insurance programs and social assistance programs, which are characterized as contributory or non-contributory, respectively. As far as social assistance programs go, *dibao* (guarantees) have played a dominant role in terms of both the coverage and the benefits being transferred, and while the social insurance system in urban areas is quite complete, in rural areas, participants only receive limited benefits compared to those of urban programs.

Due to the gradual pace of the construction of social protection policies, the current system is far from complete and is subject to adjustment, improvement, and further reform. Several characteristics of this system are worth noting.

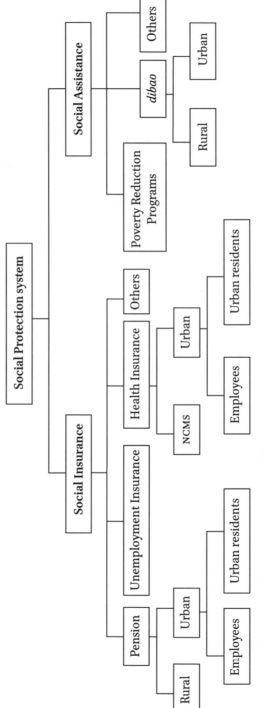

FIGURE 7.3 *The structure of social protection system in China*

The most significant feature of China's current social protection system is the significant gap that exists between rural and urban areas. Although some new programs—for instance, the New Cooperative Medical System, the Rural Pension System, etc.—have been implemented, disparities in social protections between rural and urban areas remain. To a certain extent, rural residents have been better off since new social protection programs were introduced in rural China, but at the same time, China is increasingly faced with the challenge of how to integrate different systems and reduce the gaps in benefits between different groups. This schism in the welfare system may result into further job vulnerability, as we will see later on in this paper.

A second focus of systematic disparity is across the various branches of government. As China starts to prioritize social protection, different government agencies have begun to implement the functions associated with their respective social protection programs, which has led to the emergence of new policy-based divisions for social protection systems and increased coordination costs. For example, the rural medical system is run by the Ministry of Health, while the urban health care system is administered by the Ministry of Human Resources and Social Security. Further examples include the fact that, in addition to overseeing rural pension programs, the Commission on Population and Family Planning is responsible for special programs aiming to support the parents of single children.

In this vein, the interaction between central and local governments in the construction of a cohesive social protection system is worth noting. Most social protection programs are funded by both the central and local governments. Given the disparities in economic development across regions, it is easy to understand why people in poor areas are less protected due to the constraints of limited fiscal capacity at the local level. Furthermore, it leads to segmentation across regions because the rich areas tend to retain their local benefit. This economic disparity may also result in variations in job vulnerability across regions.

Labor Market Institutions

As a result of sustainable and rapid economic development coupled with an aging population, China no longer enjoys an era of unlimited labor supply. Consequently, structural labor shortages have emerged, providing the opportunity to protect lawful rights and the interests of laborers. Under these circumstances, China has accelerated the construction of labor market institutions. A series of institutions for and policies on China's labor market have been enacted recently, which include the Employment Contract Law, the Labor Disputes Mediation and Arbitration Law, the Wage Guideline System, the Minimum Wage Regulations, and the Employment Promotion Law. In addition, the Chinese government has proposed both active and passive labor market policies to respond to labor market fluctuations.

In general, recent reforms in labor market institutions are inclined towards stricter regulations with a focus on employment protection, job security, and formalizing employment. Although it is too early to evaluate the impact of those institutional changes in the labor market, the regulations have had a noticeable effect on labor protection policies, as evidenced by the increasing coverage of social insurance and increased contract-signing.

III   Measuring the Vulnerability of the Urban Labor Market

As noted earlier in this paper, the trend of informality has been changing in the Chinese urban labor market. No matter what definition of informality is used, however, informality is always a binary variable, which is to say, a particular position either is or is not informal; it cannot be both formal and informal. This measurement of job vulnerability is subject to the following flaws.

First of all, there exits great heterogeneity among jobs defined as either formal or informal. Unfortunately, measurements of informality cannot distinguish within the same group. In other words, the vulnerability that workers face within the labor market varies among workers, but has not been observed in measurements of informality as a whole. Second of all, both the difference in job security and in social security could lead to variations in vulnerability, but current informality measurements cannot tell the sources of vulnerability, which weakens its relevance as a policy tool. Thirdly, China has been characterized by economic transition over the past three decades, including institutional changes in the labor market. A good measurement should be able to identify the source of vulnerability in the labor market during the transition, but in this case, we have to introduce some new tools.

In the following paragraphs, we will present methods for measuring informality as a binary variable, but also introduce a multidimensional method of measuring job quality.

Two Components of Vulnerability

A job's given level of vulnerability stems from two sources. First of all, a secure and stable job is of great importance for a worker's wellbeing. In many cases, job insecurity can be a source of vulnerability, but is not well reflected by existing definitions of informality. Secondly, social protection is often linked with employment, and is widely accepted by the current definitions of informality

(ILO, 2002). Therefore, social security is treated as one of the components of job vulnerability.

The Chinese government has taken great efforts to increase the security coverage of contract workers in recent years. In particular, the Employment Contract Law, which was enacted in 2008, has promoted coverage of contract workers. This change could increase job security even if it does not improve social protection. A measurement taken without considering this change may not effectively reflect the reality of the labor market.

For the above reasons, we measure job vulnerability through the following two dimensions. One is social protection, the other is job security. Here, social security protections are measured utilizing China's main social insurance programs as the focal point. For employment security, the characteristics of both employee and employer are considered. The former is reflected by the types of contract the employee signed and the latter is indicated by the characteristics of working place and the size of a given firm. The framework is presented in Figure 7.4.

Analyzing the Job Characteristics
Taking advantage of the China Urban Labor Survey conducted by the Institute of Population and Labor Economics at the Chinese Academy of Social Sciences in 2010, this paper measures individual job quality in two dimensions as noted

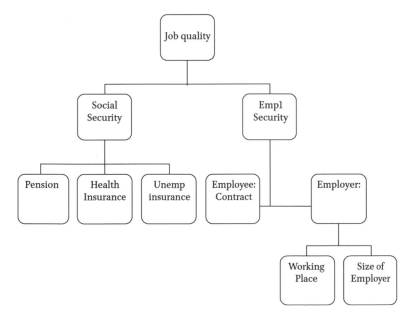

FIGURE 7.4 *Framework of scoring job vulnerability*

earlier. The China Urban Labor Survey (hereafter CULS) was implemented in five cities: Shanghai, Wuhan, Shenyang, Xi'an, and Fuzhou. The first two rounds were conducted in 2001 and 2005, respectively. In each city, 700 local resident households and 600 migrant households were surveyed. A 3-stage Proportional Probability Sampling (PPS) of urban sub-districts, neighbourhoods, and households was used. For each neighbourhood, detailed information of all dwellings is enumerated. For the purpose of this study, only the local resident sample is used. The survey provides information at both the household and individual levels. Detailed questions are designed to measure job characteristics and social security.

Firstly, we look at aspects of social security. Current social insurance programs include pensions, health insurance, and unemployment insurance. Based on the benefits that participants get from each specific program, we score each type of social security to which the workers have access. The more protection a social security program provides, the higher score it would be given. Maximum job vulnerability is scored 10 points. It consists of 5 points from scoring social security and 5 points from scoring job security. Table 7.1 gives details of the scores of social security.

As noted in Figure 7.1, there exists a significant division between migrant workers and local workers in current social security programs. The split lies in two aspects: migrant workers without a local *hukou* are not entitled to urban social insurance programs, and the benefits migrant workers can get from their programs are significantly less than those of local workers. For these reasons, the points allocated to migrant workers who are excluded from urban social insurance programs are significantly less than those of urban local workers.

TABLE 7.1   *Scoring social security in the urban labor market*

		Urban Local Workers	Migrant Workers
Pension			0.5
	Urban Worker Basic Pension	2	
	Urban Resident Pension	1	
Health Insurance			0.5
	Urban Worker Basic HI	2	
	Urban Resident HI	1	
Unemployment Insurance		1	1

Additionally, differences even exist among local workers. In some cases, the social protection for urban local workers is not attached to employers, instead, local governments provide urban resident with security programs. Given that workers have to contribute from their own pocket, the scores for these types of programs are less than those attached to employers.

The second aspect of job vulnerability is reflected by job security. We measure job security based on the types of contract the workers signed and the characteristics of stable employers, including characteristics of working place and the total size of firms. Regarding the types of contract, several aspects are worth noting here. First of all, the Employment Contract Law has not yet been applied to government employees, so federal workers receive a maximum score even without any form of contract. Secondly, for fixed-term or dispatched contract, we assume that a contract of long duration is associated with a stable job and high quality working conditions.

Employers' characteristics affect employment vulnerability, too. In this measurement, we assume that employees in large firms tend to have more stable jobs than those in small firms. Also, decent working places are given high points, referring to the relative stability of their jobs.

In the following section, we observe the pattern of job quality and analyze its determinants based on the above definitions.

IV   Observing the Vulnerability of Jobs in the Urban Labor Market

Applying the above method to CULS data, we may asses the vulnerability of each individual worker. In observing vulnerability in the urban labor market, several perspectives are worth noting here. First of all, the difference between migrant workers and local workers is of great interest in policy making. Second of all, observing the vulnerability within informal/formal group is also of importance. Finally, we can break down the variations of vulnerability into contributing factors based on regression results on the determinants of vulnerability.

Differences in Employment Vulnerability between Migrant and Local Workers

Under the current institutional circumstances, the greatest variations in employment vulnerability between migrant workers and local workers are due to insufficient reforms in the *hukou* system. Based on our measurements, comparisons between the two groups of workers are of significance for the following reasons.

TABLE 7.2   *Scoring the employment security*

		Points
Types of contract		
Formal jobs in government		5
Open-ended contract		5
Fixed term contract		
	More than 3 years	4
	1~3 years	3
	Less than one year	2
Dispatched Contract/ Contract signed for certain work		
	More than 3 years	2
	1~3 years	1
	Less than one year	0.5
Characteristics of working place		
Office or Store		2
Building Site		1
Outdoor Place		0.5
Total size of employees		
More than 20		3
7–19 employees		2
2–6 employees		1

To begin with, it is necessary for the implementation of effective employment policy to compare the level of employment vulnerability between migrant workers and local workers. As noted earlier in this paper, migrant workers tend to work more informally than local workers. Taking advantage of our new measurement in employment vulnerability, it is possible to know the degree of difference between the two groups of workers and act accordingly.

Following this, it is also politically significant to understand from whence the gap of vulnerability between the two groups of workers stems. In this case, observing the differences in employment quality and the difference in social protection is of relevance.

Figure 7.5 displays the findings of vulnerability between migrant workers and local workers. On average, local workers receive 5.4 points based on our measurement in job quality, 1.52 times higher than migrant workers. Breaking down the total scores into their two components, it is easy to see that most of the difference results from the social protection gap between the two groups of workers. For social protection, migrant workers are scored 1.3 points on average, one third of their urban local counterparts. As for their job security score, both groups received very low ratings, with only a score of 0.78 for migrant workers and 1.5 for urban local workers.

The figure also indicates that overall job quality in the labor market is still low. The average job quality score for all workers in the sample is 4.68 points, while the total score possible for this measurement is 10 points. Compared to social security, employment for most workers is not secure, as the average employment security score is only 1.35 for the whole sample.

The Relationship between Individual Characteristics

Given the heterogeneity of workers in the urban labor market, it is necessary to observe which group or type of individuals is the most vulnerable. To achieve this goal, we analyze job quality by individual characteristics, including residence, age, and gender.

The first observation is based on the life-cycle effect of job quality. Figure 7.6 depicts both employment security and social security for migrant workers and local workers, respectively, with different patterns appearing between migrants and local residents. For local workers, job quality is improved with age, but for migrant workers, a significant inverted-U shape is found for both

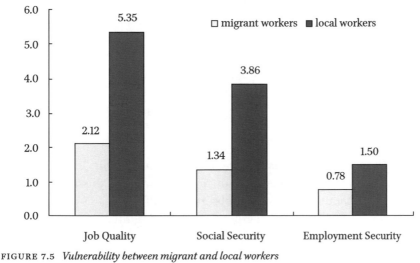

FIGURE 7.5 *Vulnerability between migrant and local workers*
SOURCE: AUTHOR'S CALCULATION FROM CULS DATA.

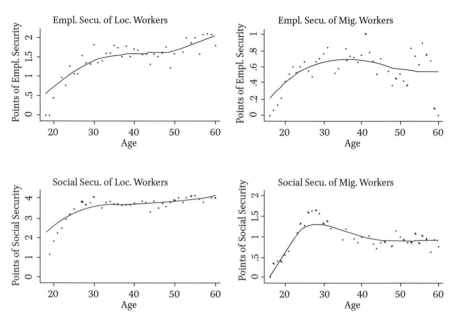

FIGURE 7.6 *Job quality changes over time*
SOURCE: AUTHOR'S CALCULATION FROM CULS DATA.

employment security and social security. Therefore, to improve the well-being of migrant workers, policy should be implemented addressing both new generation of migrants and the old migrant workers.

Table 7.3 describes the vulnerability from a gender perspective. It seems that, without controlling for other individual characteristics, migrant workers have a slightly larger gap in job stability between males and females than their urban local counterpart, where the difference is mainly from employment security. But this could be due to the fact that neither male nor female migrant workers are well protected by the current social protection system. Further analysis of the role of gender in determining vulnerability needs to control for the other factors affecting job quality, which we will examine in the next section.

Observing Variations in Vulnerability within Groups
As noted earlier in this paper, one of the advantages of this new measurement in job quality is that we can observe the differences in job quality for workers within formal/informal groups, while the informality definition treats them the same. Therefore, we can measure the differences between the newly-defined formal and informal employment groups in terms of vulnerability. We

TABLE 7.3   *Vulnerability by gender*

	Vulnerability	Social Security	Employment Security
Migrant Workers			
Males (a)	2.27	1.39	0.88
Females (b)	1.95	1.29	0.66
b/a	0.86	0.93	0.75
Local Workers			
Males (a)	5.54	3.96	1.59
Females (b)	5.10	3.73	1.37
b/a	0.92	0.94	0.86

Source: Author's calculation from CULS data.

use this definition to analyze overall job quality by age for both migrant workers and local workers, as Figure 7.7 shows.

Among those working informally, both local workers and migrant workers display an inverted-U shape in job quality over their lifespan. Through our new measurement, we know that both young workers and elderly workers approaching retirement encounter more insecurity in the labor market than other workers, while the informality measurement is not able to tell this difference. However, despite a similar trajectory over the life-cycle, it seems that local workers are subject to more variations across differing factors than are workers with different ages.

The Sources of Vulnerability

The above analysis indicates that both individual characteristics and residence status determine the quality of jobs. Generally speaking, in a competitive market, individual variations (especially human capital) determine labor market performance, while the household registration status of workers is largely a manifestation of institutional factors. To follow up, we performed a regression analysis of the quality of jobs correlating with variables of individual characteristics, including age, squared age, years of schooling, gender, self-reported health status, status of residence, and cities. Based on the regression results, the methodology of factor analysis proposed by Fields (2002) is applied to the dataset in order to analyze the contributions of determinants to job quality.

Table 7.4 presents the regression results where vulnerability, social security, and job security are taken as dependent variables. As for overall measurement

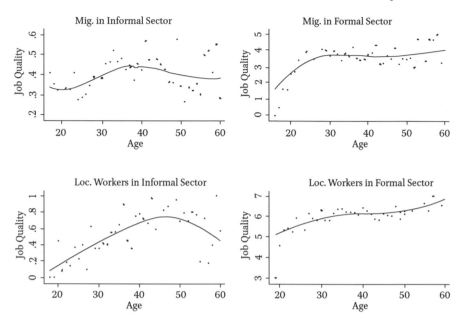

FIGURE 7.7 *Vulnerability informal and informal sectors*
SOURCE: AUTHOR'S CALCULATION FROM CULS DATA.

in job quality, all the individual characteristic variables and residence variable are statistically significant. As indicated in Figure 7.5, the estimation results show an inverted-U shape over the life-cycle. Not surprisingly, people with higher educational achievements or workers in good health tended to work in higher-quality jobs. When controlling for other characteristics, males experience less job vulnerability. Given that other variables are constant, workers with local *hukou* find it easier to get quality jobs than migrant workers.

The last two columns give the estimation results of two components of job quality, from which we may get more information on where the variations in job quality stem. Compared to the regression of total scores, the effect of residence status on job security is much smaller than on social security, which implies that the welfare gap between migrant and local workers are mainly from those institutional arrangements attached to *hukou*.

Table 7.5 presents the breakdown of results by sources contributing to variations in vulnerability. The contributions from both individual characteristics and city variables are aggregated. Residence status accounted for 28.2 percent of variations of social security, but less than 1 percent in explaining job security. This strongly suggests that, when aiming to improve job quality, reforming the social protections attached to the *hukou* system is a pressing issue in China.

TABLE 7.4   *The determinants of vulnerability*

	Vulnerability	Social Security	Job Security
Age	0.146 (7.96)	0.087 (8.17)	0.059 (4.39)
Squared Age (/100)	−0.085 (3.69)	−0.070 (5.24)	−0.0150 (0.89)
Years of Schooling	0.407 (42.45)	0.220 (39.52)	0.187 (26.70)
Gender (male = 1)	0.137 (2.51)	0.089 (2.82)	0.047 (1.19)
Health	0.131 (3.27)	−0.009 (0.38)	0.122 (4.18)
Residence (migrant = 1)	−2.180 (29.54)	−2.05 (47.79)	−0.128 (2.37)
City Variables	Yes	Yes	Yes
Adj. R^2	0.30	0.38	0.099
No. of Observations	11113	11113	11113

Note: the absolute value of t statistics in parenthesis.
Source: Author's calculation from CULS data.

V   Creating Quality Jobs

This article uses the authors' new metric to observe vulnerability in the urban labor market. By forgoing binary measurements of informality, this method of measuring job security and social security as two components can be used in calculating vulnerability. The new measurement allows variations within informal/formal groups, which reflects more information than the traditional metric for measuring employment quality.

In the final analysis, the overall job quality of the urban labor market is quite low. As discussed earlier in this paper, the average scores for job quality are 5.35 for local workers and 2.12 for migrant workers, while the total score possible on this scale is 10 points. On one hand, it is expected that the changing labor market situation will facilitate an improvement in job quality for workers; on the other hand, the government may be expected to make more of an effort towards enhancing the quality of employment and to reduce the risk of engaging with the labor market risk.

With the current substantial transition still ongoing in the labor market, China has witnessed significant changes in to its labor market both in terms of outcomes and institutions in recent years. The empirical analysis of this paper indicates significant gaps in employment quality between migrant and urban local workers, with the major difference coming from disparities in social protection.

TABLE 7.5   *Fields' breakdown of the factors contributing to vulnerability (%)*

	Vulnerability	Social Security	Job Security
Individual characteristics	21.79	18.02	10.60
Residence status	16.88	28.18	0.74
Regional factors	0.89	1.65	0.76
Residual	60.44	52.15	88.00
Total	100	100	100

Source: Author's calculation from CULS data.

TABLE 7.6   *Comparison of social insurance programs coverage rates in 2009*

	Urban workers (%)	Migrant workers (%)
Basic pension	57.0	9.8
Basic health care	52.7	13.1
Unemployment insurance	40.9	3.7
Work injury insurance	47.9	24.1
Maternity insurance	34.9	2.0

Source: NBS (2009); Sheng (2009).

As a result, improving social protection through an expansion of governmental effort ought to be one of the key strategies to achieving inclusive growth in China. Due to their vulnerability within the current social protection system, migrant workers should be the focus of this policy expansion.

Increasing the scope of social protection, especially for migrants, is of great importance to achieving inclusive growth under the current economic situation. Due to the instability of migrants' employment and the high contribution rates of various social security programs, there is a lack of incentive for both migrant workers and their employers to participate in those programs, giving rise to their low coverage (Table 7.6). Those being excluded from labor market institutions and social protection policies are in a position of being exposed to labor market risks and are prevented from serving stably in the main force of the urban labor market. Migrant workers' needs should thus be at the center of labor market institutions and social security system building.

(This article was originally published in Chinese in 2012.)

References

Cai, Fang. 2007. *Lewis Turning Point in China and Its Policy Challenges*. Beijing: Social Science Academic Press.

Cai, Fang, and Wang, D. 1999. "The Sustainability of Economic Growth in China and Labor Contributions." *Journal of Economic Research* 10.

Cai, Fang, Yang Du, and Meiyan Wang. 2011. *Migration and Poverty Reduction in China*, Report submitted to China International Poverty Alleviation Center.

Du Yang, Cai Fang, Wang Meiyan. 2009. "Labor Market Informalization and the Implications for Sustainable Growth." In *China, India, and Beyond*, edited by Natalia Dinello and Wang ShaoguangEdward Elgar Publishing. The World Bank. 1998. *China in 2020: Challenges in New Century*. Beijing: China Finance Press.

Fields, Gary. 2002. "Accounting for Income Inequality and Its Change: A New Method, with Application to the Distribution of Earnings in the United States." Working paper at http://www.ilr.cornell.edu/extension/files/20021024104432-pub785.pdf.

CHAPTER 8

Employment Elasticity and Its Implications for Employment Policy in the "12th Five-Year Period"

Qu Xiaobo

Since the 1990s, a number of domestic and foreign scholars have made empirical studies and interpretations of China's employment elasticity and changes to employment growth. Due to misunderstandings of Chinese employment growth statistics, many of these studies have found relatively strong non-uniformity between China's economic growth and changes in employment or unemployment, and that economic growth does not bring about a corresponding increase in employment. The main reason for this misjudgment and the differences in estimation is insufficiently accurate assessment of the development of the Chinese labor market, insufficiently accurate understanding of the implications of Chinese employment statistics, and thus improper use of macro data. If we cannot properly understand and interpret changes in employment elasticity, this may lead to an inappropriate grasp of employment policy priorities and implications. Therefore, we must systematically analyze research on changes to employment elasticity in order to clarify rational discussion and the interpretation of changes to employment elasticity. This paper aims to discuss the policy implications of changes to employment elasticity during the 12th Five-year Plan.

I Discussion of Employment Elasticity and Its Interpretations

As a rapidly growing developing country, China's employment elasticity and its changes have received widespread attention from academia and many observers, and much domestic and foreign empirical research has calculated and analyzed it. Table 8.1 arranges the relevant research by use of data, research methods, main findings, and the reasons for their deviations. According to the summary of Table 8.1, there are the following discussions, analysis, and main conclusions regarding changes to China's employment elasticity.

1)   The majority of studies on changes in employment elasticity find that China's employment elasticity began to show a clear downward trend

starting in the 1990s, that China's rapid economic growth has not led to a corresponding increase in employment, and that there is significant non-uniformity between employment growth and economic growth (e.g., Qi Jianguo, 2000; Gong Yuquan and Yuan Zhigang, 2002; Zhang Taiqiu, 2004, etc.) The reason is that most studies estimate China's employment elasticity from 1979 to 1978 to have been around 0.3 and that from 1990 to 2004 as around 0.1. Even using panel data estimation and analysis, studies still find a clear downward trend (e.g. Wu Hongluo and Yao Xiqin, 2004; Liu Hongjun, 2003; Xu Xiuchuan, 2005; Li Hongsong, 2003, etc.).

2) Redundant workers at state-owned enterprises (SOEs) and hidden unemployment in rural areas are difficulties in calculating employment elasticity and focal issues, and calculating their size is a technical processing difficulty. Some scholars (Jian Xinhua and Yu Jiang, 2007; Deng Zhiwang et al., 2002) have found that changes to employment elasticity must take into consideration the impact of superfluous staff. Due to SOE reform and other macroeconomic factors, a large number of workers were laid off between 1995 and 2002, and there are obviously redundant workers in China, and the scale of hidden urban and rural unemployment has a large effect on employment elasticity. After considering redundant workers and hidden unemployment, employment elasticity does not exhibit a sharp downturn. Although using the number of laid-off workers to calculate the number of redundant workers and calculate the scale of rural hidden unemployment, the deviation in calculating employment elasticity is relatively small, assuming the method of calculating the scale of hidden unemployment is too strict, it is clear that there are obvious errors.

3) The research finds that there is no typical Okun's law between changes to the publicized unemployment rate (the unemployment rate of the registered urban population) and actual output growth (e.g. Jiang Wei and Liu Shicheng, 2005; Gong Yuquan and Yuan Zhigang, 2002). Employment elasticity values divided into three industries also decreased significantly. There are significant differences in the employment elasticity of the three main economic areas of eastern, central, and western China, and the non-farm employment elasticity of the three areas are markedly higher than overall unemployment elasticity (Zhang Jiangxue, 2003). If we consider the effects of changes to output on employment, after considering the delayed effects produced by China's non-farm industry employment elasticity, employment elasticity will exhibit a considerable increase (Ding Shouhai, 2009). The differences in employment elasticity by three industries are quite large, reflecting the differing abilities of the three industries to absorb employment as the economy grows.

TABLE 8.1   *Discussion of employment elasticity and economic growth estimates and their changes*

Authors	Data	Research Methods
Wu Hongluo and Yao Xiqin (2004)	Total GDP and total employment from "China Statistical Yearbook 1980–2002"	Direct calculation of overall employment elasticity: employment (total) growth rate / total GDP growth rate
Jiang Wei and Liu Shicheng (2005)	Employment numbers and GDP index for the primary, secondary, and tertiary industries published by the National Bureau of Statistics	By building employment growth models for the primary, secondary, and tertiary industries, and by estimating employment growth through regression.
Rawski (2001)	GDP and employment data from "China Statistical Yearbook" and "China Statistical Abstract" for the corresponding years.	Direct calculation of the growth rate of urban formal sector employment.
Chang Jinxiong (2004)	Employment, GDP, industrial output, wages, and price indices from the "China Statistical Yearbook 2003" and "China Labor Statistical Yearbook 2003."	GDP employment elasticity = employment growth rate / GDP growth rate; non-farm employment elasticity = non-farm employment growth rate / GDP growth rate; urban employment

Main Results	Commentary
From 1978–2001, alongside sustained and rapid economic growth, employment elasticity exhibited a downward trend. For example, from 1985–1990, the economic growth rate was 7.89%, while employment elasticity was 0.305; from 1991–1995, the GDP growth rate was 11.6%, while employment elasticity was 0.134.	Because what is reflected is the growth relationship between overall urban and rural employment and total GDP, statistically, agriculture plays the role of an employment reservoir. Thus, it is limited in changes to the amount of employment growth (elasticity).
There is no typical Okun's law between changes to China's publicized unemployment rate (the unemployment rate of registered urban residents) and the actual output growth rate.	The unemployment figures released by the National Bureau of Statistics are only the registered unemployment rate, and this reflects very different content than the unemployment rate used in market economies.
From 1987 to 1991, urban employment grew a cumulative 23.2%. From 1997 to 2001, urban employment grew a cumulative 0.8%, which is used as evidence for doubting that China's real economic growth rate.	The reason that employment growth is underestimated is China's diversified economic sectors. Major changes have occurred to the employment structure, and only looking at changes in employment at state-owned and collective economic units not only does not reflect employment growth, but results in erroneous judgment.
Employment elasticity has declined, and China's economic growth has not brought about a corresponding increase in employment; the reform of the employment system for laid-off workers of state-owned and collective enterprises reduced employment activities; declining	(1) The three different types of employment elasticities use the same GDP growth, expanding the denominator effect; (2) using the proportion of workers to total urban employment to express reform of the labor employment system overlooks the significant increase in

(*Continued*)

TABLE 8.1 (*Continued*)

Authors	Data	Research Methods
		elasticity = urban employment growth rate / GDP growth rate.
Gong Yuquan and Yuan Zhigang (2002); Tang Kuang and Liu Yongjun (2003); Xu Xiuchuan (2005)	Corresponding data from the "China Statistical Yearbook" from 1999 to 2001.	Total employment elasticity = total employment growth rate / GDP growth rate; dividing the economic growth model by industry to estimate employment elasticity
Qi Jianguo (2000); Wang Lei and Wu Shuang (2003)	"China Statistical Yearbook" for the corresponding years	Calculates total employment elasticity and industrial employment elasticity based on the definition of employment elasticity.
Li Hongsong (2003); Zhang Chewei (2002)	Corresponding data from the "China Statistical Yearbook" from 1999 to 2001.	Li uses the differentiated formula method of employment elasticity and the economic growth model method to estimate through regression. Zhang uses the definition of employment elasticity for his calculations.

Main Results	Commentary
employment elasticity is the result of increasing labor productivity.	employment outside of work units; (3) urban employment elasticity > non-farm employment elasticity > than total employment elasticity signifies that increases in labor productivity have not reduced employment elasticity.
Since reform and opening, employment elasticity values across the primary, secondary, and tertiary industries have decreased significantly, and the relationship between economic growth and changes in employment has exhibited strong non-uniformity.	The reason for the underestimation is that total employment elasticity uses overall urban and rural employment numbers, reducing the effect of employment growth coming mainly from cities and towns. Employment data for the primary, secondary, and tertiary industries is reported rather than coming from surveys of urban households, and therefore misses a lot of new jobs.
The main reason for the sharp decline in the employment elasticity of macroeconomic growth is the sharp decline of industrial employment elasticity.	Both total employment elasticity and industrial employment elasticity have been underestimated as employment numbers in the industrial sector are reported rather than the result of surveys.
From 1978–1989, average employment elasticity was 0.311, which fell to 0.124 from 1991–2001; the employment elasticity level fell markedly, and the pulling role of economic growth weakened.	The errors in Li's calculation of employment elasticity are the same as those listed above. While Zhang also underestimates employment elasticity by breaking it down by industry, by analyzing changes to the structure of employment elasticity, he finds that China's economic growth creates sufficient employment opportunities.

(*Continued*)

TABLE 8.1 (*Continued*)

Authors	Data	Research Methods
Zhang Jiangxue (2003)	"Fifty-year Collection of Statistical Materials from New China (1949–1999)," "China Statistical Yearbook 2004," "Historical Data of China Gross Domestic Product Calculations 1952–2002."	Dual panel data model to estimate the employment elasticity and non-farm employment elasticity of three major regions.
Cai Fang, Du Yang, and Gao Wenshu (2004)	Data from "China Statistical Yearbook" and "China Town and Township Enterprises Yearbook" for the corresponding years.	Urban employment elasticity: annual growth rate of urban employment / urban GDP growth rate.
Jian Xinhua and Yu Jiang (2007)	Two sets of data from the "China Labor and Social Security Yearbook" and "China Statistical Summary 2002" for the relevant years.	Regression calculation by building a model of the employment elasticity of redundant workers.
Deng Zhiwang, Cai Xiaofan, and Zheng Dihua (2002)	"China Statistical Yearbook" from 1991, 1996, and 2000.	Calculates the scale of urban and rural hidden unemployment considering the employment elasticity coefficient of hidden unemployment.

Main Results	Commentary
There are significant differences between the employment elasticity of eastern, central, and western China. From 1978–2003, eastern China was the highest at 0.135, which exceeded the average national level, while central and western regions were below the national average at 0.116 and 0.126, respectively. Non-farm employment elasticity was markedly higher than total employment elasticity in the economy.	While the employment elasticity divided into eastern, central, and western China in this research is slightly higher than similar research, there are still errors in the estimates. Because non-farm employment numbers separated by region, like employment numbers separated by industry, are derived from the reports of work units to government, they do not reflect the true employment level broken down by region.
Urban employment elasticity overall has exhibited an upward trend since the early 1990s, showing a greater economic growth employment elasticity than the results of calculating overall urban-rural employment elasticity or employment elasticity broken down by the primary, secondary, and tertiary industries.	GDP growth rate is used to calculate urban employment elasticity, which can better reflect the true employment growth situation. At the same time, calculating the natural unemployment rate can explain why economic growth has not growth employment growth.
Employment elasticity after the effects of eliminating redundant workers between 1980 and 2004 show that the ability of GDP to pull employment did not fall after 1995.	There are clearly significant errors in using the number of workers laid off due to restructuring to calculate the number of redundant workers and their effect on employment elasticity. There is still no clear verdict on how to use better data to calculate the effect of redundant workers on employment elasticity.
Besides 1985 to 1994 when the employment elasticity coefficient showed a larger fluctuation, the employment elasticity coefficient was basically unchanged and a so-called sharp decline did not occur.	Considers hidden unemployment in rural areas and takes into account the "reservoir" effect of the rural labor force; the deviation is relatively small, but the assumptions of the method of calculating the scale of hidden unemployment are too strict.

(Continued)

TABLE 8.1 (*Continued*)

Authors	Data	Research Methods
Ray Brooks & Ran Tao (2003)	"China Statistical Yearbook," "China Labor Statistical Yearbook," and CEIC database.	Employment growth rate divided by industry and province; regression estimates of fixed effects of non-farm employment divided by region.
Ding Shouhai (2009)	"China Statistical Yearbook" 2000–2006, "Statistical Yearbook" for various provinces, and "China Labor Statistical Yearbook"	Dynamic estimation model by introducing assumptions of quasi-fixed labor factor assumptions, based on panel data estimates of employment elasticity.
Fang Mingyue et al. (2010)	Data for state-owned enterprises and other enterprises above a certain size for 1999–2005.	The microscopic employment elasticity measure is derived from the production function, and the dynamic panel method (system GMM) is used for estimation.

Main Results	Commentary
Employment elasticity was only half of the GDP growth rate from 1980–2001; forecast that employment grew by 4 million jobs between 2003–2005 and 11.5 million between 2003–2010.	Overall non-farm employment reduced the effect of changes to employment growth; as data reported by work units, employment numbers by region and by industry are lower than the actual employment numbers. Employment growth forecasts for 2003 to 2005 now seem to be far lower than the actual annual employment growth rate.
If only considering the immediate effects of output changes on employment, China's non-farm employment elasticity is indeed low. But after taking into account the lagged effects of output, employment elasticity will show a considerable increase. Especially in industry in the east and the service industry in the west, employment elasticity increased to 0.3 and 0.4, respectively.	Using the modified dynamic estimation model, there is relatively little error in using the estimated long-term non-farm employment elasticity to directly calculate non-farm employment elasticity. But due to the use of provincial employment data divided by industry, there are errors in the estimated results. For example, the research shows that a greater employment impact may break out in central and western regions, which does not match with the current reality.
In terms of short-term employment elasticity, Hong Kong, Macau, Taiwan, and foreign companies have the highest elasticity, private and collective enterprises have mid-level elasticity, and state-owned and other companies have the lowest elasticity. In terms of long-term employment elasticity, Hong Kong, Macau, Taiwan, foreign, and private companies still have higher employment elasticity than state-owned and collective enterprises.	The study uses micro-enterprises data and uses the concept of macro-employment elasticity to measure changes to micro-employment elasticity. This is conducive to understanding and discovering the influence mechanisms of different enterprise ownership structures on micro-employment elasticity and has valuable policy implications and inspiration.

(Continued)

TABLE 8.1 (*Continued*)

Authors	Data	Research Methods
Douglas Zhihua Zeng (2005)	Census data from 1990 and 2000, "China Statistical Yearbook" data for the corresponding years, and China Labor Statistical Yearbook" data for the corresponding years.	Estimates official statistics, the urban unemployment rate of laid-off workers, and the formal urban unemployment rate. Divides output elasticity by industry.
Günter Schucher (2009): Bottelier (2009)	"China Statistical Yearbook" data for the corresponding years	Calculates overall nominal employment elasticity, employment (total) growth rate / total GDP growth rate.
MingLu, Jianyong Fan, Shejian Liu (2005)	"China Statistical Yearbook 2000" and "China Statistical Summary 2001"	Calculates GDP employment elasticity by industry and by primary, secondary, and tertiary industry and by industry.

Main Results	Commentary
Employment elasticity estimated by industry and by time period shows that from 1985 to 1999, employment elasticity fell in the primary and secondary industries. China's biggest challenge in acceding to the WTO was creating 1 to 3 million new jobs in a decade to absorb laid-off workers and the transferring rural labor force.	Since informal employment dominated urban unemployment growth after the 1990s, estimating only the employment rate of the formal sector will overestimate the level of unemployment. Estimating employment elasticity by industry underestimates employment growth, especially employment growth in labor-intensive, private companies in the secondary industry. Realistically, urban employment growth has already eliminated the employment challenges that the author fears.
In the 1980s, GDP employment elasticity was 0.3, which fell to 0.1 by the end of the 1990s. From 2000 to 2007, employment elasticity was 0.11.	As employment elasticity in China's overall rural farm sector has a difficult time reflecting changes to incremental employment growth, overall nominal employment elasticity underestimates actual job growth.
Since 1997, the secondary industry has had negative GDP employment elasticity. Due to its relatively high employment elasticity, the service industry has become a major job-creating sector, while manufacturing industry employment elasticity has become negative.	The numbers of employees broken down by industry and by profession does not include a large number of urban jobs not covered by the employment statistics system, resulting in an underestimation of the employment elasticity of the secondary industry and the manufacturing industry.

4)   Changes to urban employment elasticity better reflect the situation of
     changes to employment growth in the process of economic growth.
     Urban employment elasticity has exhibited an overall upward trend since
     the early 1990s, exhibiting greater economic growth employment elastic-
     ity than calculating based on the overall urban-rural method and the
     three-industries method. As the employment numbers used to calculate
     urban employment elasticity are different from those used in the calcula-
     tions of other research, the employment elasticity of economic growth
     comes from the role of employment outside of work units. In other words,
     the conclusion that economic growth has not brought employment
     reached by past research is inaccurate. It can only be said that economic
     growth has not brought overt unemployment (Cai Fang, Du Yang, Gao
     Wenshu, 2004).

5)   High investment growth has not driven employment growth at a corre-
     sponding rate. Under the same output or investment, the employment
     numbers that businesses of different types are able to attract are differ-
     ent. The researchers (Fang Mingyue et al., 2010) observed and studied the
     relationship between changes to employment elasticity and business
     type and ownership structure from a company micro perspective.
     In terms of short-term employment elasticity, Hong Kong, Macau,
     Taiwanese, and foreign companies had the highest elasticity, private and
     collective enterprises had mid-level elasticity, and state-owned and other
     enterprises had the lowest elasticity. In the long-term, Hong Kong, Macau,
     Taiwanese, foreign, and private companies still had higher employment
     elasticity than state-owned and collective enterprises. Therefore, a
     policy-making perspective, those companies that can attract more
     employment numbers and the industries in which they reside should be
     the focus of government fiscal support.

II   Mistakes in Judgment and Statistical Understanding of Employment Elasticity

How can we correctly understand the aforementioned judgments and explanations of Chinese employment elasticity and employment growth and ratio-
nally grasp the implications employment elasticity reveals and their policy
inspiration? From the comments on existing studies of employment elasticity
in Table 8.1, we can see that most studies contain a certain degree of error
and underestimate employment elasticity and are not accurate or complete

enough in their judgment and explanation of changes to employment elasticity and employment growth. These errors can be attributed to the following:

First, the changes to overall employment elasticity calculated in many studies reflect the growth relationship between changes to overall urban-rural employment and changes to GDP. Statistically, the rural labor force plays the role of a reservoir of unemployment, with agriculture taking in all jobs that the non-farm industry cannot absorb, and it has a difficult time effectively reflecting employment changes. Thus, explanations of changes to the amount of increase in employment (elasticity) are limited. For example, Wu Hongluo and Yao Xiqin (2004, Liu Hongjun (2003), Xu Xiuchuan (2005), Ji Jianguo (2000), Günter Schucher (2009), Bottelier (2009) and others evaluate using overall employment elasticity. Meanwhile, on the other hand, the employment numbers used to calculate employment elasticity broken down by sector do not include employment outside of work unit employment channels. Thus, a significant amount of employment growth outside of work units, namely employment growth in the urban informal sector, is excluded from the calculations, and employment elasticity is underestimated. Such studies include Ji Jianguo (2000) and Wang Lei and Wu Shuang (2003).

Second, China's statistical data for labor and employment on the one hand has shown a general downward trend by work unit-type and employment divided by sector. On the other hand, it has shown continuous growth in the overall number of jobs (Cai Fang, 2004). A discrepancy has formed between total non-farm employment and the number of jobs divided by sector (the average number is around 100 million, see Table 8.2), reflecting a significant disparity between sectorial and total employment. In fact, the main contributing force of sustained urban employment growth is reflected in this discrepancy (Cai Fang, 2007). Changes in the number of people and employment elasticity in formal sectors like state-owned, collective, and new-style economic work units cannot fully explain changes in total employment growth, leading to misjudgments about China's employment growth, such as by Rawski (Rawski, 2001) and Douglas Zhihua Zeng (2005). Therefore, numbers from within the statistical scope of work unit employment can no longer fully reflect the employment growth situation.

Third, due to increasingly diverse economic sectors, the employment structure has undergone great change, and the traditional statistical system is no longer able to cover all urban employment. The urban employment amount reported in the official statistics system is calculated based on surveys of city labor markets, while employment numbers by industrial type, by industry, and by region are collected from within the statistical reporting system

TABLE 8.2   *The statistical coverage situation of changes to the urban employment structure*
            unit: 10,000 people

Year	Total Urban Employment	Work Unit Employment	Private Companies and Individual Bodies	No System Statistics	Number of Migrant Workers
2000	23151	11585	3404	8162	7849
2001	23940	11123	3658	9159	8399
2002	24780	10870	4268	9642	10470
2003	25639	10809	4922	9908	11390
2004	26476	10937	5515	10024	11820
2005	27331	11225	6236	9870	12580
2006	28310	11485	6966	9859	13210
2007	29350	11801	7891	9658	13700
2008	30210	11972	8733	9505	14040
2009	31120	12323	9789	9008	14530

Source: Calculated based on relevant data from *China Statistical Yearbook 2009.*

(Cai Fang and Wang Meiyan, 2004) and are lower than the actual employment numbers. Thus, changes to employment elasticity from previous calculated using data broken down by region, by industrial type, and by industry, have in reality underestimated employment growth, such as studies by Douglas Zhihua Zeng (2005) and Ray Brooks and Ran Tao (2003). In addition, in calculating GDP employment elasticity, non-farm employment elasticity, and urban employment elasticity, some studies use the same GDP growth rate, expanding the denominator effect in calculating employment elasticity, such as Chang Jinhong (2005).

In fact, since reform, China's strong economic growth ahs been accompanied by the growth of urban employment. The employment structure has undergone great changes, and the traditional statistical system can no longer cover all urban employment. Therefore, numbers within the statistical scope of work unit employment can no longer fully reflect the employment growth situation. Even so, between 1978 and 2002, the annual urban employment growth rate was 4.1 percent, an average annual growth of 6.36 million workers (Cai Fang, 2004). From 2002 to 2009, an average of 9.06 million workers were added to the urban employment roles (Table 8.2). One can see that the employment statistics covered by the statistical system have obviously shown a relatively significant employment growth, indicating that relevant studies have misjudged China's employment growth (such as Ray Brooks & Ran Tao, 2003 in Table 8.1).

Work unit employees include those from state-owned work units, collective work units, cooperative work units, joint venture work units, limited liability work units, joint stock companies, Hong Kong, Macau, and Taiwanese-invested work units, and foreign-invested work units. Migrant worker numbers came from the "China Rural Household Survey Statistical Yearbook." Numbers for 2009 came from the "China Statistical Summary 2010" and the National Bureau of Statistics "Migrant Worker Monitoring Report 2010."

Thus, the errors in judging employment elasticity in most studies come from misunderstandings of labor statistics. Intrinsic inaccurate grasp of China's employment growth and structural changes is caused by inaccurate evaluations of the transformation and development of the labor market and inaccurate understanding of the meanings of China's employment statistics.

It should be noted that the empirical research and interpretations of changes to employment elasticity has to a certain extent provided us a proper understanding of the implications revealed by changes to employment elasticity. 1) In the economic development process, economic growth and employment growth are not necessarily synchronous, that is, economic growth does not necessarily bring with it employment in the same or greater proportion. This is closely related to the macroeconomic objectives of the economic growth process. 2) Adjustment to the economic structure is closely related to employment absorption capacity. There are large differences and changes in employment elasticity between overall employment elasticity and that calculated by industrial type, explaining the trend of employment changes in the future structural adjustment process. Figure 8.1 also shows that the differences in the changes to employment elasticity among the primary, secondary, and tertiary industries using the latest statistical data are quite significant. Among these, employment elasticity is lowest in the primary industry. The secondary industry's ability to absorb labor force is on the decline. Changes to employment elasticity in the tertiary industry have shown a higher ability to attract employment. The trend of changes to overall employment elasticity is similar to that of tertiary industry employment elasticity. 3) There are significant differences in the employment elasticity of the three major economic regions of eastern, central, and western China, with the eastern region being the main force for creating jobs. This is because the eastern region's economy is developed, and it creates significant demand for labor. On the other hand, because of the concentration of labor-intensive industry in the eastern region, the employment driven by production in the same industry is higher than the proportion mainly coming from eastern region labor-intensive industry, which is higher than

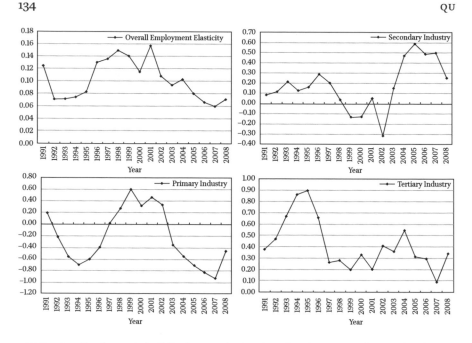

FIGURE 8.1 *Employment elasticity since 1991 broken down by primary, secondary, and tertiary industry*
SOURCE: CHINA STATISTICAL YEARBOOK 2009.

central and western regions. But with the development of the western region and the further promotion of the rise strategy of the central region, the non-farm job-creating ability of central and western regions will further increase in the future. Improving employment statistics indicators and the information collection system are essential for a true picture of employment elasticity and are also the foundation of focused promotion of employment and handling different types of unemployment. 5) Changes to urban employment reflect true changes to employment in the economic growth process. The number of employment opportunities brought on by investment and production are related to the selection of industry and the composition of industries.

III   Implications of Employment Policy during the 12th Five-year Plan Period

By reviewing and analyzing the relevant research on variations to employment elasticity, we can see that economic growth and the priority order of macro-control objectives for employment growth are closely related, as are the choices of industry in economic structural adjustment and the ability to absorb employment. The differences in the unemployment types of different labor groups, the regional differences in true employment changes reflected by urban employment growth and the employment absorbed in economic growth, etc., trigger the main sources of changes to employment elasticity and the main content revealed by changes to employment elasticity. Based on this, in the period of the 12th Five-year Plan, if China's economic growth continues, what are the employment policy implications revealed by employment elasticity and what is the focus of attention? To this end, we open the following discussion.

A   Clarify the Priority Order of Employment Targets within Macroeconomic Regulation and Optimize the Methods of Employment Regulation

First, we must rediscover the relationships between promoting employment and sustainable economic growth, maintaining price stability and achieving international balance of payments and hold up promoting employment as the primary objective of maintaining macroeconomic stability. Promoting employment must be made the primary objective of regulation because from the research on changes to employment elasticity, we can see that maintaining a certain rate of economic growth is a necessary condition for achieving full employment, but not a sufficient condition. Thus, only identifying growth targets often makes it difficult to achieve employment goals.

Second, we must clearly state employment goals, which is conducive to determining regulatory principles when conflict arises between employment and other macroeconomic objectives. For example, the employment rate and price level often move in opposite directions, and different government departments oversee the two indicators. Determining the principle of employment as a priority at a higher level is conducive to ensuring a stable employment situation when faced with complex macro-control situations.

Third, we must improve the urban employment statistical system, grasp labor market trends through scientific indicators and the information collection system, and optimize regulatory measures. Do we "need better-looking data or more accurate statistical data to guide macro regulation and employment policy?" For some time, the information distortion and negative impact of the relevant registered unemployment rate have been the subject of widespread societal concern and ample discussion. During the 12th Five-year Plan period, we should as quickly as possible use the surveyed employment rate as the main indicator for employment regulation and implementation. This would be very beneficial to the understanding of China's employment situation and the formulation of related policy.

To this end, in the period of the 12th Five-year Plan, take "giving priority to employment, controlling the level of unemployment" as an independent and priority macro-regulatory objective and further enrich, improve, and optimize the goals and methods of employment regulation.

B   *Formulate Targeted Employment Protections and Job-Promoting*
          Policies According to the Unemployment Types of Different
          Labor Groups

Changes to employment elasticity tell us that in different periods of economic development, due to institutional and policy reasons, plus the different characteristics of urban and rural laborers in age structure and human capital, when the different labor groups in cities and the countryside face different types of unemployment risks, there are differences in the vulnerabilities exposed.

First, from the perspective of the labor market, because migrant workers become the main source of labor supply, migrant workers are more vulnerable to shocks to the labor market and are more easily affected by cyclical economic factors, alternating between unemployment and shortages with changes to the macroeconomic climate. To counter their lack of coverage by social protection systems, we must break through systemic partition that the household registration system places between the labor market and public services by allowing migrant workers to enjoy unified and equal urban welfare and public services. We must promote the construction of a social protection system for migrant workers and make sure positive employment policy extends to migrant workers.

Second, the workers born in the 1940s and 1950s, who have weak human capital, are often vexed by structural, frictional, natural unemployment. For this disadvantaged group, active employment policy should focus on improving their employability and establishing a targeted unemployment mechanism for disadvantaged groups. The implementation of social protection policies will need to be more targeted and effective. At the same time, more public-welfare jobs should be created for these groups according to their culture, age, skills, physical fitness, and families.

Third, because university graduates possess specialized human capital, there is a discrepancy between their employment expectations and the demands of the labor market. Moreover, the higher the educational achievement of a worker, the higher his or her reservation wage, which makes it easier for higher-educated workers to be in a state of unemployment. Therefore, this group will face structural and frictional natural unemployment for the long-term. Moderate social protections and active job training, intermediaries, and other public employment services can reduce the time graduates of higher education spend seeking employment. Thus, during the period of the 12th Five-year Plan, we must implement a wider range of targeted, active employment policies according to the particular labor market demands for different groups of laborers.

C   Promote New-style, Urbanized Development by Focusing on Promoting the Service Industry

From empirical studies on employment elasticity, one can learn that changes to urban unemployment can better reflect true changes to employment growth in the process of economic growth, and the service-oriented tertiary industry has better employment absorption capacity than the primary and secondary industries. Thus, during the period of the 12th Five-year Plan, promoting new-style, urbanized development through a focus on promoting the service industry will bring about a greater employment-promotion effect. Because population concentrated in cities is the foundation of a large-scale service industry and a finer division of labor, the development of the urban service industry is the most important path to resolving future urban employment. For this reason, we should accelerate the modern service industry system and mechanism innovation, break up monopolies in the telecommunications, civil aviation, railroad, and posts industries to attract more private capital into the modern service industry. We should actively spur the partitioning and upgrading of traditional service industries such as home management, adapt to different levels of market demand, extend the industrial chain of the traditional service industry, and fully tap the employment potential of the traditional services sector. Meanwhile, we should absorb the lessons from the US and Europe, which were seriously affected by the financial crisis and where the employment situation was grim. In the process of urbanization, we should maintain the manufacturing sector in a certain proportion in cities (including megacity areas like Beijing and Shanghai) to satisfy multiple levels of employment demand (Yusuf, 2008).

D   Respect the Objective Laws of Industrial Development and Bring Regional Comparative Advantages into Play

The regional differences in changes in employment elasticity reflect that, because different comparative advantages across regions attract very different job numbers, promoting employment should respect the rules of industrial development in the process of economic development and bring regional comparative advantages into play. With the adjustment and transformation of the economic and industrial structures of eastern China, labor-intensive manufacturing industry and low-end service industry will gradually move toward central and western regions. Fostering the development of labor-intensive industries in central and western regions, avoiding deviation from the comparative advantage of labor-intensive industry, allowing central and western regions to play a greater role in attracting rural population to cities and towns.

However, labor-intensive industry is not driving the current rise of central and western regions. The degree of capital intensity in manufacturing in central and western China has increased rapidly since 2000, at a speed much faster than coastal areas, to the point where it is already higher than coastal areas. This capital-intensive phenomenon mainly originates from the government-led and investment-driven nature of accelerated industrialization in central and western China.

Therefore, we should adjust the regional development strategy and pull central and western region back to a development path of comparative advantage immediately. In terms of industrial structure policy, we should adhere to the principle of continuing eastern labor-intensive industry in central and western regions. In terms of regional policy, we should persist in bringing the labor-resources comparative advantage of central and western regions into play rather than the government-led, investment-driven, accelerated industrialization model.

E   *Improve the Basic Public Service System and Establish Mechanisms to Protect Employment*

Under the same output and investment, because the system is imperfect and the public service system is unsound, it will have a significant repressive role on spurring employment. A basic public service system can provide effective information support to address frictional unemployment, reduce the impact of economic fluctuations on employment, and increase the stability of employment. The specific content of a basic public services system includes public employment services, social security including various types of basic social protections and social assistance, basic medical and public health services, basic education, affordable housing, and public safety. The Fifth plenary session of the 17th Central Committee of the CPC stated that China must gradually improve a basic public service system that suits national conditions, is relatively comprehensive, covers both city and countryside, and is sustainable, namely, focusing on designing a routine, long-acting, financially guaranteed system to cover all citizens rather than just urban residents and adapted to China's current stage of economic development, which guarantees the basic public service needs of the main areas of basic people's livelihood.

From the perspective of promoting employment, the focus of improving the public service system needs to be on improving the government's guarantee, separating basic social protections from the type of employer and ownership structure, push forward equal access to basic public services so that laborers have the same access to public services as they move to different jobs throughout the country. As employment contradictions shift from contradictions based on the overall number of jobs to structural contradictions, we must improve the public services system and establish a guaranteed employment system, establish and improve a unified employment information system and service platform, strengthen information services, employment introduction, and job training for rural laborers, and reduce the real costs and opportunity costs of labor force employment.

(This article was originally published in Chinese in 2011.)

References

Brooks, Ray and Ran Tao. "China's Labor Market Performance and Challenges." *IMF Working Paper*, WP/03/210.

Cai Fang. 2004. "The Consistency of China's Employment Statistics: Facts and Publicy Implications." *Chinese Journal of Population Science*, Vol. 3, 2004.

Cai Fang. 2007. "China's Employment Growth and Structural Changes." *Social Science Management and Review*, Vol. 2, 2007.

Cai Fang, Du Yang, and Gao Wenshu. 2004. "Employment Elasticity, Natural Unemployment, and Macroeconomic Policy—Why Has Economic Growth Not Brought Overt Employment?" *Economic Research*, Vol. 9, 2004.

Cai Fang and Wang Meiyan. 2004. "Informal Employment and Labor Market Development—Reading Chinese Urban Employment Growth." *Economic Perspectives*, Vol. 1, 2004.

Chang Jinxiong. 2005. "China's Employment Elasticity Determinants and Employment Effects." *Journal of Finance and Economics*, Vol. 3, 2005.

Choi, Chang kon. 2007. "The Employment Effect of Economic Growth: Identifying Determinants of Employment Elasticity." faculty.washington.edu/karyiu/confer/busan07/papers/jin.pdf

Deng Zhiwang, Cai Xiaofan, and Zheng Dihua. 2002. "Sharp Decline in the Employment Elasticity Coefficient: Fact or Illusion." *Population and Economy*, Vol. 5, 2002.

Ding Shouhai. 2009. "How Big Is China's Employment Elasticity?—Also on the Impact of the Financial Crisis on Employment." *Management World*, Vol. 5, 2009.

Fang Mingyue, Nie Huihua, Jiang Ting, and Tan Songtao. 2010. "Estimates of the Employment Elasticity of Chinese Industrial Enterprises." *World Economy*, Vol. 8, 2010.

Gong Yuquan and Yuan Zhigang. 2002. "The Non-conformance of China's Economic Growth and Employment Growth and Their Formation Mechanisms." Economic Perspectives, Vol. 10, 2002.

Islam, Iyanatul and Suahasil Nazara. 2000. "Estimating Employment Elasticity for the Indonesian Economy." ILO 2000.

Jian Xinhua and Yu Jiang. 2007. "Estimates of Chinese Employment Elasticity Based on Redundant Workers." *Economic Research*, Vol. 6, 2007.

Jiang Wei and Liu Shicheng. 2005. "Okun Model and China (1978–2004)." *Economics and Decision-making*, Vol. 12, 2005.

Kapsos, S. "The employment intensity of growth: Trends and macroeconomic determinants." Employment Strategy Paper, No. 12 (Geneva, ILO, 2005).

Li Hongsong. 2003. "Study of China's Economic Growth and Employment Elasticity Issues." *Journal of Finance and Economics*, Vol. 6, 2003.

Padalino, S. and Vivarelli M. 1997. "The Employment Intensity of Economic Growth in G7 Countries." *International Labour Review*, Vol. 136, no. 2, p. 211.

Piacentini, Paolo and Paolo Pini. 2000. "Growth and Employment: Productivity Gains and Demand Constraints." In M. Pianta and M. Vivarelli (eds.), *The Employment Impact of Innovation: Evidence and Policies*, London: Routledge.

Qi Jianguo. 2000. "2000: The Biggest Threat to China's Economy Is a Sharp Decline in Employment Elasticity." *World Economy*, Vol. 3, 2000.

Rawski, Thomas G. 2001. "What is happening to China's GDP statistics?" *China Economic Review*.

Rangarajan, C. 2007. "Employment and Growth." *ICRA Bulletin-Money & Finance*.

Tang Kuang and Liu Yongjun. 2003. "Research, Review, Summary, and Commentary on the Inconsistency of Chinese Economic Growth and Changes to Employment Elasticity." *Market & Demographic Analysis*, Vol. 6, 2003.

Wang Lei and Wu Shuang. 2003. "A Summary of Research on Economic Growth, Employment Growth, and Employment Elasticity." *China Human Resources*, 2003.

World Bank. 2009. "From Poor Areas to Poor People: Assessing Poverty and Inequality in China," research report.

Wu Hongluo and Yao Xiqin. 2004. "China's Economic Growth and Employment Growth in Transition." *Fuzhou University Journal* (Philosophy and Social Sciences Edition), Vol. 3, 2004.

Xu Xiuchuan. 2005. "Selection of Methods for Calculating Employment Elasticity and Empirical Analysis Based on Chinese Data." *Southwest Agricultural University Journal*, Vol. 3, 2005.

Yusuf, Shahid and Nabeshinma, K. 2008. "Optimizing Urban Development", in Yusuf and Saich ed., *China Urbanizes Consequences, Strategies, and Policies.* The World Bank, Washington, D.C.

Zeng, Douglas Zhihua. 2005. "China's Employment Challenges and Strategies after the WTO Accession." *World Bank Policy Research Working Paper* 3522, February 2005.

Zhang Chewei and Cai Fang. 2002. "The Trends of Changes to Employment Elasticity." *China Industrial Economics*, Vol. 5, 2002.

Zhang Jiangxue. 2005. "Comparison of Employment Elasticity in China's Three Major Economic Regions—Based on Panel Data Model Empirical Research." *Quantitative and Technical Economics*, Vol. 10, 2005.

Zhang Taiqiu. 2004. "Analysis of the Inconsistency between China's Economic Growth and Job Growth." *Nanjing University of Finance and Economics Journal*, Vol. 3, 2004.

CHAPTER 9

Changes to the Industrial Structure and Regional Migration during the 12th Five-Year Plan Period

Wu Yaowu

In the process of market-oriented reform and opening, Chinese companies made full use of their comparative advantage of abundant labor and selected and developed labor-intensive industries. While creating rapid economic growth, this also created a large number of non-farm jobs, which fundamentally changed the old dual employment structure. By analyzing the regional and structural particularities of employment growth, this essay makes predictions as to the direction and scale of future job growth, then analyzes the migration of farm labor to non-farm industry to assess the possible constraints faced in the next stage of economic growth. Credible predictions depend on the following conditions: high-quality data, correct model-setting, and assumed conditions that are close to reality. In order to improve the quality of predictions, this essay makes cautious choices and detailed discussion in data use and model design. One can see that when using different data, the resulting employment elasticity is steady and consistent. This signifies that under the existing industrial structure, the economic growth has a strong ability to create jobs. As long as a moderate growth rate is maintained, a large number of non-farm employment opportunities will be created during the 12th Five-year Plan period.

Due to large disparities in regional economic development in China, when a shortage of labor begins to appear, manufacturers in different regions will make different choices. In economically developed eastern regions, salary levels are already higher than in central and western regions. Manufacturers are better able to withstand labor shortages and rising wage levels, and they make two choices. First is industrial upgrading, that is, using capital to replace unskilled labor. Second is to relocate labor-intensive industry to central or western regions where wages are lower. As a result, the demand for unskilled labor among eastern manufacturers falls, and as industry moves to central and western regions, so do job opportunities. Not only can central and western regions take on this relocated, labor-intensive industry, but original labor-intensive manufacturers can, by further expanding, occupy the market given up by eastern manufacturers. Labor from central and western regions is an important component in the eastern manufacturing market. Those laborers may be more inclined to return to their hometowns for employment once new opportunities emerge there, no longer migrating eastward. This change in direction of the flow of labor triggered by changes to the industrial structure will undoubtedly alter the structure of the labor market.

I   Non-farm Employment Is Growing Rapidly, and Job Creation Is Increasingly Concentrated in Urban Areas

China's economic growth has created a large number of non-farm employment opportunities, and these job opportunities have emerged in both urban and rural areas. But non-farm job opportunities created in urban areas are both more numerous and more stable. From 1998 to 2002 was a key period of state-owned enterprise reform in China. Although more than 60 million workers were laid off due to restructuring, more than 8 million jobs were created in cities and towns each year. In this period, new non-farm job opportunities in rural areas remained almost stagnant.[1] After 2003, rural non-farm employment growth resumed, while urban non-farm employment growth increased to around 10 million jobs annually. In urban and rural areas combined, more than 16 million jobs were created between 2005 and 2006, which explains why a nationwide labor shortage began as soon as the SOE layoff process was complete. See Figure 9.1. If not limited by labor supply constraints, more and more companies would be unable to find the labor they require each year, the gap between labor supply and demand would grow, and the actual job growth numbers would significantly increase.

Looking at the performance of urban and rural non-farm employment, non-farm jobs in urban areas have grown steadily, while non-farm jobs in rural regions have fluctuated, and growth there has slowed since 2006. If the economic growth trend is considered, it can be expected that new non-farm jobs will mainly occur in urban areas.

Due to the discrepancy in incomes between the agricultural and non-farm sectors, in the process of economic growth, the rural labor force has been migrating to the non-farm sector. While this process has fluctuated with the economic environment, the overall trend has never changed. But it is precisely this characteristic of the migration between labor sectors that has deceived

---

1   This period was the most difficult time for urban jobs, but it was also the time of the greatest urban job growth numbers in China. After making up for the destruction of more than 60 million jobs, China still achieved net job growth of 8 million positions annually.

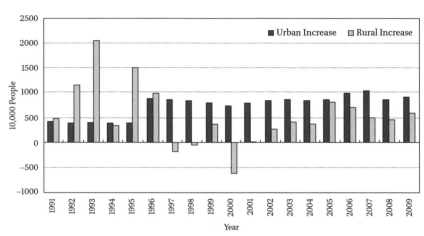

FIGURE 9.1 *Urban and rural non-farm employment in recent years*
SOURCE: CHINA STATISTICAL YEARBOOK 2010

many scholars not familiar with economic reality. Even though complaints of
"difficulty recruiting workers" pervade the entire country and have persisted
for eight years, these scholars claim that there is still great pressure on employment in China. Their evidence is the low elasticity value of economic growth
to employment growth, which in recent years has often been less than 0.1.[2] See
Figure 9.1.

Behind this low overall employment elasticity is actually a numbers trick:
under rapid economic development, as long as overall employment grows
slowly, total employment elasticity will be low. But behind this phenomenon
are the persistent reduction of the primary industry labor force and the rapid
growth of the secondary and tertiary industry labor forces. This is the proper
meaning of "industrialization," which is the development goal that we have so
diligently sought. Since 2003, employment elasticity in the secondary industry
has remained between 0.25 and 0.6 (an average of 0.41), and in the tertiary
industry it has fluctuated between 0.1 and 0.55 (an average of 0.32). This indicates that when the rate of economic development is maintained at around
10%, the rate of job growth in the secondary industry is 4.1%, and that in the
tertiary industry is 3.2%. This far exceeds population growth and labor force
growth, so the gap between demand and supply of labor in the secondary and

---

2   The average from 2003–2008 is 0.078. This chapter has selected data since 2003 based on
    two considerations. First, data closer to today has a greater impact on the future. Second,
    from 1998–2002, China was in a state of radical SOE reform. In order to make up for employ-
    ment growth after job losses, the compiled data underestimates the true situation of job
    creation.

tertiary industries can only be filled with workers transferring from the primary industry. The number of people with jobs in the primary industry has fallen rapidly, and employment elasticity in the primary industry is −0.64.

The growth of the number of urban and rural non-farm employees and the growth of the numbers of workers in the secondary and tertiary industries provide a consistent message from different angles. The Chinese economy, led by labor-intensive industry, has created a large number of non-farm jobs in the process of rapid growth.

With nationwide labor shortages and rising wages, companies are responding by increasing their technical levels and capital intensity. Nevertheless, the basic characteristic of China's industrial structure, dominated by labor-intensive industry, will not change in the short term. Even if the industrial structure begins to adjust, the market adjustment process is a gradual one. Thus, as long as economic growth during the 12th Five-year Plan period is maintained at a relatively high pace, there will be no fundamental change in the strong ability of China's economy to create non-farm jobs. Combining the aforementioned analysis, the analysis of this chapter will mainly concentrate on the urban labor market.

II   Estimates of Employment Elasticity

If data reflecting economic reality are authentic, the employment elasticity values derived from different methods of estimation will not be significantly different. This chapter begins by aggregating data, then extends to micro-level enterprise survey data. The employment elasticity information for the primary, secondary, and tertiary industries in Figure 9.1 is derived from simple calculations using aggregated data: calendar-year employment growth rate divided by GDP growth rate. In order to build predictions of future employment growth on a more accurate foundation, this chapter further uses the latest corporate survey data to estimate employment elasticity in different industries and different regions. On the one hand, we can verify whether this is consistent with employment elasticity derived from aggregate data. On the other hand, research objective of this chapter determines the need to predict multiple dimensions of employment elasticity, which is something the aggregate data cannot provide. Different data accurately reflecting the relationship between economic growth and employment growth will result in similar estimates. Results obtained from erroneous data will usually vary substantially. This basic fact is helpful in evaluating the credibility of different employment elasticity estimates.

This chapter uses two sets of micro data to calculate employment elasticity by industry and by region. The first is data from a survey of 1,536 private companies conducted between July and September 2009 by the National Federation of Industry and the Chinese Academy of Social Sciences Institute of Population and Labor Economics. The second is data from a survey of 2,058 companies in eight provinces conducted by the Chinese central bank in October 2009. These two sets of data have a common point in that they designed retrospective information into their questionnaires, asking companies about their operating conditions between 2007 and 2009. This data structure is easily converted into three (years) of (quasi-)panel data.

Islam and Nazara (2000) suggested methods of calculating employment elasticity under the panel data structure. According to these methods, the authors calculated results under pooled OLS estimates, the fixed effects model, and the random effects model. First, they estimated the value of the relationship between fixed effects (u) and the error term (v) and discovered that differences between different (detailed) industries fell roughly between 0.65 and 0.95 (Finkel, 2004). This suggests that there is a significant difference between the pooled OLS estimation and the random effects model, and the authors excluded pooled OLS estimation results. Second, by estimating the random effects model and fixed effects model, the authors discovered large differences between the two elasticity coefficients. Both theoretically and empirically, it is difficult to judge the difference between a priori explanatory variables and fixed effects (u). The more secure method is to use the generalized least squares (GLS). In general, its results are closer to the estimation values of the random effects model.

As the National Federation of Industry and the CASS Institute of Population and Labor Economics sample covers all industries, we will first observe the employment elasticity of this data. This employment elasticity is the elasticity between a company's calendar year number of employees and its sales. See Table 9.1.

Although the financial crisis occurred in this period, the elasticity coefficient calculated from the total sample is as high as 0.54, signifying that an increase in a company's sales of 1 percent will result in 0.54 points of job growth. In all industries, excluding sports, culture, and the arts, employment elasticity is relatively small. Employment elasticity in the vast majority of industries is above 0.2, and this reaches 0.73 in the highest industries. Manufacturing is the largest job-creating sector, and the employment elasticity of private companies in the manufacturing sector is 0.55. It can be said that this is consistent with people's experience: the manufacturing industry has a strong ability to absorb employment.

TABLE 9.1 *Employment elasticity by industry (2007–2009; private company sample)* (*GLS results*)

Industry	Coefficient	Standard Deviation	Observed Values
Agriculture, forestry, animal husbandry and fishery	0.625	0.013	227
Extractive	0.487	0.021	110
Manufacturing	0.551	0.003	1797
Electricity and gas	0.506	0.027	35
Construction	0.502	0.019	218
Geological prospecting	0.454	0.012	3
Transportation	0.486	0.026	34
Telecommunications	0.245	0.052	21
Wholesale and retail trade	0.456	0.005	579
Finance and insurance	0.495	0.017	13
Real estate	0.329	0.014	380
Social services	0.426	0.017	119
Medical health and hygiene	0.528	0.030	62
Sports	0.014	0.058	3
Social welfare	0.207	0.015	6
Education	0.591	0.050	21
Research and comprehensive technical services	0.731	0.034	71
Art and culture	0.016	0.140	12
Total	0.538	0.002	3771

Source: National Federation of Trade and CASS Institute of Population and Labor Economics survey of private enterprises (2009).

The companies surveyed by the People's Bank of China are mainly concentrated in the manufacturing sector, but breaking these down further we can identify 31 categories. This survey data and that of the National Federation of Enterprises can complement and confirm each other. Following the same statistical caliber, we first calculate the employment elasticity of the three years from 2007 to 2009 and expand the calculation of elasticity to the elasticity of employment and enterprise output and the elasticity of employment and the equity of enterprise owners. The former is consistent with the elasticity coefficient caliber of Table 9.1, while the latter expands the evaluation of elasticity.

The employment (to output) elasticity of all manufacturing industry was 0.566, almost equal to the manufacturing industry elasticity in Table 9.1. Breaking it down into sub-industries, besides the "tobacco industry" where the sample of companies is too small to calculate, the vast majority of manufacturing companies in other sub-industries all have employment elasticity above 0.4. That is, not only is the employment elasticity of manufacturing enterprises large, but it is very strong. All manufacturing industry has a strong capacity to create jobs.

III   The Quantity and Regional Distribution of New Job Growth

When we use existing data to predict the future, it is built on the basis of two assumptions. First, the social economy is inherently stable and not prone to sudden reversal (North, 1994). Second, when using multiple imperfect data to measure the same result, the deviations may offset each other, and we can hope to obtain a more satisfactory result (Murray, 2006). Thus, when forecasting future employment totals and regional distributions, we may use multiple data, and by comparing these estimation results, obtain a more realistic judgment. This is the empirical strategy of this chapter.

A   *Quantitative Forecasts of New Job Growth*
Using existing employee numbers for the secondary and tertiary industries and the average employment elasticity for 2003 to 2008 and making an assumption about the rate of growth during the 12th Five-year Plan period, we can forecast the number of employees in the secondary and tertiary industries during the 12th Five-year Plan period. During the 12th Five-year Plan period we assume a low-growth scenario of 7%, a medium-growth scenario of 8%, and a high-growth scenario of 9%. Under these three growth assumptions, secondary industry will grow 10.4%, 11.9%, and 13.4%, respectively. Tertiary industry will grow 6.9%, 7.9%, and 8.9%, respectively. Employment elasticity for secondary industry is assumed to be 0.41, and that of the tertiary 0.32.

According to these assumptions, the number of employees in the secondary and tertiary industries will have grown in the following way compared to before the beginning of the 12th Five-year Plan. Under the assumption of 7% economic growth and unchanged employment elasticity, the secondary industry will add 52.49 million jobs over 2010, and the tertiary industry will

TABLE 9.2   *Employment elasticity of manufacturing sub-industries (2007–2009) (GLS estimates)*

Industry	Employment/Output			Employment/Owner Equity		
	Coefficient	Standard Deviation	Observed Values	Coefficient	Standard Deviation	Observed Values
All manufacturing	0.566	0.006	6916	0.590	0.001	6971
Agro-food processing	0.497	0.010	618	0.609	0.006	619
Food	0.437	0.016	227	0.482	0.013	232
Beverage	0.356	0.014	141	0.396	0.014	141
Tobacco						
Textiles	0.646	0.011	576	0.646	0.009	551
Textile and garment, shoes, and hats	0.569	0.013	524	0.561	0.011	528
Leather, fur, feathers, and their products	0.543	0.034	112	0.621	0.037	109
Timber processing, bamboo, cane, palm fiber, and straw products	0.509	0.013	209	0.425	0.014	195
Home furnishings	0.493	0.018	123	0.506	0.009	125
Paper and paper products	0.533	0.021	163	0.622	0.012	164
Printing and reproduction of recorded media	0.610	0.022	130	0.543	0.008	129
Educational and sports good	0.800	0.027	63	0.719	0.026	64
Petroleum processing, coking, and nuclear fuel	0.452	0.014	50	0.620	0.031	48
Chemical raw materials and products	0.642	0.013	380	0.579	0.010	378
Medicine	0.452	0.015	178	0.505	0.016	179
Chemical fibers	0.523	0.038	74	0.716	0.032	74
Rubber	0.760	0.030	62	0.721	0.009	62

(Continued)

TABLE 9.2 (*Continued*)

Industry	Employment/Output			Employment/Owner Equity		
	Coefficient	Standard Deviation	Observed Values	Coefficient	Standard Deviation	Observed Values
Plastics	0.661	0.014	361	0.653	0.009	362
Non-ferrous metals	0.513	0.010	352	0.535	0.010	370
Ferrous metals smelting, rolling, and processing	0.523	0.016	142	0.629	0.018	142
Non-ferrous metals smelting, rolling, and processing	0.431	0.017	122	0.455	0.016	119
Metal products	0.546	0.011	412	0.538	0.006	427
General equipment	0.607	0.010	435	0.669	0.006	441
Specialized equipment	0.557	0.013	232	0.521	0.007	236
Transportation equipment	0.716	0.012	276	0.797	0.010	277
Electrical machinery and equipment	0.634	0.012	387	0.644	0.007	402
Telecommunications equipment, computers, and other electronic equipment	0.537	0.009	210	0.587	0.014	220
Instrumentation and cultural and office machinery	0.584	0.037	50	0.752	0.032	53
Artwork and other manufacturing	0.524	0.013	262	0.479	0.011	272
Recycling and waste materials recycling and processing	0.430	0.030	41	0.416	0.030	40

Source: People's Bank of China Enterprise Survey (2009).

add 31.37 million, for a total of 83.86 million new jobs. Under the 8% growth assumption, the secondary industry will add 61.16 million jobs over 2010 and the tertiary industry 36.26 million, total growth of 97.43 million jobs. Under the 9% growth assumption, the secondary industry will add 70.13 million jobs over 2010 and the tertiary industry 41.24 million, total growth of 111.38 million jobs. A report on calendar year new job growth numbers in the secondary and tertiary industries during the 12th Five-year Plan period can be seen in Table 9.1.

B   *The Geographical Distribution of New Jobs*
The employment elasticities obtained from calculations using the sets of data from the two surveys are quite similar. One can infer that the data reflect the true business situation. The People's Bank of China Enterprise Survey included 2,058 businesses from eight provinces. The private enterprise survey includes 30 provinces. When forecasting the regional distribution of job growth, we use the private enterprise survey data. When forecasting job growth in the manufacturing industry, we use data from the People's Bank of China survey.

Table 9.4 reports the employment elasticities of enterprises in different areas within the People's Bank of China survey data using all samples from 2007 to 2009. One can see that employment elasticity was 0.586 in eastern China, 0.42 in central China, and 0.544 in western China. By year, these elasticities were 0.592, 0.453, and 0.545, respectively, for 2007 to 2008, and 0.62,

TABLE 9.3   *Forecasts of nationwide secondary and tertiary industry jobs*

Year	Scenario 1		Scenario 2		Scenario 3	
	Secondary Industry	Tertiary Industry	Secondary Industry	Tertiary Industry	Secondary Industry	Tertiary Industry
2009	21684	26603	21684	26603	21684	26603
2010	22609	27190	22742	27276	22875	27361
2011	23573	27791	23852	27965	24132	28140
2012	24578	28404	25015	28672	25458	28941
2013	25626	29032	26236	29397	26857	29766
2014	26718	29673	27516	30140	28332	30613
2015	27858	30328	28858	30902	29889	31485

Source: Calculated based on data from *China Statistical Yearbook*.

TABLE 9.4   *Employment-operating revenue elasticity*

	2007–09		2007–08		2008–09	
	Coefficient	Standard Deviation	Coefficient	Standard Deviation	Coefficient	Standard Deviation
Nationwide	0.565	0.001	0.572	0.009	0.575	0.009
Eastern	0.586	0.003	0.592	0.011	0.620	0.011
Central	0.420	0.003	0.453	0.025	0.404	0.024
Western	0.544	0.004	0.545	0.025	0.562	0.025
Low capital intensity	0.581	0.002	0.606	0.015	0.587	0.015
Medium capital intensity	0.566	0.002	0.566	0.014	0.584	0.014
High capital intensity	0.535	0.006	0.540	0.017	0.555	0.017

Source: People's Bank of China Enterprise Survey data.

0.404, 0.562, respectively, for 2008 to 2009. Looking within the manufacturing industry, employment elasticities were also very close between capital-intensive sub-industries and non-capital-intensive sub-industries.

Employment elasticities for 2007 to 2008 are very close to those from 2008 to 2009. Combining this information with the effects of the financial crisis since August 2008 and the arrival of the Lewisian turning point, we can make two important judgments. First, the employment model of Chinese businesses has not changed notably due to the effects of the financial crisis, and the ability of the Chinese economy to create jobs is very robust. It has not been as we feared initially, with the impact of external events resulting in widespread unemployment. Second, many scholars have worried that after the arrival of the Lewisian turning point, companies would rapidly increase capital intensity and thus have a negative impact on job creation. Enterprise employment elasticity indicates no significant change. The adjustment of the industrial structure is a gradual process and will not seriously affect employment.

In terms of the goal of this study, that is, to predict future job growth, the stability of employment elasticity undoubtedly reduces the risks of prediction.

We first predict the geographical distribution of economic growth. The greatest difficulty in forecasting the geographical distribution of employment growth is the divergence between the broken-down and total numbers published by China's statistical authorities. For example, in 2008, the National Bureau of Statistics put the number of urban employees at 302.1 million nationwide. But adding up the but adding up the employment numbers for China's 31 provinces, municipalities, and autonomous regions, one obtains a total of 207 million, only two thirds of the compiled total. If this discrepancy cannot be resolved, an error of one-third makes predictive results unconvincing.

Supposing that the census data captures all non-farm payrolls, we can use the 2004 economic census data and the 2005 population census data to build a benchmark for the regional distribution of urban non-farm payrolls. Because the years of these two censuses are close together, the resulting number of non-farm jobs and the regional distribution are also very close, and we can average the shares of the employees of each province and municipality among the total number of employees. We can assume that 2009 urban employees still follow this regional distribution and allocate the 411.2 million non-farm payrolls to the various provinces and municipalities. At this point, we have constructed the actual geographical distribution of urban employment for 2008. By calculating the proportion of each province's proportion of urban non-farm payrolls to the national total, we find that of the total of 411.17 million urban, non-farm workers, 230 million are located in eastern China, 103.72 in central China, and 77.44 in western China. Employment elasticity is 0.535 for eastern China, 0.543 in central China, and 0.505 in western China. Assuming equal growth rates in the three regions, 7%, 8%, and 9%, respectively, we can predict the number of jobs during the 12th Five-year Plan period.

If the growth rate during the 12th Five-year Plan period remains at 7%, by 2015, eastern China will have total employment of 286.79 million, an increase of 48.16 million jobs from 2010. Central China will have 22.08 million more jobs than 2010, and western China will have an additional 152.1 million jobs. Assuming economic growth remains at 8%, eastern China will add 55.92 million jobs over 2010, central China 25.65 million, and western China 17.64 million. Assuming economic growth remains at 9%, eastern China will add 63.91 million jobs, central China 293.1 million, and western China 20.15 million. Under these three different growth rates, national urban non-farm employment will increase by 85.44 million jobs (under 7% growth), 99.2 million jobs (under 8% growth), and 113.37 million jobs (under 9% growth).

Comparing with the preceding job growth numbers for the secondary and tertiary industries, we find that the results obtained from the two calculations are quite close.

TABLE 9.5   *Calculating non-farm employment growth based on employment elasticity from the survey of private companies*

Year	2009	2010	2011	2012	2013	2014	2015
Method 1							
Eastern	23001	23863	24757	25684	26646	27643	28679
Central	10372	10766	11175	11600	12041	12498	12973
Western	7744	8018	8301	8595	8898	9213	9539
Method 2							
Eastern	23001	23986	25013	26083	27199	28364	29578
Central	10372	10822	11292	11783	12295	12829	13386
Western	7744	8057	8382	8721	9073	9440	9821
Method 3							
Eastern	23001	24109	25270	26487	27762	29099	30500
Central	10372	10878	11410	11968	12553	13166	13809
Western	7744	8096	8464	8848	9251	9671	10111

C   *Manufacturing Industry Job Growth*

Qu Wan (2010) divides 31 manufacturing industry subcategories into three types according to the per capita capital of large-scale manufacturing enterprises: high capital intensity, medium capital intensity, and low capital intensity. We use the same classifications in this paper. Based on 2005 census data, we calculate the job numbers of each category of manufacturing then use the data from the People's Bank of China Enterprise Survey to calculate employment elasticity and predict employment numbers for the three categories of manufacturing industry during the 12th Five-year Plan period (see Table 9.6).

The prediction method is as follows. Data from the 2005 census show that manufacturing industry employees account for 29.2% of total non-farm employees. Using this proportion to calculate the industry distribution of urban jobs in 2009, we arrive at 120.77 million manufacturing jobs. Similarly dividing the manufacturing industry jobs from the 2005 census into the three categories of manufacturing industry, we arrive at 41.6% for low capital intensity, 33.7% for medium capital intensity, and 24.6% for high capital intensity. Based on this ratio, we can divide up the 120.77 manufacturing industry jobs into 50.28 million in low capital intensity industry, 40.74 million in medium capital intensity industry, and 29.75 million in low capital intensity industry.

TABLE 9.6   *Job numbers for manufacturing of different capital intensities*

Capital Intensity	2009	2010	2011	2012	2013	2014	2015
Method 1							
Low	5028	5331	5654	5995	6357	6742	7149
Medium	4074	4314	4568	4837	5122	5423	5742
High	2975	3141	3316	3500	3695	3900	4117
Method 2							
Low	5028	5375	5747	6144	6569	7023	7509
Medium	4074	4349	4642	4954	5288	5644	6024
High	2975	3165	3366	3581	3809	4051	4309
Method 3							
Low	5028	5419	5841	6296	6786	7314	7884
Medium	4074	4383	4716	5073	5458	5872	6317
High	2975	3189	3417	3662	3925	4206	4508

Continuing with the 7%, 8%, and 9% growth assumptions, manufacturing industry is the main body of the secondary industry. Assume its growth rate is consistent with that of the secondary industry, which would be 10.4%, 11.9%, and 13.4%. Table 9.6 shows manufacturing industry job growth under the three assumptions. According to Method 1, by the end of the 12th Five-year Plan, jobs across the three categories of manufacturing industry will have grown by 18.18 million, 14.28 million, and 9.77 million from 2010, or a total of 42.22 million jobs. According to Method 2, jobs across the three categories of manufacturing industry will have grown by 21.34 million, 16.76 million, and 11.44 million, or a total of 49.53 million jobs. According to Method 3, jobs across the three categories of manufacturing industry will have grown by 24.65 million, 19.34 million, and 13.19 million, or a total of 57.18 million jobs.

Clearly, rapid and sustained job growth will continue for both high capital intensity and low capital intensity manufacturing industry.

D   Brief Assessment of the Predictions

Based on current job numbers, employment elasticity, and assumed growth rates, we have predicted the overall number of new jobs to be created during the 12th Five-year Plan period, as well as their structural and regional distributions. It should be noted that the growth at this time is "potential." It shows that the Chinese economic structure itself contains a great ability to create jobs, but some factors can still constrain the realization of this potential. The most direct constraint is whether labor supply is able to keep up with demand. In recent years, more and more companies have been unable to attract the workers they need. Thus, in order to ensure that China's economic growth creates ample jobs and ensure that the majority of people can fairly share the fruits of economic growth, we must concentrate on developing labor supply.

We are confident that we will continue to be able to maintain a high rate of growth. The greatest risk affecting the predicted results is the calculation and use of employment elasticity. During the 12th Five-year Plan period, will China's economic growth still be able to maintain such high employment elasticity? Considering the impact of the economic crisis after 2008, employment elasticity in 2008 and 2009 was not significantly lower than in 2007 and 2008. This result undoubtedly improves our confidence. China's employment elasticity is stable.

In addition to employment elasticity, are there other experiences by which we can judge job growth during the 12th Five-year Plan period? I believe there are both favorable and unfavorable factors affecting the achievement of this rate of growth. The first favorable factor is that as the urban labor shortage continues, wages will rise, which will attract more rural laborers to the city. Second, because capital intensive industry will migrate to central and western regions, central and western rural laborers who previously thought it too far to migrate to eastern cities will find the cost of migrating lower. In other words, the migration of the industrial region will develop a new pool of "surplus labor." Third, as the labor market supply and demand situation has changed in recent years, the government has intensified efforts to protect the legal rights of workers, lowering the risk of relocation, and increasing the benefits that groups on the border of migrating can expect.

But there are also severe constraints to maintaining sustained and rapid employment growth. First, with increasing wages, profit margins in labor-intensive industries have been squeezed, and companies are closer and closer to the technical limit of their survival, and they are beginning to move to central and western regions. Those companies not migrating often choose to become more technology and capital intensive, in which case their job-creating employment elasticity will fall. Second, a portion of labor-intensive businesses has closed down because of rising wages, thus rejecting workers. While these workers can find employment at those companies that have not closed their doors, this factor will clearly reduce the ability of that region's economic growth to create jobs. Third, recent data from Ministry of Human Resources and Social Security enterprise surveys show that in 2009, approximately three-quarters of companies surveyed were unable to recruit all of the workers they needed, and this barrier to job growth is intensifying (Ministry of Human Resources and Social Security, 2010). Going forward, there is significant uncertainty as to whether such "recruitment difficulties" can be resolved.

In recent years, the capital intensity in the manufacturing sector has increased. We worry that the "substitution of capital for labor" has weakened the job-creation ability of economic growth. Calculating the employment elasticities of different capital-intensive enterprises, we find that the employment elasticity of capital-intensive manufacturing industry is 0.535, while the employment elasticity of low-capital-intensity manufacturing industry is 0.581. This means that going forward, even if manufacturers increase their capital intensity, as long as rapid growth is maintained, their capacity to create jobs will still be very strong. Under the three established growth rate scenarios, we assume that if all low-capital-intensity manufacturers increased their capital intensity to the current level of capital-intensive manufactures, manufacturing industry jobs will grow by 39.27 million, 46.01 million, and 53.06 million positions during the 12th Five-year Plan period.

Data can never make their own causal inferences. To make a credible inference as to the ability of the Chinese economy to create jobs during the 12th Five-year Plan period, existing data only provide us with accessible information. Based on the rapid growth situation in recent years, as well as the industrial transfer situation, we find that all regions have formulated ambitious development plans. These regions also have self-reported growth rates higher than data ultimately published by the central government. We predict that China's economic growth has sufficient power, and job growth in the secondary and tertiary industries can be achieved.

IV   Regional Changes in Labor Force Migration

Since 2003, labor shortages have spread across the country from coastal regions and continue to this day. Rising wages have changed the cost structure for manufacturers, and labor-intensive industries are under increasing pressure. Labor-intensive industries in the eastern region have begun to move toward central and western regions where wages are lower and the workforce can still be developed. This industrial transfer has been seen as a "V-formation Model" between domestic regions. Due to the unavailability of the latest data, a comprehensive analysis of the regional changes in labor migration cannot be conducted in this data. We can only make a simple analysis of the directional changes of labor migration based on a 2009 survey of migrant workers from the National Bureau of Statistics.

Figure 9.2 compares the proportions of migrants in the three regions. According to the characteristics of the 2009 questionnaire, we divide all migrants into two categories: "old migrants" refers to those migrants who had moved out to labor or engage in business in the previous year and who are still doing so this year; "new migrants" refers to those who had not moved out to labor or engage in business the previous year but who have in the current year. To a certain extent, the latter group is representative of the recently added migrant population.

One can see that in eastern areas, migrants migrate within the region (within their own provinces or within eastern provinces) in proportions of 95.9% and 96.8%, respectively. Clearly, when laborers in eastern regions migrate across provinces, they have other eastern provinces as their goal. But the change in central and western regions is distinct. In the central region, 34.5% of "old migrants" migrated to the same region or other provinces. But new 57.7% of new migrants migrated in their own region or two another province. In the west, these proportions were 45.6% and 63.3%, respectively. From the direction of the migration of new migrants from central and western regions, we can infer that non-farm employment opportunities are increasing rapidly there, and those regions are thereby absorbing local migrant workers.

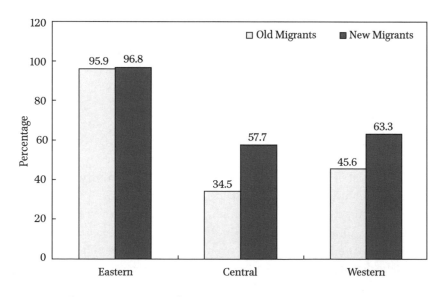

FIGURE 9.2 *Changes in intra-regional migration*
SOURCE: QUOTED FROM "MIGRANT WORKERS MONITORING SURVEY REPORT."

It can be said that new laborers joining the migrant ranks from central and western regions are now mainly migrating within their own area, within their own province, or to neighboring provinces.

Does central and western China have sufficient labor to respond to industrial transfer? This article uses several large batches of data from different times to analyze the non-farm employment situation of rural labor in different regions. Since 2000, young rural laborers have been more likely to occupy non-farm jobs, but the proportion in non-farm jobs in eastern regions is higher. In recent years, the proportion of non-farm jobs has increased rapidly. In 2000, the proportion of 16 to 34-year-old rural laborers engaged in non-farm labor was 25–32%. In 2005, this proportion had risen to 36 to 45%. After 2005, non-farm wages grew rapidly, and the proportion of 16–34-year-old laborers working in non-farm jobs increased to 62–67%.

The National Bureau of Statistics 2009 Migrant Worker Monitoring Survey shows that because workers who have not left their hometowns for work may still engage in non-farm business or labor there, a portion of rural laborers still claim to be engaged in the "agriculture, forestry, animal husbandry, and fishery industry." If this population were counted as having non-farm jobs, the non-farm employment proportion in Table 9.7 would be 10 percentage points higher. The proportion of 35 to 44-year-old rural laborers engaged in non-farm jobs would rise to 43–47% (see Figure 9.2). This means that if the proportion of non-farm jobs in central and western regions could rise to the level of eastern regions, central and western regions can continue to transfer a portion of the labor force from the agricultural industry when labor-intensive industry from eastern regions moves west. However, these new non-farm laborers will increasingly be concentrated in the older-age portion of the labor force. Thus, the labor shortage faced by manufacturers will remain a serious problem.

V   Conclusions

In this chapter, we calculated the employment elasticities of the secondary and tertiary industries, different industries, and different regions according to compiled data and the data from two corporate surveys and found that China's economy has a strong ability to create non-farm jobs. This characteristic will not change suddenly. Therefore, as long as rapid growth is maintained, in the 12th Five-year Plan period, trends like transfer from the primary industry to secondary and tertiary industries and rapid urbanization will not change fundamentally. Since 2003, a shortage of ordinary workers has spread throughout

TABLE 9.7   *Proportion of rural labor engaged in non-farm jobs*
             unit: %

Age Group	2000			2005			2009		
	Eastern	Central	Western	Eastern	Central	Western	Eastern	Central	Western
16–24	41.6	31.0	22.8	56.4	46.4	33.1	82.9	65.8	53.8
25–34	33.5	21.9	19.3	46.7	34.6	27.7	77.8	56.6	48.8
35–44	26.7	15.7	13.4	35.3	23.2	18.8	60.9	34.0	30.2
45–54	19.2	9.8	8.1	24.3	13.1	9.4	42.1	21.2	16.8
55–64	12.0	6.4	4.4	15.8	6.8	4.2	31.5	11.6	9.9
Total	28.1	18.3	15.0	35.7	25.3	19.5	56.5	36.8	31.6

Source: 2000 Census data; 2005 1% Population Sample Survey data; "Migrant Worker Monitoring Survey Report."

the country. Even in "resource cities" hard hit during SOE restructuring in the 1990s, companies have been experiencing "recruitment difficulties" and rising wages since 2005. Data from the 2009 Migrant Worker Monitoring Survey show that fewer and fewer laborers are able to transfer to cities and towns. Going forward, the labor force required cities and towns will be filled be older rural laborers. However, the transfer costs for laborers 40 years of age and older is higher. We can predict that the rate of job growth during the 12th Five Year Plan will be constrained by the rate of transfer from the primary to secondary and tertiary industries.

Based on the employment elasticities of the three regions, we reach the conclusion that eastern, central, and western regions will all experience sustained job growth. Considering that wages in eastern China are higher than in central and western regions, "recruitment difficulties" are now more serious there. However, the supply-side constraints on employment growth are also more serious there. Going forward, job growth may be most concentrated in central and western regions. Data from the National Bureau of Statistics Migrant Worker Monitoring Survey show that in 2009, the number of migrant workers in central and western regions grew markedly, while the number in the eastern region experienced an absolute reduction (National Bureau of Statistics Rural Department, 2010). This empirical fact is not accidental, but an inevitable phenomenon after the arrival of the Lewisian turning point. The gap in development level and wages between eastern China and central and western China will gradually narrow and begin to converge.

In terms of policy implications, because eastern China has a shortage of laborers, resulting increasingly in a loss of comparative advantage in labor-intensive industries, the region therefore faces escalating pressure for industrial upgrading and must quickly transform its model of development. Central and western regions still have the potential to transfer rural laborers into industry and should actively accept the transfer of labor-intensive industry from the eastern region, achieving the transfer of industry between developed regions and relatively backward regions and allowing the original development model to be extended as far as possible in order to achieve sustainability of economic growth.

(This article was originally published in Chinese in 2011.)

References

Finkel, Steven E. 2004. *Linear panel analysis*. Chapter 29, Handbook of longitudinal research. New York: Elsevier Press, 2008, forthcoming.

Islam, Iyanatul and Suahasil Nazara. 2000. *Estimating employment elasticity for the Indonesian economy.* ILO.

Ministry of Human Resources and Social Security. 2010. Spring 2010 Corporate Labor Demand and 2009 Employment Situation of Rural Migrant Laborers. "China Population and Labor Report." *Population and Labor Green Paper 2010.* Beijing: Social Sciences Press.

Murray, Michael P. *Econometrics: A Modern Introduction.* Beijing: Peking University Press, 2006.

North, Douglass. 1994. "Economic performance through time." *AER.* Vol. 84. No. 3.

National Bureau of Statistics Rural Department. 2010. "2009 Migrant Worker Monitoring Survey Report."

Addendum

ADDENDUM TABLE 9.1   *New job growth in the secondary and tertiary industry during the 12th five-year plan period*
unit: 10,000 people

Year	Method 1		Method 2		Method 3	
	Secondary	Tertiary	Secondary	Tertiary	Secondary	Tertiary
2010	925	587	1058	673	1191	758
2011	964	600	1110	690	1257	779
2012	1005	614	1164	707	1326	801
2013	1048	627	1220	725	1399	824
2014	1093	641	1280	743	1475	848
2015	1139	655	1342	762	1557	872

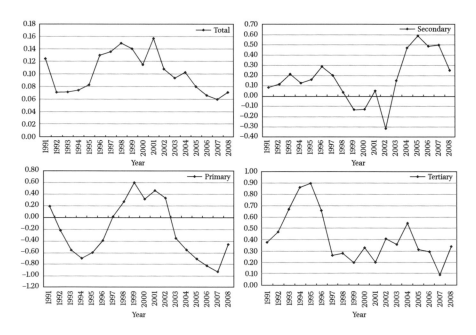

ADDENDUM FIGURE 9.1   *Primary, secondary, and tertiary industry employment elasticities since 1991*

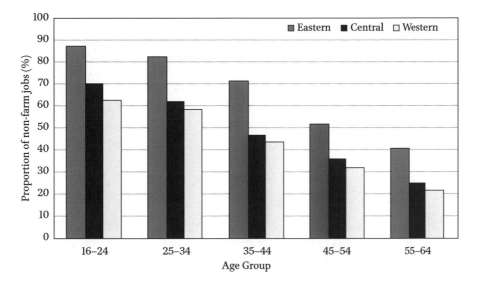

ADDENDUM FIGURE 9.2   *The situation of rural laborers in different regions engaging in non-farm jobs*
SOURCE: QUOTED FROM "MIGRANT WORKER MONITORING SURVEY REPORT"

CHAPTER 10

Wage Increase, Wage Convergence, and the Lewis Turning Point in China

Cai Fang and Du Yang

1   Introduction

In recent years, there have been multiple empirical studies arguing whether or not the Chinese economy has reached its Lewis Turning Point (for example, Minami and Ma, 2010; Yao and Zhang, 2010; Zhang and Wang, 2009; Cai, 2010a). Although those studies provide both supporting and contradicting evidence and disagreements remain, there remains room for further investigation. First of all, defining a Lewis Turning Point would help clarify the argument. Secondly, investigating the empirical results based on certain criteria of the Lewis Turning Point would help correctly interpret the data, which might otherwise lead to dissent. This paper is intended to provide more evidence on the arrival of the Lewis Turning Point based on a clearer definition of its more-or-less agreed-upon criteria.

According to Lewis (1972) and Ranis and Fei (1961), a Lewis Turning Point can be referred to as the period of time at which expansion of labor demand exceeds that of labor supply and, as a result, the wage rate of ordinary workers starts to rise while the wage of the agricultural sector is not yet determined by its marginal productivity of labor, and the difference in marginal productivity of labor between agricultural and non-agricultural sectors remains. The time when the wage rates in agricultural and non-agricultural sectors are both determined by their marginal productivity of labor while the gap in productivities disappears can be called the commercial point. Only at this time will dual economic systems end. This paper is intended only to discuss the Lewis Turning Point by examining the trends in wage changes.

Based on the Japanese experiences of achieving a turning point, Minami (2010) suggests five characteristics of wage-related changes as criteria to test the advent of the Lewis Turning Point. That is, if the Lewis Turning Point arrives, one can empirically observe that (1) wage in the subsistence sector equals the marginal product of labor, (2) wage in the subsistence sector becomes determined by marginal product of labor, (3) wages in the subsistence sector jump from a constant (or slowly increasing trend) to a rapidly increasing trend,

(4) wage differentials between unskilled and skilled workers tend to decrease, and (5) there is a trend that the elasticity of the labor supply shifts from being indefinite to be between zero and infinite.

It is obvious that Minami set those criteria to test the commercial turning point rather than the Lewis Turning Point. He himself agrees that the first criterion is too strict to directly test, and that empirical works should be devoted more to other criteria, instead. Since this paper aims to define the Lewis Turning Point in a different way, we will focus on discussing the third and fourth criteria—namely, the increase of ordinary workers' wages and the wage convergence between unskilled and skilled workers.

In the development of a dual economy characterized by an unlimited supply of labor, the wage rate of ordinary workers typically remains at a constant subsistence level above marginal productivity of labor in agriculture.[1] The reallocation of an agricultural surplus labor force to non-agricultural sectors begins with the introduction of a household responsibility system in the farming sector, which in China has made extraordinary progress as the institutional barriers deterring labor mobility were eliminated in the urban labor market. In the country's 30-year period of reform, rural surplus laborers have experienced a shift from agricultural to rural non-agricultural sectors, a mass migration from rural to urban sectors, and from the central and western regions to the coastal regions. As the labor policies adjust to be more tolerant and friendlier towards labor mobility across regions and sectors, migrant workers have become a significant component of employees and residents in urban areas. In 2009, the stock of rural laborers having migrated beyond township boundaries reached 145 million, a figure which significantly mitigated the extent of the labor surplus in China's agricultural sector. Meanwhile, China's demographic transition has reached the phase at which the increase in the working age population is diminishing. Given the continuously increasing demand of the overall economic growth for a labor force, a scenario is appearing in which the growth of labor demand exceeds the growth of labor supply.

Accordingly, a shortage of labor, especially a shortage of migrant workers, appeared in the coastal areas in 2003 and then became widespread throughout the country. As can be expected from the turning point theory, wages of migrant workers substantially increased with an annual growth rate of 10.2 percent in the period of 2003 to 2009. In addition, the wage rates of hired workers in agricultural sectors have also increased, indicating a consistency among the

---

1   The wage constancy is only an abstract expression in theory. Because the subsistence standard changes over time, subsistence wage rates change as well, which has, however, no nexus with marginal productivity of labor.

decrease of surplus labor in agriculture, shortage of unskilled workers in urban areas, and induced wage rise in all sectors (Wang, 2010). According to Lewis (1954), all those phenomena indicate the advent of the Lewis Turning Point in the Chinese economy (Cai and Wang, 2010). This paper is intended to examine the changing trend of wages as a test of the Lewis Turning Point and to discuss their implications for the economic growth of China in the near future.

During China's thirty-year reform period, the persistent wage differentials among workers in China's labor market are attributable to two factors. First, they are caused by differences in human capital, which reflects the differentiated educational attainments and skills of workers. Studies show that as the labor market develops, human capital tends to increase, which leads to a more significant divide in wages among workers (for example, Zhang et al., 2005). Secondly, they are caused by the discrimination in wage determination against migrant workers and female workers. The contribution of this factor to wage differential has been reduced over time as the labor market matures (Wang and Cai, 2008; Wang, 2007).

In addition to the labor market development, the changed relationship between demand for and supply of labor also tends to weaken the contributions of the above factors to gaps in wages. In the pre-Lewis Turning Point period, there were an abundance of unskilled laborers and a scarcity of skilled workers. When the labor market started to work, therefore, workforce recruitment bottlenecked with skilled workers and the wage gap between unskilled and skilled workers widened. Furthermore, not constrained by a labor shortage, employers tended to pay migrant workers at a wage rate lower than their marginal contribution to production by taking advantage of then-existing discriminatory institutions against workers without an urban permanent residence permit, or *hukou* (Knight and Song, 2005, p. 108). While those institutional ingredients discriminating against migrant workers are gradually being eliminated with increasing employment policy and *hukou* policy reforms, wage discrimination and other mistreatment of migrant workers persists under the condition of unlimited supply of labor.

As the Lewis Turning Point is reached, there appears to be a shortage of unskilled workers. The effect of the changed relationship between demand for and supply of labor on the declining wage gap begins to exert greater influence, which leads to wages convergence despite the factors causing wages differentials still existing. In addition, as labor shortage becomes a constraint to enterprises' production and causes substitution of physical capital for labor in agriculture, the marginal productivity of labor begins to play a role in determining wages. In conclusion, after arriving at the Lewis Turning Point, society's changed situation in labor market should logically induce changes in wage rate and wage differentials.

2   The Trend of Ordinary Workers' Wage Increase

The typical dual economy development of China began in the early 1980s, during which time economic reforms were initiated and began to spur rapid economic growth. It ended in 2003, which—due to a host of changes characterizing the turning point taking place—is referred to as a representative year of the Lewis Turning Point. This dual economy development was also accompanied by a transition from a planned economy to a market economy, which still bore the legacy of a planned employment system. That is, during that period, the Chinese economy was characterized not only by its abundant agricultural laborers but also by overstaffing in urban enterprises, which later transitioned to massive layoffs and unemployment in urban areas. Therefore, the oversupply in the labor force was a normal condition at the time.

During the course of rapid economic growth, which has also been accompanied by swift social transformation, institutional obstacles deterring labor mobility between rural and urban sectors have been gradually removed, and labor migration has brought about a significant decline in the agricultural share of total employment. In the meantime, the reform of employment policy and development of the urban labor market have put an end to overstaffing in urban enterprises and reallocated the laid off and unemployed through labor market mechanisms.

In the same period, China has experienced a radical demographic transition. As a result, the total fertility rate dropped to below-replacement level in the 1990s, and the natural growth rate of population decreased to 0.5 percent in 2009. As with many industrialized economies in their comparable phases, demographic transition can lead to a changing pattern in labor supply— namely, the growth of the working age population experiences acceleration first, then it grows at a diminishing pace, until it eventually ceases to increase altogether. China's working age population is predicted to grow imperceptibly until 2013, when it will stop growing completely and begin to decline. These changes on the labor supply side indicate an end to the unlimited supply of labor which had characterized the dual economy.

On the other hand, the fast economic growth and its resultant employment expansion constantly create a strong demand for labor. The demographic and economic trends have together changed the relationship between supply of and demand for labor. If we consider the annual increase in the working age population aged between 16 and 64 as labor supply and the annual increase of urban employment as labor demand, the comparison between the two trends clearly demonstrates the altered situation of the labor market (Table 10.1). Since the numbers of laborers engaged in agriculture are in a declining trend and the non-agricultural sectors in rural areas are not expected to expand, the

TABLE 10.1   *Increment in demand for and supply of the labor force (in millions)*

	Migrant Workers	Urban Resident Workers	Working Age Population
2003	9.20	4.78	13.58
2004	4.33	4.34	8.48
2005	7.55	4.27	11.49
2006	6.34	5.17	11.23
2007	4.85	5.45	10.08
2008	3.44	3.56	6.85
2009	4.92	3.76	8.46

Source: Authors' own calculation based on *China Statistical Yearbook* (various years), *China Yearbook of Rural Household Survey* (various years), and *China Population Yearbook* (various years).

increase of urban employees (including migrant workers) can well represent the overall demand of the Chinese economy for labor.

By combining various sources of employment data, we find that in 2009, 12.5 percent or 39 million of 310 million reported urban employees were migrant workers. That is, the urban employment statistics do not adequately cover the migrant workers. In fact, the total amount of migrant workers, who are defined as out-migrating from their home townships for more than 6 months, increased to 145 million in 2009, of which 95.6 percent migrated to cities. With other data available, we know the annual growth of urban employment, which is the summation of the increases in urban resident employees and migrant workers, and then can compare it with the annual growth of the working age population of the country as a whole. As is shown in Table 10.1, the phenomenon of labor supply exceeding labor demand can no longer characterize the Chinese labor market after 2003.

A related change is that the average age of the working age population in rural areas is increasing as the population ages. Because labor migration from rural to urban sectors faces not only physical and psychological costs but also institutional barriers, older laborers in rural areas whose human capital endowment is relatively weak tend to be less capable of and less willing to migrate than their younger counterparts (Du and Wang, 2010). As a result, while people can still observe the existence of surplus laborers in rural sectors, the diminishing actual supply of labor in rural areas and unremitting demand for labor in urban sectors causes the shortage of migrant workers.

The rapid inflation of ordinary workers' wages is indicative of such a change in the labor supply and demand relationship, characterizing the present labor market and confirming the advent of the Lewis Turning Point in China. To illustrate the new trend in unskilled workers' wages, this study will present three selected categories of wages data—namely, wages in the sectors employing mainly unskilled and semi-skilled workers, wages of migrant workers, and wages in paid agricultural workers, instead of using data on urban sectors' wages aggregately presented in statistical yearbooks. The reason is twofold. First of all, urban employees, particularly in the state sector, are more or less protected in terms of wages (Knight and Song, 2005, p. 108), and data of wages in these formal sectors are too aggregated, thus the wage movement in those sectors is not particularly representative of unskilled workers. Secondly, the regular statistics on wages often omit wages of informal urban workers and migrant workers, so it is necessary to seek out the wages of migrant workers as proxy of unskilled workers' wages.

Various officially-conducted surveys show that not only have the wages in manufacturing and construction increased constantly (mainly reflecting the general trend of wages since they do not specifically represent migrant workers' wages), migrant workers' wages in real terms have been catching up (Table 10.2). A new survey conducted by the National Bureau of Statistics (NBS) shows that the real monthly wage of migrant workers was 1221 *yuan* in 2009, 90 percent higher than in 2001.

While disagreements still exist as to whether there is actually a significant increase in migrant workers' wages as well as what could cause the increase, there have been few scholarly written papers to present evidence to support the opinions that either assert there is no significant increase in migrants' wages, or that factors other than labor supply and demand change cause the increase in wages. To counter these disagreements, we offer relatively general arguments instead of specific discussions.

First, we attempt to respond to the proposition that the inflation of migrant workers' wage is insignificant. Apart from the NBS source present in Table 10.2, there are other individual surveys and new reports, which assert even higher levels and faster growth of migrants' wages. As an example, a survey conducted by the People's Bank of China in early 2010 shows that the average wage of migrant workers was 1783.2 *yuan* in 2009, a 17.8 percent increase compared to the previous year (DSS-PBC, 2010, p. 40).

In fact, to compare local and migrant workers' wages requires combining wage rates with working hours, because they work in different ways. According to a survey conducted in 2010 (the China Urban Labor Survey, or CULS),[2]

---

2 The China Urban Labor Survey, or CULS, is a series of surveys conducted by the Institute of Population and Labor Economics, Chinese Academy of Social Sciences, in 2001, 2005, and 2010, respectively. It representatively sampled laborers in urban households and migrant

TABLE 10.2 *Real Wages and their Growth Rates by Sector (yuan, %)*

	Farm Workers (Daily Wages)			Non-Agricultural Sectors (Monthly Wages)		
	Grains	Pig Farm	Cotton	Manuf.	Constr.	Migrants
1998	18.43	9.60	19.70	589	621	
1999	14.26	9.64	11.83	658	674	
2000	19.00	10.13	19.72	733	732	
2001	18.25	10.49	18.35	813	789	643
2002	18.32	11.06	17.71	924	864	664
2003	18.73	11.21	18.43	1041	956	701
2004	21.40	18.63	25.81	1131	1029	755
2005	24.04	18.88	27.14	1250	1138	820
2006	27.73	22.36	27.77	1404	1282	887
2007	30.95	26.58	30.30	1562	1403	951
2008	37.85	29.52	32.09	1714	1525	1138
Annual growth rate	15.1	21.4	11.7	10.5	9.8	10.2

Source: Daily wages of grains, cotton, and pig farms with a size of over 50 are from the Compilation of National Farm Product Cost-benefit Data; monthly wages of manufacturing and construction are from China Labor Statistics (various years); monthly wages of migrant workers are from NBS Statistical Reports (various years).

migrant workers work 27 percent more hours a week than do urban local workers. That is, migrants have to work longer in order to get higher monthly wages. In fact, the same survey shows that while migrants' wages were only 88.2 percent of local urban workers', the monthly wages of the former were slightly higher than that of the latter (5.6 percent higher) after adjusting for the difference in weekly working hours. As the migrants' demographic characteristics change, the new generations of migrant workers tend to work fewer hours than did their older counterparts. The results of CULS show that migrant workers worked nearly 12.4 hours fewer than did their predecessors in 2005. That is, the growth of migrants' wages and their convergence with urban locals' (shown in Table 10.2) can imply a larger surge of actual wage rate (e.g. if measured by hourly wage rate).

---

households and surveyed both individual laborers and households in Shanghai, Wuhan, Shenyang, Fuzhou, and Xi'an.

Secondly, we try to respond to the propositions asserting that the scarcity of migrant workers is caused by other factors, such as the existing *hukou* system or the enhanced education attainments of the new generations of migrants, rather than by a changed relationship between labor demand and labor supply. As for institutional barriers deterring labor mobility, they have been present at all times throughout the planned and reform periods. In fact, the policies restricting labor mobility have been reformed rather rapidly and intensely in recent years, particularly since 2003 (see Cai, 2010). In terms of migrants' education attainments, they always have been continually improving, not just since 2003. Instead of its contribution to the increase of wage rate, this study in fact finds that the contribution of education attainments to wages differentials has declined in recent years, as is discussed in the next section. Further strengthening the argument that it is the change in labor demand and supply that causes the wage inflation, refer to the figures of the rapid increase in paid workers in selected agricultural sectors in Table 10.2.

3   Wage Convergence in the Labor Market

The wages of ordinary workers are in essence determined differently in pre- and post-Lewis Turning Point periods. Under the dual economy, the nature of unlimited labor supply determined that wages for migrant workers moving from agriculture to non-agricultural sectors in urban areas are not determined by their marginal product of labor. When passing through the LTP, the changing situations between labor supply and employment demand start affecting the wages for various groups, i.e., a relatively unchanged scarcity of skilled workers and increasing scarcity of unskilled workers. The determinant for migrants' wage begins to shift from subsistence wages to marginal productivity of labor. Hence, wage convergence is expected to take place during this particular period of time.

In the case of the Chinese labor market, as the LTP arrives, it is expected that wages will converge between skilled and unskilled workers, between migrants and local residents, and across regions. By making use of the data from three waves of CULS, we found an overall trend in wage convergence in the urban labor market. Pooling together both urban resident workers and migrant workers in urban areas, the calculated Gini coefficient of urban wages was 0.37 in 2001, but had been reduced to 0.33 in 2010. The calculated Theil Entropy index was also reduced from 0.25 to 0.19 in the same period. The existing wage inequality measured by other indices was to a certain extent declined as well. The rest of this section reveals the wage convergence by group of workers.

Wage Convergence among Migrant Workers

Although migrant workers as a whole represent unskilled workers, variations exist among migrant workers in terms of human capital. For example, among the 145 million migrant workers in 2009, 11.7 percent only completed primary schooling or were illiterate, 64.8 percent finished junior high school, 13.1 percent finished senior high school, and 10.4 percent graduated from technical secondary school or above (DRS-NBS, 2010, p. 5). In other words, three fourths of migrant workers are unskilled workers with junior high school diploma or below. Migrants would be unable to match local workers' wage rates unless those unskilled workers attained a faster wage growth. Analysis from CULS data indicates that the Gini coefficients for migrant workers alone have been decreasing, from 0.396 in 2001 to 0.334 in 2005 and 0.319 in 2010.

In addition, migrants' wage growth by education group can be observed in Figure 10.1, where each dot represents real wage growth for a group of workers with same education attainment, the horizontal axis is wage level in base year (2001 and 2005 respectively), and the vertical axis is wage growth from the base year to 2010. Although workers with higher education attainments made more earnings in all three rounds of surveys, Figure 10.1 clearly indicates workers with a lower education and lower wage rate in the base years have faster wage growth during the subsequent period observed.

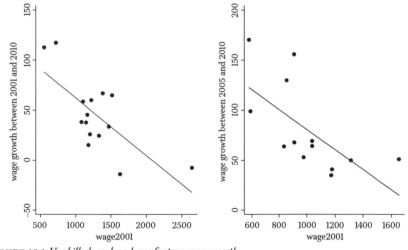

FIGURE 10.1 *Unskilled workers have faster wage growth*
SOURCE: AUTHORS' CALCULATION FROM CULS DATA.

To further understand the wage convergence within migrant workers and the driving forces of wage growth for unskilled workers, we investigated the returns on education for skilled migrant workers relative to unskilled migrant workers using the CULS data. The estimation explains why, after the LTP, the unskilled workers experience a faster wage growth, which narrows the gap of returns on education between skilled and unskilled migrant workers. A typical Mincer regression is applied and the equation is shown as follows:

$$\ln y_i = \alpha_0 + \alpha_1 edug_i^j + \alpha_2 ex_i + \alpha_3 ex_i^2 + ged_i + city + \varepsilon_i$$

The left variable is the hourly earnings in logarithmic terms, and explanatory variables include the levels of last education, categorized by primary school or below, senior high school, above senior high school, labor market experience and its squared term, gender, and city variables.

As noted earlier, migrant workers who finished junior high school dominate the labor market, so this group is taken as a reference group when observing the relative returns on education of the two groups with higher levels of education. The regression results (Table 10.3) show that the relative returns on education for workers with above senior high school dropped from 80.4 percent in 2001 to 75.3 percent in 2005 and 57.1 percent in 2010, and that the relative returns on education for workers who just finished senior high school dropped

TABLE 10.3 *Relative Returns on Education for Migrant Workers*

	CULS2001	CULS2005	CULS2010
Prim. School and Below	−0.116 (0.039)	−0.119 (0.287)	−0.093 (0.032)
Sen. High School	0.259 (0.040)***	0.173 (0.030) ***	0.169 (0.024) ***
Above Sen. High	0.804 (0.084) ***	0.753 (0.085) ***	0.571(0.041) ***
Gender (male = 1)	0.179 (0.031)	0.204 (0.022)	0.23 (0.019)
Experience	0.039 (0.044)	−0.0039 (0.0012)	0.022 (0.0029)
Squared Experience	−0.00078 (0.0001)	−4.85e−07(1.48e−07)	−0.00058 (0.00006)
City Variables	Yes	Yes	Yes
No. of Obs	2283	3263	3499
Adj-R²	0.197	0.162	0.238

Note: standard errors in parenthesis, *** significant at 1%.

from 25.9 percent in 2001 to 17.3 percent in 2005 and 16.9 percent in 2010. The declining trends of relative returns on education indicate that as the unlimited supply of labor ends, the marginal productivity of labor starts playing a role in the wage formation of unskilled workers, whose lower education attainments reap relatively higher returns on the labor market.

Wage Convergence between Local and Migrant Workers

Prior to the advent of the LTP, a surplus of mass rural labor is the fundamental constraint holding back migrant workers' wage from going up. In the meantime, the institutional segmentation of the urban labor market impedes migrant workers' access to work in formal sectors. Therefore, the institutional segmentation distinguishing between migrant and local workers entails two different mechanisms of wage determination corresponding to the two groups of people. On one hand, the condition of unlimited supply of labor suppresses any increase in migrant workers' wages. On the other hand, the labor market segmentation protects local workers while discriminating against migrant workers.[3]

After the LTP has been reached, a substantial change takes place in the relationship between supply of and demand for migrant workers. That is, the shortage of unskilled workers generates a wage inflation for migrant workers, who are at the low end of wage distribution. Meanwhile, the institutionally-determined wage is quickly eliminated. These two factors drive the wage increase of migrant workers and thus the wages convergence between local and migrant workers.

Figure 10.2 shows the wage growth rates at each decile of wage distribution for both migrant workers and local workers during the period of 2001 to 2010. It is easy to find that local workers witnessed more balanced wage growth, whereas migrant workers had a larger variation of wage growth. First of all, migrant workers at the bottom end of wage distribution in 2001 experienced faster wage growth than migrant workers at the top of the wage distribution continuum. Secondly, migrant workers at the bottom end of wage distribution in 2001 tended to experience faster wage growth than local workers at the same deciles in the subsequent years, as evidenced by at the six lowest deciles of migrant workers having higher growth rates than their local worker counterparts. These trends indicate that, with the gradual removal of institutional

---

3   By comparing wage rates and marginal products of labor, Knight and Song (2005, p. 108) find that there coexisted underestimation on migrant workers' wage and overestimation on local workers' wage in the Chinese urban labor market.

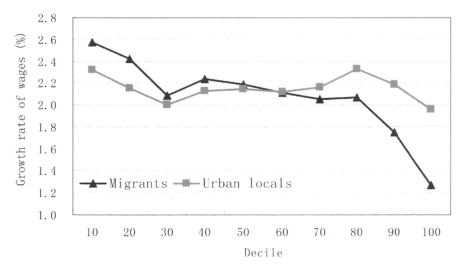

FIGURE 10.2 *Wage growth rates by decile of 2001 (2001–2010)*
SOURCE: AUTHORS' CALCULATION FROM CULS DATA.

barriers, the forces of the labor market force are already major mechanisms in wage determination.

To further examine the wage convergence between migrant workers and local workers, we pooled the samples of both migrants and local workers together to observe the changing role that *hukou* status plays in wage determination over time, while controlling for individual characteristics and localities of labor markets (city variables). The estimation results (Table 10.4) show a diminishing effect of *hukou* identity on wage determination. When controlling for other variables, urban residence variables explain 11 percent of the wage difference in 2001, 9 percent in 2005, and 5 percent in 2010. Considering that migration flow has been increasing and the total number of migrant workers in 2009 was 1.73 times as much as in 2001, the wage convergence between local and migrant workers is set to narrow.

Wage Convergence across Regions

As wages converge between migrant and local workers and barriers within the labor market are gradually eliminated, more extensive and integrated labor mobility across regions is expected to bring about a reduction in regional wage differentials. A previous study (Cai, et al., 2007) finds that, after controlling for individual and migratory characteristics, migrant workers' wages across regions tend to converge. Following the same methodology—namely, by following a suitable inequality index based on wage regression, while controlling

TABLE 10.4   *The* Hukou's *role in wage determination*

	CULS2001	CULS2005	CULS2010
Residence (migrants = 1)	−0.107 (3.85) ***	−0.087 (2.95) ***	−0.048 (2.38) **
Years of Schooling	0.102 (25.21)	0.098 (20.60)	0.11 (30.98)
Work Experience	0.005 (1.89)	−0.001 (1.09)	0.018(6.48)
Squared Experience	−0.0 (−1.20)	−0.0 (1.12)	−0.0 (−5.13)
Gender (male = 1)	0.21 (10.50)	0.24 (11.07)	0.18 (11.05)
City Variables	Yes	Yes	Yes
Number of obs.	6260	6535	7940
Adj-R²	0.31	0.42	0.37

Note: t statistics in parenthesis, *** significant at 1%, ** significant at 5%.

for individual characteristics and *hukou* status, we can explore the impact of regional factors on wages differentials.

Compared to conventional techniques, the regression-based breakdown is of merit (Fields, 1998; Bourgignon et al., 1998; Morduch and Sicular, 2002). For one thing, it allows us to avoid the endogeneity that often appears when doing inequality breakdowns by category. In addition, it also makes it possible to examine the sources of inequality from continuous variables.

Following Shorrocks equations (1982), the inequality index could be written as a summation weighted by wage.

$$I(\mathbf{y}) = \sum a_i(\mathbf{y})y_i \tag{1}$$

$I(\mathbf{y})$ is the overall inequality index, for example, Theil entropy, Gini coefficient, or coefficient of variations, etc., y_i is the wage for worker i, and $a_i(\mathbf{y})$ is the weight applied to each individual, which varies across different inequality indicators. Each regressor in the regression equation contributes to the inequality index. The share in overall inequality measurement from factor k (explanatory variables or residual) is s^k, which is expressed as:

$$s^k = \frac{\sum_{i=1}^{n} a_i(\mathbf{y})y_i^k}{I(\mathbf{y})} \tag{2}$$

Since (2) is determined by the regression coefficient $\hat{\beta}_k$ and the level of the factor x_i^k, the regression based breakdown could be expressed as

$$s^k = \hat{\beta}_k \frac{\sum_{i=1}^{n} a_i(y)x_i^k}{I(\mathbf{y})} \tag{3}$$

Regarding the inequality index used in the Theil entropy of this paper, the index could be broken down as the following format:

$$I_{TT}(\mathbf{y}) = \frac{1}{n}\sum_{i=1}^{n} \frac{y_i}{\mu} \ln \frac{y_i}{\mu} \tag{4}$$

and

$$s_{TT}^k = \frac{\frac{1}{n}\sum_{i=1}^{n} y_i^k \ln \frac{y_i}{\mu}}{\frac{1}{n}\sum_{i=1}^{n} y_i \ln \frac{y_i}{\mu}}$$

Hence, according to the estimated results of Table 10.4, we can break down the Theil entropy of wages by the source of their inequality and the regional factors in Figure 10.3. The contribution of regional factors to inequality increased from 0.144 in 2001 to 0.175 in 2005, whereas it declined to 0.093 in 2010, and it was significantly lower than that in 2001. In addition, the portion of regional factors that explains wage inequality declined from 56 percent in 2001 to 51 percent in 2010.

4   Conclusions and Policy Implications

The development process of the Chinese dual economy has been accelerated by the accomplishment of a demographic transition that slows the increase in labor supply, and by the fast growth of an economy that sustains a strong demand for labor. The changed relationship between labor demand and labor supply, as well as its resulting wage increase, symbolizes the advent of the Lewis Turning Point in China. While different perspectives remain, the vast majority recognize that China's demographic transition will not be reversed, and in the short term, China's economic growth promises to continue its upward trend.

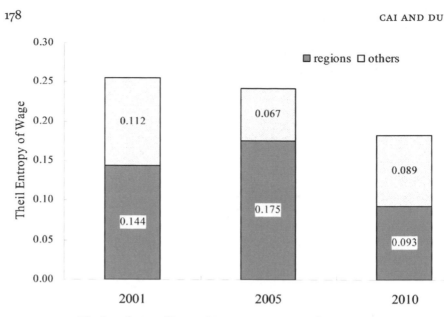

FIGURE 10.3   *The Contribution of Regional Factors to Wage Inequality*
SOURCE: AUTHORS' CALCULATION FROM CULS DATA.

Additionally, it is difficult to deny that the key identifier of a Lewis Turning Point—that of reduced labor supply coupled with increasing labor demand—is a fact in the modern Chinese economic growth model.

The essential point of the policy implications is that, as labor becomes relatively scarce, the Chinese economy begins to move towards a pattern framed by the neoclassical theory of growth. That is, further growth can only be sustained by an increase in total factor productivity (TFP), not on a simple increase in physical capital and labor. Moreover, since wage convergence between unskilled and skilled workers is one of the most important features of the Lewis Turning Point—namely, that low income group tends to benefit more from the general trend of wage inflation—the conditions for a Kuznets turning point, at which income inequality stops widening and then begins decreasing, become more likely.[4] The improvement of income distribution, however, is not spontaneous, but dependent on the effective function of labor market institutions and social protection mechanisms. The most fascinating outcome of the turning point would be that, with their new increase in income, migrant workers contribute greatly to overall consumption and thus contribute to the

---

4   The Japanese experience shows that in the pre-Lewis Turning Point period, the existence of mass surplus labor force drove labor income share in national income to decline (Minami and Ono, 1981). It implies that in the pre-Lewis Turning Point period, as the surplus labor force decreases, the conditions for improving income distribution gradually increase.

sustainability of its further growth. In the following paragraphs, we illustrate three challenges facing China as it meets the Lewis Turning Point.

Shifting the Economic Growth Model

The neoclassical theory of growth assumes a diminishing return on capital because of labor scarcity. That is, without the enhancement of TFP, economic growth cannot be sustained by factors of production alone. When Krugman (1994), Young (1992), and others criticized the "East Asian miracle," they did not apprehend the unique features of the region; with an unlimited supply of labor at the time, and with predictions based on neoclassical assumptions, they mistakenly foretold an unsustainable future for the growth of those economies. As the Chinese economy gradually moves away from a scenario of unlimited supply of labor, however, those skeptical arguments may serve as a wakeup call for China in the sustainability of its economic growth.

In their prominent study on the lost decade of the Japanese economy, Hayashi and Prescott (2002) suggest that it was low growth in productivity that caused and is still causing the economy's stagnation. In 1990, when the population window closed in Japan, it was already one of the richest countries of the world. However, in 2013, when the demographic dividend ends, China will be faced with a unique challenge—"aging before affluence," in which case, China should do everything possible to shift of growth model to a TFP-driven one. What follows are two of the major challenges facing China in raising its productivity in manufacturing.

First, China's development strategy tends to be detrimental to the effects resources reallocation that are potentially to be gained in its structural adjustment. In the course of implementing regional strategies, namely, the "Go-West" movement, the "Rejuvenation of Northeast China and Other Old Industrial Bases," and the "Rise of the Central Regions," the central government has used various policy measures to encourage favorable and subsidized investments in the central and western regions. While this policy has reduced regional disparities by artificially counterpoising investments in infrastructure and industries among the eastern, central, and western regions, these types of subsidies and favorable loans have obliterated the distinction between competitive and inefficient investments. Those investments deviating from the comparative advantages of the central and western regions have led to the heavy reliance of some enterprises on governmental support. In the period from 2000 to 2007, the annual growth rates of capital-labor ratio in the central and western provinces, were, on average, 9.2 percent and 8.1 percent, respectively—much higher than the average 4.2 percent growth rate in the eastern provinces. In 2007, the capital-labor ratios of the central and western regions were 20.1 percent and

25.9 percent higher than that in eastern regions, respectively (Cai, Wang, and Qu, 2009).

Secondly, China's labor shortage and the convergence of wages between unskilled and skilled workers tends to create a disincentive for schooling, thus weakening future human capital accumulation. The rapid structural change of the Chinese economy, however, is increasing the demand for work skills gained through education and training, yet the rapid surge of demand for unskilled labor and the resulting rise of unskilled workers' wages temporarily weakens family motivation to have their children stay in schools, since they now have a better opportunity for employment and higher pay in labor market while also facing increased cost of schooling.

As is shown in previous studies, an overwhelming portion of the urban sectors' need for labor has been fulfilled by labor migration from rural areas, while the human capital rural migrant workers are relatively low but increasing over time (Wang, 2009). If the human capital accumulation process is halted, even just temporarily, it will not only impede the structural upgrade of Chinese industry, but also generate employment difficulties for some groups of workers in the near future. To avert such a risk, government intervention in subsidizing secondary education, vocational education, and on-the-job-training is urgently needed.

Building Labor Market Institutions

Although a meeting between the Lewis Turning Point and the Kuznets turning point can be theoretically expected—and has in fact been confirmed in some countries—any improvement in income distribution is not a spontaneous result of the Lewis Turning Point, but is a condition of institutional restructuring in both primary distribution and redistribution. The advent of the Lewis Turning Point changes the relationship between demand for and supply of labor market institutions, giving rise to the potential formation of public policies favorable towards ordinary workers and low-income families in the labor market.

As laborers and migrant workers are faced with more employment opportunities, they actually obtain the power to "exit" or the right to "vote with their feet"—namely, more choices in the job market. How they use such power depends on their current jobs. In some scenarios, they may simply choose to quit if they are not satisfied with a job in a small, futureless enterprise, since it is largely possible for them to find a job elsewhere. In other scenarios, they are more likely to take action to voice their demands in front of employers, such as complaints, collective bargaining, and in more extreme cases, strikes. If they are dissatisfied with their current status but reluctant to leave the firms, which

have the advantage in terms of size, fame, and development potential,[5] workers may strike in order to seek higher pay and better working conditions., In
recent years (particularly after 2008, when Chinese labor laws were updated),
labor disputes have intensified. That is not a sign of the aggravation of labor
relations, but an indication of stronger demand for labor market institutions.

After their economies arrived at the Lewis Turning Point, Japan and Korea
utilized different approaches to dealing with the surge in demand for wage
increases. When Japan arrived at its turning point around 1960 (Minami, 1968),
the government responded seriously to labor disputes by playing an active
role in collective bargaining and helping to form a harmonious labor relationship. As a result, income distribution quickly improved following the Lewis
Turning Point, and the country enjoys little income inequality (see Minami,
1998; Moriguchi and Saez, 2008). When Korea, on the other hand, arrived at
its turning point around 1970, the role of trade unions was strictly restricted
by the government, and workers were unsatisfied with their wages. The consequence was not only a slower improvement of income distribution compared
to Japan's, but also a disastrous political cost—namely, a more than decade-
long collapse of social cohesion (see Freeman, 1993). In short, the time lag
between the Lewis Turning Point and Kuznets turning point was much longer
in Korea than in Japan, because of different approaches to building labor market institutions.

Fostering New Consumers

Creating new consumers out of ordinary workers and low-income families,
who benefit the most from the wage increase and wage convergence occurring
at the Lewis Turning Point, is critical for the transformation of Chinese growth
from an export- and investment-driven model to a consumption-driven model.
Migrant workers are central to this concern. While they work and live in cities,
migrant workers cannot normally spend what they earn like their native counterparts do, because without an urban *hukou,* they are not included within the
urban social security programs, and because their employment is unsecured,
they are thus subjected to cyclical unemployment.

According to a study conducted by the Asian Development Bank (Chun,
2010), the Chinese middle class—namely, those whose daily income is between
two and 20 US dollars—while making up 66 percent of the total population,

---

5   In his most prominent work, Hirschman (1970) uses three expressions—namely, exit, voice,
    and loyalty—to illustrate the mechanisms by which citizens, consumers, and workers
    express their dissatisfaction. Here, we borrow those expressions to understand the labor
    market changes as a result of the passage of the Lewis Turning Point.

is responsible for 79.2 percent of the total consumption of China. The same study divides the Chinese middle class into three groups—the lower middle class, with a daily income of between two and four USD, the mid middle class, with a daily income of between four and ten USD, and the upper middle class, with a daily income of between ten and 20 USD. Based on such a categorization, we find that the rural households, whose average daily income is 3.6 USD, the migrant households, whose average daily income is 9.4 USD, and urban resident households, whose daily income is 11.9 USD, fall into lower, middle, and upper middle class groups, respectively. That is, not only can poverty alleviation increase households' consumption level, but labor mobility and, more significantly, the obtaining of urban citizenship, can increase consumption levels. In this case, when households escape from poverty—specifically, once their daily income jumps from lower than 1.25 USD to the 1.25 to 2 USD range, their consumption increases by 120.5 percent; when households enter the lower middle class, their consumption increases by 17.5 percent; when rural households migrate and become migrant households, their consumption increases by 80.1 percent; and when migrant households obtain an urban *hukou*, their consumption significantly increases by 117.8 percent.

(This article was originally published in Chinese in 2011.)

References

Bai, Moo-ki. 1982. "The Turning Point in the Korean Economy." *Developing Economies* 2: 117–140.

Bourgignon, Francois, Fournier, M., and Gurgrand, M. 1998. "Distribution, Development, and Education: Taiwan, 1979–1994," paper presented at LACEA Conference, Buenos Aires.

Cai, Fang. 2010. "The Turning Point and Reorientation of Public Policy in Chinese Economic Growth." *Social Sciences in China.*

———. 2010. "Demographic Transition, Demographic Dividend, and Lewis Turning Point in China." *China Economic Journal,* 3(2): 107–119.

Cai, Fang and Meiyan Wang. 2010. "Growth and Structural Changes in Employment in Transition China." *Journal of Comparative Economics* 38: 71–81.

Cai, Fang, Meiyan Wang, and Yue Qu. 2009 "Industrial and Labor Relocations among Chinese Regions." *The Chinese Industrial Economics* 8.

Cai, Fang, Yang Du and Changbao Zhao. 2007 "Regional Labour Market Integration since China's World Trade Organization Entry: Evidence from Household-level

Data, in Garnaut, Ross and Ligang Song (eds)." *China—Linking Markets for Growth.* Canberra: Asia Pacific Press, pp. 133–150.

Chun, Natalie. 2010. "Middle Class Size in the Past, Present, and Future: A Description of Trends in Asia." *ADB Working Paper Series* 217: September.

Department of Rural Survey of National Bureau of Statistics (DRS-NBS). 2010. "A Monitoring Survey Report on Migrant Workers in 2009." In *Report on China's Population and Labor (No. 11): Labor Market Challenges in the Post-crisis Era*, edited by Cai Fang. Beijing: Social Sciences Academic Press (China).

Department of Survey and Statistics, People's Bank of China (DSS-PBC). 2010. "The 5th Monitoring Report on Migrant Workers." In *Report on China's Population and Labor (No. 11): Labor Market Challenges in the Post-crisis Era*, edited by Cai Fang. Beijing: Social Sciences Academic Press (China).

Du, Yang and Meiyan Wang. 2010. "New Estimate of Surplus Rural Labor Force and Its Implications." *Journal of Guangzhou University* (Social Science Edition) 9 (4): 17–24.

Fields, Gary S. (1998) Accounting for Income Inequality and its Change, Mimeo, Cornell University.

Freeman, Richard. 1993. "Labor Market and Institutions in Economic Development." *AEA Papers and Proceedings* 403–408.

Hayashi, Fumio and Edward C. Prescott. 2002. "The 1990s in Japan: A Lost Decade." *Review of Economic Dynamics* 5 (1): 206–235.

Hirschman, Albert O. 1970. *Exit, Voice, and Loyalty: Responses to Decline in Firms, Organizations, and State.* Cambridge, MA: Harvard University Press.

Knight, John and Lina Song. 2005. *Towards a Labour Market in China*, New York: Oxford University Press.

Krugman, Paul. 1994. "The Myth of Asia's Miracle." *Foreign Affairs* (November/ December).

Lewis, Arthur. 1954. "Economic Development with Unlimited Supplies of Labour." *The Manchester School of Economic and Social Studies* 22: 139–191.

————. 1972. "Reflections on Unlimited Labour." On *International Economics and Development* edited by L. Di Marco, New York, Academic Press, 75–96.

Minami Ryoshi. 1998. "Economic Development and Income Distribution in Japan: An Assessment of the Kuznets Hypothesis." *Cambridge Journal of Economics* 22 (1): 39–58.

Minami, Ryoshi and Xinxin Ma. 2010. "The Turning Point of Chinese Economy: Comparison with Japanese Experience." *China Economic Journal* 3 (2): 163–179.

Minami, Ryoshin. 1968. "The Turning Point in the Japanese Economy." *The Quarterly Journal of Economics* 82 (3): 380–402.

————. 2010. Turning Point in the Japanese Economy, presented at the Workshop in the Project of Institute of Asian Cultures Toyo University "The Discussion on the Changes in East Asia Labor Market Based on Lewisian Turning Point Theory." Tokyo, July 18–19.

Minami, Ryoshin and Akira Ono. 1981. "Behavior of Income Shares in a Labor Surplus Economy: Japan's Experience." *Economic Development and Cultural Change* 29 (2): 309–324.

Morduch, Jonathan and Terry Sicular. 2002. "Rethinking Inequality Decomposition, with Evidence from Rural China." *Economic Journal* 112 (476): 93–106.

Moriguchi, Chiaki and Emmanuel Saez. 2008. *The Review of Economics and Statistics* 90 (4): 713–734.

Ranis, Gustav and Fei, John C.H. 1961. "A Theory of Economic Development." *The American Economic Review* 51 (4): 533–565.

Wang, Meiyan. 2007. "Changes of Discrimination against Migrant Workers in China's Urban Labor Market." *China Labor Economics (Zhongguo Laodong Jingjixue)* 4 (1): 109–119.

———. 2009. "Educational Return and Educational Resource Allocation between Rural and Urban Areas—An Empirical Analysis Using China's Urban Labor Survey Data." *World Economy (Shijie Jingji)* 5: 3–17.

———. 2010. "The Rise of Labor Cost and the Fall of Labor Input: Has China Reached Lewis Turning Point?" *China Economic Journal* 3 (2): 139–155.

Wang, Meiyan and Fang Cai. 2008 "Gender Earnings Differential in Urban China." *Review of Development Economics* 12 (2):

Yao, Yang and Ke Zhang. 2010. "Has China Passed the Lewis Turning Point? A Structural Estimation Based on Provincial Data." *China Economic Journal* 3 (2): 155–162.

Young, Alwyn. 1992. "A Tale of Two Cities: Factor Accumulation and Technical Change in Hong Kong and Singapore." In *NBER Macroeconomics Annual*, edited by Olivier Blanchard and Stanley Fischer. Cambridge, Mass.: MIT Press.

Zhang, Junsen, Yaohui Zhao, Albert Park and Xiaoqing Song. 2005. "Economic Returns to Schooling in Urban China, 1988 to 2001." *Journal of Comparative Economics* 33: 730–752.

Zhang, Xiaobo, Jin Yang, and Shenglin Wang. 2009. "China Has Reached the Lewis Turning Point." *Journal of Zhejiang University (Edition of Humanities and Social Sciences* 9).

CHAPTER 11

Intensified Reform of the Labor Market and Abolishment of the Rural-Urban Divide

Zhang Zhanxin and Hou Huili

Over the years, social scientists have paid attention to and attempted to interpret the issues surrounding the fact that rural migrants suffer from unfavorable labor market inequalities and discrimination in public services relative to the local residents. Since the 1990s, studies have centered on the Rural-Urban Divide system, and as a result, have developed a number of viewpoints. The rural-urban permanent residence permit, or *hukou,* divides rural and urban residents into two types of social status with different basic rights; under this dualist partition, rural labor transfer to cities indicates "peasant workers' mobility rather than permanent migration (Sun 2003). Without urban *hukou,* rural migrants moving into cities could only get jobs in the secondary labor market, becoming the "third group" between peasants and urban citizens— the "bottom elite" (Li 2004). With the exclusion of rights for rural migrants and the symbolic establishment of "peasant worker" status, the rural-urban system has been copied and propagated in cities, with a dual-society in urban China composed of urban citizens and rural migrants (Chan 2005).

Since 2000, the central government has implemented a series of policies in favor of rural migrants and pushed forward *hukou* reform, labor system reform, and social security reform. Under these circumstances, has the Rural-Urban Divide system been declining? To this question, recent literature has addressed three different answers. Some scholars clearly argue that the Rural-Urban Divide system persists or is reinforced. This view holds that local governments having obtained more power to reform the *hukou* system in their jurisdiction has made it more difficult for rural migrants to get urban *hukou;* consequently, the *hukou* system dividing rural and urban populations remains potent and intact, and the situation of rural migrants in cities not only will not improve, but may in fact worsen (Chan, and Buckingham, 2008). Some even consider that, because big cities tend to resist the central government's guidelines regarding *hukou* reform and insist on the Rural-Urban Divide, differential citizenship based on rural and urban *hukou* is both the precondition of China's reform and its byproduct (Wu 2010). The second viewpoint is that the rural-urban system, which has persisted since the beginning of reform, has started to show some signs of change, but that it is not enough to know if the system is weakened or not (Whyte 2010). The third viewpoint claims that, as a set of formal institutions, the rural-urban system has to a large extent already ended in the first decade of the new millennium (Zhang 2007).

Whether the Rural-Urban Divide system persists or declines is related to several basic points about labor market reform in the new century. In the early 1990s, the objectives for reform of the socialist market economy was established, within which building contractual labor relations and cultivating the labor market were two key elements. In practice, however, reform measures in this period were focused on state-owned enterprises. State enterprises' workers needed time to be marketized, and the newly emerging labor market inevitably retained divisive segmentation. Differences between local workers and rural migrants in employment, income, and other aspects were the main forms of urban labor market segmentation, and indicated the Rural-Urban Divide's persistence.

In the first decade of the new century, has the rural-urban labor market integration been successful? Or has there been little progress? This topic can also be approached from a different angle. A basic point persisting in recent arguments of rural-urban dualism is the fact that rural migrants cannot obtain an urban *hukou*. This approach raises a crucial question: up to now, to what extent does *hukou* resident status still play a role in dividing the rural and urban population? Is the *hukou* system still important to building the structure of an urban labor market?

Discussions about the Rural-Urban Divide are also relevant to the ongoing debate about China's stage of economic development regarding the Lewis Turning Point. Some scholars claim that China no longer has a dual-economy with unlimited surplus rural laborers, and has instead reached the Lewis Turning Point (Cai 2008). According to Lewis (1979) and others (Fields 2004), in developing countries, there exists a barrier of labor market segmentation. Unlike most developing countries, China's huge amount of surplus labor in the countryside before the reform resulted from its unique systematic arrangement—the Rural-Urban Divide (Cai and Lin 2003). Therefore, the decline of the Rural-Urban Divide should be one of the preconditions for China's dual economy to realize the Lewis Turning Point. If formal institutions for dividing rural and urban people still exist, or if the labor market continues to be segmented, rural migrants to cities will have to bear systematic exclusions. In this case, arguments about the Lewis Turning Point will be questioned in view of an institutional arrangement.

Based on the perspective of institutional change, this paper addresses the decline of the Rural-Urban Divide and other issues related to rural-migrants' socio-economic positions. The basic points are: (1) intensified labor market reform in the new decade has led to the end of the Rural-Urban Divide system, (2) major factors affecting migrants' rights and interests have shifted to local institutions and policies due to the nature of regional segmentation, and (3) *hukou* status inequality on the whole is shrinking, but population pressure in big cities may slow down the process of overall *hukou* system reform.

The System of Rural-Urban Divide and the Impact of Early Reform

The Rural-Urban Divide system consists of several related institutions, in which the *hukou* system and urban labor system are basic arrangements. After the new state was founded, China quickly initiated the *hukou* system, but it began as merely a mechanism of residential recording. Later on, rural and urban populations were clearly defined, and control of migration, especially to cities from the countryside, was strengthened incrementally. In the 1960s, a complete administrative system based on rural and urban *hukou* status was finally formed. The main functions of the *hukou* system were population management and control, while labor management and control were basically realized through the dual-labor system for rural and urban residents. Urban laborers were assigned jobs by the state, whereas rural laborers had to participate in agricultural production in the People's Communes (人民公社, rénmín gōngshè). According to regulations regarding *hukou* administration at that time, rural residents could transfer from agricultural *hukou* to non-agricultural *hukou* when being recruited by urban government labor departments. However, due to a heavy industry oriented development strategy, solo public ownership structure, and life-time employment system, those cities' governments with employment burdens were unable to absorb many rural surplus laborers. Rural laborers informally working in urban enterprises with the status of temporary workers or seasonal workers could not be registered as urban *hukou*. In addition, if rural residents without a transferred *hukou* lived in cities, they were permitted to do so as "temporary population" only, and their usual permission was for no more than three months. Rural people, therefore, could neither get transfer to urban *hukou* nor move to cities; they were actually restricted to the countryside and agriculture. The Rural-Urban Divide system manifested itself in other ways as well. For instance, there were different supply mechanisms for food and other necessities for urban and rural residents. In urban state and collective work units, workers and staff assigned by government plans were eligible to have labor insurance such as pension and healthcare. The Rural-Urban Divide system essentially defined differential citizenship rights for rural and urban people insofar as residence, employment, social security, and social services, based on their different *hukou* status.

Since 1978, China's reform and opening-up (改革开放) has been impacting on the Rural-Urban Divide system. During this period of rural reform, peasants received economic rights in job searching and doing independent business, hence it became possible for them to leave agriculture and go into cities. In urban China, the emergence and growth of non-public economies gave rise to a variety of flexible systems of labor employment, which enlarged labor demand and provided room for rural surplus laborers to transfer to non-agricultural sectors. Under these circumstances, the rural-urban barrier limiting the exodus of the rural population and labor to cities was gradually relaxed. In 1984, a new policy allowed peasants to settle in market towns with food for themselves, which was the first step for them in leaving the countryside. In 1985, the limit of a three-month-residence for migrants were stopped, and instead, a "temporary residence permit" system was instituted, which began to permit longer periods of habitation in cities for the floating population. These changes led to the emergence of a significant "temporary population," of which the rural floating population made up the majority. Thereafter, more and more rural laborers moving to cities joined the pattern of "floating but not (*hukou*) migrating," (Hou and Zhang 2010) whereas in the urban areas, a labor market "outside the formal system" open to rural workers was in formation. Rural migrants' leaving their home towns and the agricultural sector, moving into cities, and working in the industrial sector were breakthrough changes for the Rural-Urban Divide system established in the central planning period.

However, rural migrants have not yet obtained equal rights in the employment, social security, and public services provided to urban citizens. Many studies in the 1990s focusing on the large floating population from the countryside indicated that, due to *hukou*-based institutional discrimination, rural migrants in the urban labor market occupied a distinctly unequal socio-economic level. As "migrant laborers," rural migrants were restricted to certain industries and jobs, with most of them employed in dirty, difficult, and dangerous work that local laborers were not willing to do. Even when rural migrants obtained jobs in the formal sector, their employment status was still "informal," and compared with local workers, they did same works but with lower payment, longer working hours, and different rights. Rural migrants did not enjoy the same social security treatment as local workers, such as pension and healthcare. The systematic and institutional discrimination towards rural migrants were a main sign of the persistence of the Rural-Urban Divide.

In 1993, the central government determined its strategic target—establishing a socialist market economy, which meant the equal employment of urban and rural labor and denied any forms of labor market segmentation. However, in the execution of this reform, the central authority had to take into consideration the effects on cities and state-owned enterprises. Unemployment and re-employment policies and the construction of social security services were emphasized in order to provide some protection to workers, and policies of restricting rural migrants were implemented to buffer the impact of restructuring on urban employment. From 1994 to 1997, nearly half of the provinces issued by-laws or regulations stressing restrictions and control of the influx of rural migrants' employment (Li and others 2007). During this period of time, due to difficulties and the complexity of state-owned enterprises' restructuring, employment pressure in cities, and other factors, a clear distance remained between the theoretical framework of social reform and the actual institutional environment of rural migrants.

Strategic Measures to Intensify Labor Market Reform

Ten years after establishing a socialist market economy, in 2003, the central government decided to intensify reforms of the economic system. *Decisions Regarding the Completion of the Socialist Market Economy System* ("中共中央关于完善社会主义市场经济体制若干问题的决定") announced that, to complete the socialist market economy, systematic changes should be undertaken in order to alter the dual urban-rural structure, and necessitated the modernization of the market framework with uniformity, openness, competition and order. The *Decisions* put emphasis on gradually reforming rural and urban labor markets and establishing equal employment for rural and urban laborers, as well as intensifying *hukou* reform and facilitating the stable and orderly transfer of rural surplus labor. In this new period, the three important measures causing the rapid decline of the rural-urban division system were as follows: (1) designing a policy package for rural migrants: the so-called "new policies for rural migrants," (2) carrying out a *Labor contract law* to unify labor market regulations, and (3) promoting rural migrants' participation in social insurance and integrating the social insurance system.

New Policies for Rural Migrants

In January 2003, the General Office of the State Council issued *Notice about Management and Services for Peasants to Go into Cities to Work*,[1] which required that "regions and relevant departments should stop administrative examination of and approval for enterprises 'recruiting rural migrants and eliminating restrictions about occupations and the jobs of rural migrant laborers from the countryside," and that each industry and job "should equally treat rural migrants and urban residents." Later, departmental regulations and local statutes restricting rural migrants' employment were abolished one by one. For example, in February 2005, in line with the central government's requirements for improving the conditions for peasants' employment in cities and eliminating policies and regulations restricting rural migrants' work in cities, the Ministry of Labor and Social Security issued the *Notice about Abolishing 'Temporary Regulations on Management of Rural Labor across Provinces' Employment and Supplementary Documents* (The "Interim Provisions" were issued in November 1994).[2] Another example is that, in March 2005, the Standing Committee of the Beijing Municipality People's Congress abolished *Regulations on the Management of Migrants Working and Running Businesses in Beijing*, which was issued in April 1995.[3] As a result, policies and practices discriminating against and restricting rural migrants began to lose legal footing, and institutional obstacles for realizing equal treatment for rural migrants and urban citizens were erased. In March 2006, the State Council published *Several Opinions about Solving Problems of Rural Migrants*,[4] which indicated that new policies for rural migrants would be systematized. This document clearly proposed the principles outlining and a number of policies for solving rural migrants' problems, including governing the wage issues of rural migrants, improving and promoting rural migrants' labor management, employment services, social security and other points related to urban public services, *hukou* reform, rural development, and other important aspects. These policy measures, accompanied by labor institution reform and social security reform, provided a strong driving force for promoting rural migrants' socio-economic rights and positions.

---

1   http://www.gov.cn/zwgk/2005-08/12/content_21839.htm.
2   http://law.Chinalawinfo.com/ncwlaw2002/slc/slc.asp?gid=57285&db=chl.
3   http://news.sohu.com/20050223/n224391539.shtml.
4   http://www.gov.cn/gongbao/content/2006/content_244909.htm.

Enacting the *Labor Contract Law*

The *Labor Law* issued in 1994 has defined the subsequent labor contract institution in China.[5] According to this law, employers should sign a labor contract with employees. Such contractual relations can have nothing to do with the laborer's *hukou* status, employment sector, firm's ownership, or other related factors.[6] Legally speaking, the *Labor Law* denied any such Rural-Urban Divided labor system. At this time, the basic idea of implementing the law was to provide conditions for the state sector's restructuring; the employment of those rural migrants who had moved to cities was restricted by department regulations and local statutes, and these laborers could not, as defined under the *Labor Law*, become legally-defined actors. For these reasons, contractual labor relationships did not cover rural migrants. This situation had lasted for many years. In 2004, a survey conducted by the Ministry of Labor and Social Security in 40 cities showed that only 12.5 percentage of rural migrants had contracted with their employers.[7]

New policies for rural migrants clearly state rural migrants' status as the subject of a contractual labor relationship, and require all enterprises to sign and implement a labor contract when recruiting rural migrants and to establish labor relationships with defined rights and obligations. After the *Labor contract law*'s passing in 2007, the percentage of rural migrants who signed labor contracts grew quickly, and millions of rural migrants become the subject of labor contracts and hence received equal labor rights. In 2009, about 136 million rural migrants were employed, of whom 42.8% (over 58 millions) signed labor contracts with their employers.[8] Rural migrants thus become one of the groups covered by the labor contract system. In view of citizenship rights, rural migrants obtained equal labor rights with other laborers. This also meant that a uniform institutional framework had emerged onto the urban labor market.

---

5   http://hr.tju.edu.cn/new/rsc/rlzy/gzzc/200911/P020091110556944292044.pdf.
6   Clause 2 of this law stipulates that this law is applicable to all kinds of employers and laborers with employment relations among them.
7   Research team of Research Office, State Council (2006), p. 13.
8   Cai Fang ed. (2010), pp. 2–9.

Promoting the Participation of Rural Migrants in the Social Insurance System through the Enactment of the *Social Insurance Law*

Allowing for more and more rural migrants to be covered by employment-related social insurance was one of the primary aims of the new policies, along with deepening social security reforms. Since 1997, reform plans regarding enterprise workers' pensions, medical-care, and unemployment insurance were methodically enforced, indicating the first stage of social security reform. At this time, the main target group was workers within the state sector, so the new social security coverage was limited to state-owned enterprises, and did not include workers in foreign companies and domestic private firms or rural migrants. After 2000, there was a breakthrough in rural migrants taking part in urban social security when, in January 2004, the *Regulations on Work-related Injury Insurance* was enacted.[9] Shortly after its announcement, the authorities made it clear that this regulation was totally applicable to rural migrants employed by enterprises.[10] This meant that possessing a rural *hukou* was no longer a status barrier to this insurance, i.e., the new insurance scheme did not feature a discriminatory Rural-Urban Divide.

Rural migrants' participating in urban pension and medical-care plans were more complicated, for such schemes hinged upon the willingness of rural migrants to participate, and inter-regional applicability of insurance rights proved complex. For these reasons, at the beginning, policy initiatives to promote rural migrants' participation in these programs were "to urgently address the medical problems of migrant workers, especially those related to serious illnesses," and "to explore the pension insurance methods suitable for rural migrants".[11] Provincial and city governments adopted different policies to promote rural migrants' participation based on local conditions. For instance, Guangdong applied the same programs for rural migrants as were available to local workers, while in Shanghai and Chengdu, special social insurance schemes were designed solely for rural migrants. Although there remained problems of a segmented system for rural migrants participating in pension and medical-care insurance, the institutionalized exclusion of this social group had passed. Promoting rural migrants' inclusion in work-related social insur-

---

9   http://www.gov.cn/zwgk/2005-05/20/content_144.htm.

10   The Ministry of Labor and Social Security on June 1, 2004, issued the *Notice about Rural Migrants' Participation to Work-related Insurance* (http://trs.molss.gov.cn/was40/mainframe.htm).

11   See Several Opinions about Solving Problems of Rural Migrants.

TABLE 11.1   *Rural migrants' Participation Rates in Social insurance* (%)

	Medical Care	Pension	Unemployment	Work-Related Injury
2006	17.9	10.7		19.2
2007	22.9	13.5	8.4	29.1
2008	30.4	17.2	11.0	35.2

Source: http://www.mohrss.gov.cn.

ance achieved measureable results. Table 11.1 shows that, from 2006 to 2009, rural migrants' participation rates in social insurance were increasing rapidly.

After 2008, legislative reform of social security also made measurable progresses. Two new regulations—*Temporary Methods for Transferring Urban Enterprise Workers' Basic Pension Insurance* and *Temporary Methods for Transferring and Continuing Temporary Workers' Basic Medical Insurance*—were published, which was a substantial step towards eliminating regional segmentation within the social insurance system. More importantly, following over three years' of discussions and revision, the *Social insurance Law* was issued on October 28, 2010, and enforced on July 1, 2011.[12] The *Social insurance Law* regulated social insurance programs such as basic pensions, basic medical care, work-related injuries, unemployment, and maternity insurance, and by providing clear terms for transferring insurance plans, enhancing insurance quality levels, and other changes. In particular, one of the supplementary articles stipulates that "rural residents working in cities" participate in social insurance in accordance with the law.[13] This means that rural migrants' legal position and institutional rules are the same as those of other laborers in cities. In other words, the new work-related social insurance institutions have *de jure* erased the legal features of the Rural-Urban Divide. In this sense, the *Social insurance Law* serves as a landmark for social insurance's integration crossing of regions and of crossing the rural and urban areas.[14] From "new policies for rural migrants" to the *Social insurance Law*, rural migrants' equal participation

---

12   http://www.gov.cn/flfg/2010-10/28/content_1732767.htm.

13   The fact that rural migrants' rights regarding social insurance are defined by such a special clause is worth noting. This means that, in the past, if social insurance plans were written without special provisions for rural migrants' applicability, "workers" did not include rural migrants.

14   http://finance.qq.com/a/20101029/000471.htm.

in urban social insurance has been enhanced everywhere from government policies to state law.

The Significance of Reform in the First Decade of the New Millennium

In the first decade of the new century, rural migrants have obtained equal labor rights and work-related social insurance rights by means of three reform measures aimed at facilitating equal employment in the rural and urban areas and composed of implementing new policies for rural migrants, enforcing labor contractual system, and integrating social insurance. This signifies that rural migrants have become key figures in the urban labor market with positions equal to other laborers. The difference between urban and rural *hukou* status no longer generates labor market segmentation and inequality. In reexamining the process of intensifying labor market reform, people may find that these reform measures were not directly relevant to *hukou* reform. Before 1992, *hukou* reform was under consideration in terms of removing the dual nature of rural and urban *hukou* status and setting up a registration system based on location of actual residence. *Hukou* reform in small town started in 1997. In some mid-size cities, experiments in *hukou* reform were undertaken. Up until now, however, in big cities attracting large floating populations, there was no real breakthrough in *hukou* reform. Despite the fact that *hukou* reform was stagnant, the decline of the Rural-Urban Divide continued. The significance of intensifying labor market reform is through defining universal labor rights and social insurance rights without changes to laborers' *hukou* status, which weakened the role of *hukou* status in segmenting urban and rural labor markets.

These observations are helpful to further discussions about whether the Rural-Urban Divide is in decline or not. Scholars arguing the persistence of the Rural-Urban Divide pay much attention to the fact that rural migrants cannot be registered under an urban *hukou* in their destination cities while ignoring an essential feature of the recent labor market reform that redefined the rights of individual laborers so that their *hukou* status became irrelevant. This assumption that *hukou* status rights and positions are unchangeable is losing its basis in reality. While the dual *hukou* system for urban and rural populations is one of the basic conditions of Rural-Urban Divide, the *hukou* system merely classifies urban and rural citizens, not defines citizenship rights. Differential citizenship rights are determined by the labor system, urban welfare system, and other related systems. If new institutional arrangements are designed according to a consistent universal principle that does not discriminate against rural migrants, *hukou* status will lose its implication of "social closure"-segmenting rural and urban people. Intensified reform in the urban labor market is in the process of unifying citizenship rights for rural and urban populations in spite of the fact that urban and rural *hukou* statuses have not changed.

The recent reform measures of the labor market are ongoing, refining and completing the labor and social security reform started in the 1990s that was aimed at establishing a socialist market economy. In the 1993 reform guidelines and the 1994 Labor Law, the theoretical foundation and legal basis were in support of new policies for rural migrants, and a system for contractual labor and a uniform social insurance system could be found across rural and urban areas. These three steps—the initial impact to the Rural-Urban Divide system in the 1980s, the shock to the foundation of the Rural-Urban Divide in the 1990s, and the intensified reform after 2000—have constituted a course of institutional change leading to the decline of the Rural-Urban Divide. The Rural-Urban Divide, in the sense of a formal, institutional arrangement, no longer defines individuals' basic economic and social rights in labor employment and social insurance based on their agricultural and non-agricultural *hukou* status.

The conclusion that intensified labor market reform has caused the decline of the Rural-Urban Divide may be questioned by the following points. First, in labor employment, although local regulations discriminating against migrants were abolished, some urban sectors (mainly the public sector) continue to require a local *hukou* when recruiting; second, the urban social security treatments that are not related to employment, such as the Minimum Life Security System and rural and urban residents' pension systems, are still restricted to local *hukou* holders; third, some urban public services (i.e., schools) are not fully open to migrants; and finally, in some communities with a significant concentration of migrant workers, locals enjoy generous benefits and employment opportunities that are not made available to migrants.

To understand these phenomena and respond accordingly, it is necessary to discuss the issue of regional segmentation. Regional segmentation, generally speaking, refers to the institutional arrangement or policy design of creating boundaries of economic opportunities, social welfare, and public services to local *hukou* status of administrative jurisdictions. A direct consequence of regional segmentation is that those suburban migrants without a local *hukou*, no matter the rural migrants and migrants from other cities (with urban *hukou* of other cities), all suffer social exclusions by local institutions or policies. Here, the function of *hukou* status has moved from dividing rural and urban population to segmenting locals and migrants. The cause of inequalities that migrants bear is no longer that of a nationwide rural urban divide, but two forms of regional segmentation—"local-migrant" segmentation at the city and community level.

"Local-Migrant" Segmentation at the City and Community Level

Similar to the Rural-Urban Divide of population and labor, "local-migrant" segmentation is related the *hukou* system. The difference is that the Rural-Urban Divide is based on classification of urban and rural *hukou*, while "local-migrant" segmentation is based on the locality of *hukou* registration, which distinguishes between a local *hukou* population and non-local *hukou* population. At different levels of administration, such as a province, a city, or a community (administrative village), local and non-local populations can be identified. "local-migrant" segmentation divides the locals and non-locals and then exclusively provides local citizens with socio-economic rights.

Formation and Development of the "Local-Migrant" Split at the City Level

With the government-led decline of the Rural-Urban Divide in the mid-1990s, regional segmentation led by local governments formed and developed. During the reform and opening-up period, local governments obtained great autonomy and assumed more duties towards the stability and prosperousness of their jurisdictions. It was therefore possible for local governments to make regulations and policies in favor of local residents' employment, security, and welfare. Now, due to regions' different stages of economic growth, population pressure, and other factors, different administrative areas' local regulations and policies are quite different, which makes regional segmentation observable. Within cities there are differences in rights and benefits between local residents and migrants, which is representative of the "local-migrant" segmentation reflecting regional segmentation.

In cities with a large floating population of migrants and open cities along the coastal areas, the pattern of "local-migrant" segmentation has changed from employment protection for local workers to the exclusion of migrants from the social security system. Since 1995, some cities had implemented numerous restrictions on migrant workers related to the Rural-Urban Divide, but which also began to have some features of regional exclusion. For example, at that time, Beijing's administration of labor employment prioritized "urban first, then rural, local first, then migrant,"[15] indicating that the employment of local residents was more important than that of migrants. Since 2000, the major form of "local-migrant" segmentation in cities has shifted to social security.

---

15   Li Ruojian, Yan Zhigang et al. (2007), p. 47.

At the beginning, the policy design of social security followed the principle of "local responsibility:" work-related social insurance was managed by local governments, while other social security schemes (such as Minimum Living Security) were funded by local finances. Within this framework, departments and officials of local governments tended to provide high social security benefits to the locals in order to provide a tangible increase in statistics. This is necessary to deal with local public opinion and pressure from the members of the local people's congress, and a requirement of regional competition. In a city with a considerable number of migrants, when these migrants are included social security schemes, the welfare of local residents will be lowered. Therefore, when designing social security institutions, city governments may set *hukou* restrictions (such as Urban Minimum Living Security), or permit migrants' participation but limit the transferability of benefits across regions (such as workers' pension, medical care, etc.). The inability to transfer benefits makes it difficult for migrants to really enjoy local social insurance, and at the same time reserves more social security funds for the city. This means there is a clear exclusion of migrants in local social security's policy design and operation. Due to unbalanced regional development, decentralization of public finance, and local management of social security, "local-migrant" segmentation of urban social security is inevitable (Zhang and et al. 2007).

Another difference from the nationwide Rural-Urban Divide it that "local-migrant" segmentation in urban areas demonstrates great variation among different cities. Big cities and open coastal cities usually enjoy better social security benefits, have a larger, concentrated number of migrants, and segmentation or exclusion tends to be more obvious than in the mid-sized and small cities of the country's interior. In interior cities and small towns, the thresholds of *hukou* transfer are relatively low, so some migrants are able to participate in local social security by obtaining local *hukou* registration. The social security levels in these areas are usually not high, therefore, even without a transfer to the local *hukou*, not being included in social security may not be a big problem. In cities' public sector, staff favors recruiting local *hukou* holders, so this job market is segmented. However, the major group suffering from this segmentation is those with high education and without local *hukou*, not rural migrants.

Recently, the "local-migrant" segmentation in cities has undergone certain changes. With the enforcement of the *Social insurance Law*, problems in the cross-regional transfer of work-related social insurance may be resolved. In some areas, local governments have developed pension schemes for urban and rural residents (divided or integrated), but these insurance schemes are restricted to the local population. In some cities, especially mid-sized and small cities without excessive population pressure, public services are increasingly open to migrants, and the threshold for *hukou* transfer is being lowered. Overall, in China, institutional change facilitating population migration and social integration is taking place. Such institutional change is, to a certain degree, mandatory, for the central government leads the process through the implementation of national guidelines, laws, and regulations. Such institutional change is somehow induced, for local governments or agencies of some cities and communities will take active roles in improving management to enhance migrants' integration, as well as constructing a harmonious city or community against a backdrop of demand for talent and the changing supply and demand of labor.

Native Villagers and Migrants in Changing Communities

In cities with a heavy concentration of migrants, "local-migrant" segmentation is observed in communities undergoing a rural to urban transformation. Some transforming communities, driven by urbanization, are usually included as part of a nearby city's extension, such as the "urban villages" within big cities. Transforming communities driven by rural industrialization, or so-called industrialized new rural villages, are commonly located in the surrounding areas of cities. Transforming communities gathering in an area, which features rural industrialization and urbanization, may be at a distance from the traditional urban center.[16] Although such phenomenon were present in the 1980s, the wide formation of "local-migrant" segmentation in communities didn't occur until the 1990s, when the number of floating populations in cities were quickly increasing. In terms of space distribution, this form of segmentation can be easily seen in big cities and the surrounding areas of open, coastal cities.

In changing communities, the division between locals and migrants is quite different from what is seen with the Rural-Urban Divide. In the residential areas of a city, the committees of old neighborhood communities very much reflect the traditional "urban biased" policies. Now, however, in this kind of community, local residents have lost most of their advantages over migrants except for some "legacies," such as work units for their past employment and reformed housing. Transforming communities differ. Studies on "urban villages" (Li Junfu 2004; Li Peilin 2004) suggest that in "urban villages," villagers have residential land on which they are able to build houses for renting and

---

16   For the examples of "urban village," new village and new town of rural industrialization, see Zhang, Hou et al. (2009), pp. 36–39.

are eligible for welfare redistribution from the village's collective economies, while migrants do not have such rights. In rural industrialized new villages or newly industrialized cities, the locals are more likely to take upper- and mid-management positions in local enterprises, whereas migrants from outside are usually tasked with menial jobs.

In transitional communities (villages), the villager status mechanism is central to excluding migrants (Wang 2003). Villager status is based on the local *hukou* of a community. While *hukou* status can be transferred to a local registration from outside, in some areas, the concept of "village membership" has formed to protect the interests of the original villagers, and those with a transitional *hukou* may or may not be included in villager population counts. Thus residents in a transitional community are divided into two groups of villagers, one with villager status and the other without—migrants. Additionally, there are other types of segmentation and stratification within a transitioning community.[17] The mechanism for determining a villager's status is an internal rule of the changing community, not a law or a legal regulation, but this mechanism rests on a firm basis of rural collective ownership in land and assets and the villager committee system.

Comparisons between "Local-Migrant" Segmentation at the Urban and Community Level

"Local-migrant" segmentation at the urban and community levels are similar, but different in certain important aspects. The following are comparisons between these two forms in terms of the implementing bodies, the protected, the excluded, the basis, the operating procedures, variations, and tendencies.

(1) The Implementing Bodies
The implementing body of the "local-migrant" divide at the city level is the city government, while that at the community level is the administrative agent of the transitioning community. Such an agent may be the village committee, or one normally being reorganized in the form of neighborhood committee, but to a large extent the village committee administration continues to operate. In rural towns or townships in the process of broad industrialization, administrative agents of transitioning communities include both village committees and the town administrative bodies.

---

17   See the example of Huxi village, Jiangyin City of Jiangsu province. http://www.Chinadaily. com.cn/hqcj/2010-01/21/content_9356643_2.htm.

(2) People being Protected

"Local-migrant" segmentation at the city level protects local residents in cities, whereas at the community level, it protects local villagers (with local agricultural *hukou* or villager status). These exclusive rights designed by city governments may vary between local urban and rural residents, or be the same. For instance, the residential pension system recently introduced in some cities are uniform: local residents with both an urban *hukou* and rural *hukou* are eligible to enroll.

(3) Groups being Excluded

"Local-migrant" segmentation at both the city level and at the community level exclude migrants without local *hukou*, regardless of their urban or rural *hukou* status. Concerning the "local-migrant" segmentation at the community level, in addition to non-local *hukou* groups, some with local *hukou* but without village status may be excluded from some rights.

(4) Basis of Segmentation.

"Local-migrant" segmentation at the city level is based on local financial autonomy and the persistence of serious regional differences, while segmentation at the community level is based on rural collective ownership (land, assets, etc.) established before the reform and further developed in the following years.

(5) Operating Procedures

"Local-migrant" segmentation at city level operates in accordance to local regulations and policies, whereas "local-migrant" segmentation at the community level is controlled by village policies or agreements among villagers.

(6) Variations of Segmentation

As far as the "local-migrant" segmentation at city level, there exist multiple variations: big cities and open cities in the coastal regions have the most serious problem, but variations in "local-migrant" segmentation among communities are greater: such segmentation does not exist in traditional urban communities, is (to some degree) observable in those involved in urbanization, and is most serious in industrialized rural communities.

(7) Changing Tendencies

In cities, as social insurance becomes transferable across regions, the segmentation of work-related social insurance will weaken, but social security, welfare, and public services based on local finance will continue to exist. In transitioning communities, "local-migrant" segmentation will exist for a much longer time, but further reforms to rural collective ownership and the villager committee system may lead to its decline.

The Decreasing Inequality of *Hukou* Status

Against the background of the Rural-Urban Divide's ending and the formation of regional segmentation, *hukou*-related inequality and social stratification in cities is changing. At present, the effect of *hukou* status has shifted from "*hukou* stratification*" to "*hukou* inequality," and the significance of a given *hukou* status is diminishing. In the heyday of China's Rural-Urban Divide, besides rural-urban inequality being common in developing countries, rural populations did not have access to urban society due to the institutional barriers erected between cities and the countryside. Rural-urban inequality was thus fixed and enhanced; peasants became poor and a low-caste class.[18] The reform and opening-up gave rise to population migration and provided opportunities for rural residents to migrate to cities. Rural populations, however, continued to suffer from systematic discrimination and exclusion, and rural migrant laborers became the bottom class in the new dual-urban society. Due to a redefinition of rights in the course of the new decade's intensified labor market reform, rural migrants managed to obtain equal rights in labor employment and social insurance, and their socio-economic positions was correspondingly greatly promoted. So far, the difference between a rural *hukou* and urban *hukou* no longer causes institutional segmentation and stratification.

With the conclusion of the systematized Rural-Urban Divide, some vestige of the system remains, and there are still some inequalities between rural migrants and urban *hukou* holders. For example, because of the lack of long-term investment in education, the human capital of rural migrants and hence their employment opportunities are relatively low. Formal discrimination has disappeared, but there may still exist some discriminatory ideas and practice leveled against and excluding rural migrants in cities and enterprises. In labor contracts and work-related social insurance, although the institutions have been designed to offer full coverage and uniformity, rural migrants' participation rates may remain relatively low due to the focus of institutions' on formal sectors, while rural migrants make up a high parentage of the informal sector. Rural migrants do not have a developed social network in their destination cities. Generally speaking, despite the institutional framework of Rural-Urban Divide being abolished, society still needs time to develop a sound, balanced rural-urban system and to construct new social relations. The institutional legacy of differences between migrants and local citizens is due to nationwide Rural-Urban Divide, such as rural migrants' educational levels; some are related

---

18   Whyte (2010).

to local features, such as variations among cities in attracting rural migrants to participate in social insurance plans. These differences are not based on formal institutions and tend to diminish over time, and so are not fixed and are therefore unable to produce social class inequality.

On the other hand, with the decline of the Rural-Urban Divide and emergence of regional segmentation, differences between migrants to cities and local residents have been made manifest. Incoming migrants—including both rural migrants and migrants from other cities—almost all encounter differences in rights and discrimination of one form or another. These "local-migrant" segmentations display considerable variations among cities, but nevertheless, do not have the same nationwide social stratification effect as the past Rural-Urban Divide system. Compared with the "local-migrant" segmentation at the city level, the segmentation of the community is much smaller in terms of its impact. In some transitioning communities, differences in rights and interests between the locals and migrants are considerable, but the migrants still have access to the same basic socio-economic rights as the locals due to national institutions and local policies controlling the communities. Therefore, relative to the segmentation of the city, the influence of "local-migrant" division is low. Overall, regional segmentation brings about some inequality, but does not create a new social class.

In cities, the general trend has been for the segmentation and inequality effects of *hukou* status to diminish over time. The legacies of the Rural-Urban Divide are weakening. Much progress has been achieved in the integration of work-related social insurance across rural and urban areas and different regions, and nationwide implementation of new institutions will speed up the solidarity of the labor market. The extent of regional segmentation has been restricted to residential social security and public services sponsored by local governments. This raises the question: is it already or near the right time to implement comprehensive *hukou* reform? This is to say, is it possible to consider erasing the difference between rural and urban *hukou* and revising the rules of *hukou* registration, thus getting the *hukou* system back to being simply a tool for residential registration management?

As for prospective reform of the *hukou* system, we are cautiously optimistic: this reform will continue, but it will take time to complete. The main reason for that is that the imbalance between rural and urban areas and among regions are a basic condition of China, which require a long time to change. Due to the size of the rural population, it is not possible in a short time to unify rural and urban public services (including social security) or to open an urban service system. At this stage, therefore, uniform *hukou* status without the rural-urban difference is difficult.[19] For cities, opening public services will be met by heavy population pressure, especially for the biggest cities (Guo 2010). Recently, in Beijing, Shanghai, and other metropolises, some policies limiting the non-local *hukou* population have emerged in regards to the housing market, car purchasing, and other areas, and a local *hukou* thus seems to be more valuable than before, making *hukou* reform more difficult. Here, a similar logic can been seen: in the 1950s and 1960s, cities were affected by an inflow of rural populations, and the dual-*hukou* administration for rural and urban people was hence strengthened. Today, high pressure on the population, resources, and environment of metropolises has led to the re-emergence of exclusive *hukou* segmentation against migrants. Therefore, complete reform of the *hukou* system and free mobility and equal rights for populations and labor are, to a large extent, not a simple issue of redefining the rules of the game, but instead relate to weakening and eliminating big cities' monopolies over economic and social resources, reducing their extraordinary growth, and realizing a balanced development between rural and urban areas and among regions.

Conclusions and Discussion

Is the persistence of the Rural-Urban Divide system still a decisive feature of the labor market and migrants' socio-economic positions? Several recent studies have provided positive views on these issues. This article addresses another possibility: following intensified labor market reform in the new decade, the Rural-Urban Divide system has been completely abolished. This conclusion is significant when considering formal institutional arrangements. In some informal aspects, such as social relations, ideas, and conventions, there are some observable "signs" of the Rural-Urban Divide, which as a historical legacy may, in the long run, affect the rights and interests, status, and prestige of rural peasants migrating to the cities. This conclusion is not relevant to the general discussion of rural-urban inequality. The Rural-Urban Divide system is unique to China and a few other countries, while rural-urban disparity and rural poverty are common phenomena in almost all developing countries. The essence of the end to the Rural-Urban Divide system is that, when considered alongside labor migration, the basic socio-economic rights of employment and social security are no longer defined in accordance with rural and urban *hukou*

---

19   Recently, in some areas, peasants refused to transfer their rural *hukou* to urban ones, which is another problem of *hukou* reform.

status. The end of the Rural-Urban Divide system represents a great change in China's fundamental social structure. In the past, this system generated a peasant class with an unchangeable socio-economic fate. In the early stages of reform, this system prevented rural migrants from joining urban society, and made it difficult for them to move up from their original position. As the system came to an end, the difference between rural and urban *hukou* no longer necessarily means an unchangeable social status and disparate economic fate. In this sense, the road for China's rural population to migrate to cities and achieve upwards mobility has begun to open, and hence, China is no longer a dual society with institutional barriers between rural and urban areas.

With the systematic decline of the Rural-Urban Divide in cities and transforming communities, "local-migrant" segmentation has formed and continues to develop. These new forms of segmentation feature institutional exclusions against both rural migrants and migrants from other cities, creating difficulties for the social integration of these migrant groups in their destination cities. On the other hand, those being protected by "local-migrant" segmentation are not limited to local urban *hukou*-holding residents who benefited from past urban-biased policies. Nevertheless, these localized discriminatory divisions are not comparable to the previous Rural-Urban Divide and are unable to generate new social classes. Rural migrants and migrants from other cities may have to bear some discriminatory treatments and differences in rights and interests, but they are not new special groups in the urban social stratification structure.

Relative to inter-city migrants, rural migrants and their family members are likely to suffer more inequalities and greater difficulties in integrating into urban society. These problems are partially derived from the common impact of local segmentation on migrants and partially from the special influence of the remaining legacies of the Rural-Urban Divide. Rural migrants are no long the sole focus of urban exclusion and their issues have been reduced considerably. Later, with the completion of related policies, changes in social attitudes, and the self-development of rural migrants, the number of inequalities between local citizens and migrants across cities and rural migrants will continue to decrease.

The institutional change of the Rural-Urban Divide has something to do with the economic transformation of the "Lewis Turning Point." On one hand, although the end of the Rural-Urban Divide as an institutional modification cannot serve as direct evidence of the Lewis Turning Point, it at least shows that the transfer of rural labor to cities does not have to overcome the systematic barriers that limited rural populations in the past. In this sense, the end of the divide has provided a basic condition for the flourishing of the Lewis

Turning Point. On the other hand, the Lewis Turning Point brings changes in the relationship between labor supply and demand, which have facilitated and encouraged the decline of the Rural-Urban Divide and are helpful in weakening the legacies of the divide.

The end of China's Rural-Urban Divide and the formation of a dual-level "local-migrant" segmentation calls for improvement on the empirical research being done on migrants to cities. First, the research should extend its range of subjects. The previously-common "two-group" testing between rural-migrants and local workers (citizens) may generate logical mistakes. "Three-group" testing should be used instead, in which migrants from other cites serve as a key variable for estimating the extent and strength of the legacies of the Rural-Urban Divide and studying the effects of "local-migrant" segmentation in cities. Local rural *hukou*-holding populations may be included insofar as it is possible. Second, the sampled area should be larger. Current studies on urban migrants usually obtain samples from urban neighborhood committees while neglecting administrative villages surrounding the central areas of cities, so migrants living in transitional communities are not be considered. This may lead to a bias in the sample's representativeness, and hence migrants in such communities and the inequalities these migrants face will be missed in research. It is therefore necessary to extend the sampling space from the neighborhood committees of core urban areas to rural communities which are located at the peripheries of cities but have actually urbanized. Finally, the general approach and specific case studies should be combined. Institutional backgrounds and population pressure among cities may vary considerably, and variations of segmentation in different transforming communities can subsequently be observed. Therefore, random sampling and background examinations of cities and communities within a given survey should be mutual supplementary, and caution should be applied when pooling together samples from different cities and communities.

(This article was originally published in Chinese in 2011.)

References

Cai Fang. 2008. *Lewis Turning Point: new phrase of China's economic development.* Social Sciences Academic Press.

———. 2007. *Green Book of Population and Labor, 2007.* Social Sciences Academic Press.

―――. 2010. *Green Book of Population and Labor, 2010*. Social Sciences Academic Press.

Cai Fang and Lin Yifu. 2003. *Chinese Economy*. Chinese Finance and Economy Press.

Chan, Kam Wing and Will Buckingham. 2008. "Is China Abolishing the *Hukou* System?" *The China Quarterly* 195: 582–606.

Chen Yingfang. 2005. "'Peasant Workers' Institutional Arrangements and Status Identification." *Sociological Studies* 2005, no. 3.

Fields, Gary. 2004. "Dualism in the Labor market: a Perspective on the Lewis Model after half a Century." *The Manchester School* 72: 724–735.

Guo Xiuyun. 2010. "Difficulties of *Hukou* Reform in Big Cities and the Possibility of Policies in the Future." *Population and Development* 2010, no. 6.

Hou Yafei and Zhang Zhanxin. 2010. *Urban Inclusion to the Floating population: Perspectives on Individuals, Families, and Communities, and Research on Institutional Change*. China Economic Publishing House.

Lewis, W. Arthur. 1979. "The Dual Economy Revised." *The Manchester School* 47: 211–229.

Li Junfu. 2004. *Restructuring of Urban villages*. Science Press.

Li Peilin. 2004. *The End of Village: a Story of Guangzhou Villages*. The Commercial Press.

Li Qiang. 2004. *Rural migrants and China's Social Stratification*. Social Sciences Academic Press.

Li Rujian, Yan Zhigang, et al. 2007. *Toward Order: Research on Local Regulations about Migrants Management*. Social Sciences Academic Press.

Martin King Whyte. 2010. "The Paradoxes of Rural-Urban Inequality in Contemporary China," in *One Country, Two Societies: Rural-Urban Inequality in Contemporary China*, edited by Martin King Whyte, 1–25. Cambridge: Harvard University Press.

Research Team, Research Office of the State Council. 2006. *Survey Reports on China's Rural migrants*. Zhongguo Yanshi Press.

Sun Liping. "The 'New Dual-Structure' between Rural and Urban Areas and Rural migrants' Movement," in *Rural migrants—Economic and Social Studies on China's Rural migrants to Cities*, edited by Li Peilin. Social Sciences Academic Press, 2003.

Wang Xiaoyi. "Coming to Villages," in *Rural migrants—Economic and Social Studies on China's Rural migrants to Cities*, edited by Li Peilin. Social Sciences Academic Press, 2003.

Wu, Jieh-min. 2010. "Rural Migrant Workers and China's Differential Citizenship: A Comparative Institutional Analysis," in *One Country, Two Societies: Rural-Urban Inequality in Contemporary China*, edited by Martin Ling Whyte, 55–81. Cambridge: Harvard University Press.

Zhang Zhanxin. 2007. "From the Rural-Urban Divide to Regional segmentation," *Population Research* 2007, no. 6.

Zhang Zhanxin et al. 2007. "The Rural-Urban Divide, Regional segmentation, and Lack of Access to Social Security for Migrants to Cities—Evidence from Shanghai and Four other Cities." *Chinese Population Science* 2007, no. 6.

Zhang Zhanxin, Hou Yafei et al. *Floating population in Urban Communities: Surveys in Beijing and Other Five Cities*. Social Sciences Academic Press, 2009.

Index